SOCIAL SERVICE
in Hawaii

SOCIAL SERVICE
in Hawaii

By
MARGARET M. L. CATTON

Pacific **PB** *Books*

Publishers
PALO ALTO, CALIFORNIA

COPYRIGHT © 1959 BY MARGARET M. L. CATTON
LIBRARY OF CONGRESS CATALOG CARD NUMBER 58-14378
PRINTED AND BOUND IN THE UNITED STATES OF AMERICA
PUBLISHED BY PACIFIC BOOKS, PALO ALTO, CALIFORNIA.

DEDICATED
TO RENNY,
MY SISTER

Introductory

When the idea of a history of social service in Hawaii first took shape in my mind, I envisaged an all-inclusive one. The history would cover all the islands and include both case-work and group-work agencies—the Young Men's and Young Women's Christian Associations, Palama Settlement, the Salvation Army, and community organizations (e.g., the Honolulu Council of Social Agencies and the various island community chests). I should have known better. This was too big an order for one assignment.

In consultation with Dr. Arthur L. Dean,[1] I decided to revise the original plan and to limit the history to casework agencies. An exception is made in chapter XII, "The Neighbor Islands," since social welfare outside Oahu was centered in community or group work.

As I proceeded I was forced to another decision. There is a paucity of data concerning the early years of Hawaii's older organizations. Some had no official headquarters and few kept records. The majority of executives of agencies founded before the beginning and in the early years of this century have died or have left the Islands, and not one of their organizations had in narrative form any account of its formation and continuing functions.

This lack of historical data, and the time which definitive writing of histories would involve, led to the decision to write this book in two parts. Part I contains summarized histories of all our casework agencies since the founding of the first one in 1852. To do even this much meant extensive searching through numerous reports and files and some correspondence with former social workers who have since left Hawaii. (The

---

[1] Dr. Dean was the second president of the College of Hawaii, 1914–1919, remaining in office after it became the University of Hawaii until 1927. He took a leading role in the development of scientific, educational, and social welfare programs in the Territory. Dr. Dean died in Honolulu on March 1, 1952.

term "casework" is used in a very broad sense, viz., to include organizations which devoted themselves to helping individuals in their social and personal needs long before social service became the profession it is today.)

Under the title of each chapter in Part I, with one exception, is the year in which a particular agency was founded. The exception is chapter XII, "The Neighbor Islands." For reasons apparent in it, no beginning date is given. Otherwise, both the year in which an organization was established and the deadline of my writing of it is stated under each title as "Period Included." Where agencies have become extinct, the date of establishment and the date of dissolution are noted.

Part II contains exclusively the history of medical social service as developed by the Medical Social Service Association of Hawaii and its predecessor groups. Since I was for so long the executive of the organization which established medical social service in Honolulu, it has been possible to cover this subject in detail. Future historians of medical social service will not have the difficulty I had in finding factual data for Part I.

Acknowledgments

The underlying principle upon which this history is based is authenticity. A careful search was made for historical data in the files of social agencies, the Hawaiian Mission Children's Society, the Public Archives of Hawaii, and the Legislative Reference Bureau, University of Hawaii. I am grateful to their executives and staffs for according me this privilege. The names of authors and publishers who consented to my use of their publications are given in the reference notes in the respective chapters of this volume. I should indeed have been at a loss without their help.

Every chapter in the manuscript was reviewed, sometimes more than once, by persons associated in the past or the present with particular organizations. This meant sending chapters to the neighbor islands, to the mainland, and even to England. I should like to name the reviewers individually, but they are so numerous it seems impracticable; nevertheless, I wish them to know how grateful I am for their invaluable assistance in this regard.

To Professor Wayne McMillen, School of Social Service Administration, University of Chicago, I owe a very special debt of gratitude. Dr. McMillen was a visiting professor, in 1955, at the School of Social Work, University of Hawaii. He reviewed the total manuscript critically, twice; supplied the professional advice and encouragement which helped me to bring my efforts closer to publication; and then kindly wrote the Preface. Another experienced writer who gave me valuable advice is Miss Emily V. Warinner. I have her to thank for the choice of Pacific Books as publisher. And since I was dependent upon the patience and good will of a typist my thanks to Mrs. Eleanor S. Anderson, an expert, who typed and retyped the innumerable pages.

Finally, had it not been for Miss Ethel M. Damon this book would not have been written—at least not by me. Miss Damon

not only encouraged me to enter the profession of social work,
but also, when the time came to close that chapter in my life,
urged me to write a history of social service in Hawaii.

M. M. L. C.

Preface

In any profession the practitioners need a sense of their relationship both to the past and to the future. A knowledge of historical antecedents deepens their sense of obligation to preserve the heritage of the past and to hand it on, enriched, if possible, to the next generation. Students, in particular, need to acquire, as early as possible, an identification with the professional tradition. Teachers know the importance of history in accelerating this development. This explains the rows of portraits of the great jurists and the great physicians of the past inevitably found on the walls of the libraries and lecture halls of the schools of law and medicine.

Over the years the field of social work has slowly built up a body of historical literature. These studies have made a major contribution to the development of a sense of professional self-respect among social workers. They have also, as in older professions, provided teachers with means of awakening in students an awareness of the responsibilities they are assuming in accepting the status of a professional person. Their impact upon the attitudes of practitioners and of students is not, however, the total measure of their importance.

In the area of social work practice, historical studies provide a frame of reference for the professional process known as community organization. An examination of the past often reveals to the leadership groups of today the extent to which current policies, practices, and organizational structures are merely historical survivals. Once a vestigial remnant is recognized as no longer appropriate to the current level of community life something is likely to be done about it. Moreover, the comparisons provided by examining parallel historical developments are in themselves illuminating. Why, for example, did one state decide to build a public orphanage, while another preferred to subsidize private institutions, and still another left the problem exclusively in the hands of local political subdivisions? And what were the results of these diverse approaches to the problem? Historical studies, by providing such comparisons as these, afford guidance to those currently responsible for framing community welfare policies.

The pattern for historical studies in the field of social welfare was set by the monumental labors of Sidney and Beatrice Webb in their volumes on the English Poor Laws. Obviously their approach could not be imported into the United States without adaptions. In this country the public welfare structure varies from state to state. Hence historical studies have necessarily focused, not upon the national development, but upon a single state or, in some instances, upon a local political subdivision. And within a single state, the research has sometimes centered upon a single field, such as child welfare or the mental health services.

In addition to these histories of the public social services, some studies have been published in this country which trace the development of a voluntary welfare movement or of a single voluntary agency. Of the former the one that is undoubtedly best known is Watson's "History of the Charity Organization Society Movement in the United States." In the latter group are several histories of state conferences of social work and a considerable number of annals of long-established welfare agencies and institutions. Thus an over-all inventory reveals a respectable body of historical studies in the field of welfare in America, some relating to particular political entities and others to particular movements or agencies, voluntary as well as governmental.

The setting of all these studies has been in one or another of the states or political subdivisions of the continental United States. Now at last a history of welfare services has been written, the setting of which, though under the United States flag, is far from the mainland. This is, in fact, the first history of American social services in an area geographically separated from the continent. Moreover, it is the only history of American welfare developments which has its roots in a Polynesian culture and reflects the impact of an indigenous monarchy. On the mainland European traditions of philanthropy and social welfare have always exercised a predominant influence. In Hawaii these traditions encountered, not only the Polynesian mores, but also the philosophical and religious concepts of the ancient cultures of the Orient. The result has been a mutual adaptation that gives to the history of welfare services in Hawaii a content which is both colorful and unique. Unlike many histories of welfare services, this one encompasses both governmental and voluntary programs.

Margaret Mary Louise Catton was apparently destined to be the author of this first history of the social services in Hawaii. Her birth, her inherited traditions, her education, and her life experiences all contributed to provide her with the background needed for the task. She was born on the Island of Maui, the second largest island comprising the present Territory of Hawaii. Designated on the maps of that day as the Sandwich Islands, this territory was still to most of the world a half-legendary Polynesian paradise, the economic resources of which were just beginning to attract interest.

Among those drawn to the islands by the rapidly developing sugar industry were considerable numbers of Scotsmen. Robert Catton, the author's father, arrived with his bride in 1878, to represent a Scotch engineering firm. The Catton family struck its roots into the soil of Hawaii and has remained there to the present day.

The author grew up in unique surroundings. The sugar planters imported thousands of laborers during the second half of the 19th and early 20th century, chiefly from the Orient. On the plantations each racial group occupied separate living compounds. Communication among the different linguistic stocks was by "pidgin English"—a curious amalgam of Hawaiian, English, and other tongues, necessarily accompanied by an abundance of gesticulation and pantomime.

Barriers other than race and language also separated the various component groups of this pioneer society. Religion and politics in particular made for divisiveness. Congregationalism, introduced to the Sandwich Islands in 1820, gained a strong foothold. In the latter part of the 19th century France and Great Britain introduced the Roman Catholic and Anglican communions. Sectarianism grew lustily, with the result that sometimes neighboring families held no communication with one another because they were adherents of different churches. Prior to the overthrow of the Hawaiian monarchy in 1893, the islanders divided politically into pro-monarchists and anti-monarchists. Feeling ran high on this issue, sometimes causing parents to remove their children from the established schools.

Margaret Mary Louise Catton—or Mary Catton, as her

friends call her—grew up in the midst of these social conflicts. They occasioned irregularities in her education. She enrolled in several schools in Honolulu and, at one period, was taken "home"—to Scotland—by her parents to pursue her studies. Thus her early education, though unconventional, was colorful and diverse. Her professional education, on the contrary, was entirely orthodox. She matriculated at the New York School of Social Work and after completing her professional education there returned to Honolulu in 1919 to become the first woman born in the Islands to graduate as a professional social worker.

Her professional life has been devoted to the building up of modern social services in Hawaii. Her chief work was in medical social service. She is responsible for the development of casework service at The Queen's Hospital in Honolulu and she stimulated the initiation and guided the development of similar services in other hospitals in Honolulu. In appreciation of her many years of service in the health field, the Hawaii Medical Association conferred upon her its Distinguished Service Award in 1956 with the following citation: "In recognition of countless services to the medical profession and the citizens in this community above and beyond the call of routine professional responsibilities."

The last phrase of this citation merits further comment. Mary Catton's professional career in Hawaii spanned a period characterized by the most rapid integration of varied racial groups ever witnessed on this globe. Annexation by the United States in 1898 conferred American citizenship upon all persons born in the Islands, regardless of race. The resultant sharing of political rights and political controls by members of all racial stocks has produced both racial harmony and genuine integration. Not only practices, but what is far more important, *feelings,* of democratic equality are today more nearly universal in Hawaii than elsewhere in America.

Mary Catton's work contributed to this phenomenal transformation. Her voice was always raised in issues involving good professional standards, including equality of treatment. She was a leader in formulating plans and promoting programs to meet the welfare needs of Hawaii's cosmopolitan population. Much of her knowledge of the development of modern welfare services in Hawaii is therefore based upon her personal experiences.

Following her retirement in 1948, Mary Catton embarked,

with characteristic vigor, upon the task of recording the history of welfare developments in the astonishing melting pot in mid-Pacific which she knows so well. No other local history of social services in America has either a geographical or a social setting comparable to Hawaii. Likewise it seems probable that no author of a local history of American social services has ever had a more intense emotional, intellectual, and professional identification with his subject than Mary Catton. Her book, like her life, reflects her dedication to her profession and to the fabulous land in which she was born.

WAYNE MCMILLEN
University of Chicago

November 10, 1958

Contents

List of Illustrations

Part I

I

A Bit of Background

The Hawaiian Islands in the North Pacific, slightly more than
two thousand miles from the American continent, form the
northern tip of a triangle; New Zealand is its southern point
and Easter Island its eastern. Within the triangle are many
islands, the whole known as Polynesia. Toward the center of
the triangle is Tahiti, from whence the Polynesian settlers of
Hawaii probably came.

Guided "by the sun, clouds, birds, currents, and waves, and
at night by the stars," they came in canoes fashioned by stone-
age implements. In successive voyages they brought their
women, domestic animals, and plants, and settling here
thatched their huts and beat out their cloth from the inner
bark of the mulberry tree. Hawaii became home.

The Polynesians, like other ethnic groups, had class distinction. In Hawaii the highest class consisted of the *alii*, or chiefs;
second were the *kahunas*, the learned men and skilled artesians;
third were the *makaainana*, the common people or serfs. The
chiefs owned the land; the commoners tilled it by hand and
paid for its use in produce.

The religion of the Hawaiians was closely related to nature,
personified by many gods both male and female, among them
Kane, the creative parent of all living creatures, Lono, the god
of agriculture, and Ku, the god of war and power.[1] * Pele, the
goddess of fire, is still held in awe by some who attribute untoward natural occurrences to her displeasure; this is particularly true of Kilauea, the more or less active volcano on the
Island of Hawaii. The priests in early Hawaii were *kahunas*
who officiated according to prescribed rights, whether in the
building of a canoe, going into battle, or treating the sick.

---

* Footnotes will be found at the end of each chapter.

3

In the thirteenth or fourteenth century migrations of the Polynesians ceased and the people of these islands lived in almost complete isolation for five hundred years. One day in early 1778 those living at Waimea on the island of Kauai beheld a sight which filled them with utter astonishment. Out at sea, heading toward land, were two craft, the like of which they had never seen. Paddling out in their canoes, the natives set up a friendly relationship with Captain James Cook, the British naval officer and explorer in command of the vessels.

Captain Cook was treated with the deference due a chief. He wanted to replenish his stores of food and water, the natives wanted the nails and iron they saw on the ships; so, by means of barter, each was gratified. After remaining in Hawaiian waters two weeks, Captain Cook resumed his voyage of exploration in the northern Pacific. He named this tip of the Polynesian triangle the Sandwich Islands, after the Earl of Sandwich of the British Admiralty.

In January 1779 Captain Cook returned, this time anchoring in Kealakekua Bay on the Kona coast of Hawaii. Again through barter the mariners obtained food and the natives iron, tools, and daggers. After a stay of several weeks the vessels set sail but soon had to return to Kealakekua for repairs to one of the ships damaged in a storm. As a result of an altercation which arose between the natives and the foreigners, chiefly because of the theft of a boat for its metal, there was a fight in which Captain Cook was killed.

The Islands then constituted four kingdoms—Hawaii, Maui, Oahu, and Kauai—each under its ruling chief. Over the years Kamehameha I of historical fame (1758–1819) brought the entire group of islands [2] into a united kingdom under his rule.

Seven monarchs succeeded Kamehameha I. The last ruler, Queen Liliuokalani, was deposed in 1893. A Provisional Government followed from January 1893 to July 4, 1894, when the Republic of Hawaii was set up. On August 12, 1898, the Hawaiian Islands were annexed to the United States but the territorial government was not established until June 14, 1900. [3]

Captain Cook's discovery made the location of the Sandwich Islands common knowledge to explorers and traders. The

Islands had convenient harbors in which to replenish stores or to lay up for the winter. Fur traders were the first to take advantage of this knowledge. Beginning in 1785 they stopped here on their way from the northwest coast of America where they had collected furs, mainly otter skins, to trade for goods in China. In the early 1800's this trade had come to an end.

In the 1790's, men from visiting ships discovered sandalwood in the Islands and by 1811 it had become a source for trade. The chiefs coveted firearms and ships and a miscellany of goods, including much of no intrinsic value. They got them from the white man who wanted food to eat and sandalwood to trade in China. With all their natural prowess, Hawaiians could not till their land, catch their fish, make their salt, and, at the same time, gather heavy loads of sandalwood. Consequently, they neglected their regular duties and a famine threatened. Furthermore, the forced climb from the warmer temperature at sea level to the wet and cold mountainous regions where the sandalwood grew resulted in deaths from exposure. There is a story to the effect that sandalwood gathering became so arduous that the natives decided to put an end to it by killing the young shoots as they tramped over the trails. At any rate, the mountains were shorn of this tree and by 1830 the trade had collapsed.

The next influx of foreigners began with the whalers in 1819. It is estimated that at the peak of the whaling industry, between 1840 and 1860, several hundred vessels stopped in the spring and fall of each year at Honolulu on Oahu and Lahaina on Maui. But with the development of illuminating gas, oils, and lubricants from coal and petroleum, the whaling industry came to an end sometime after 1876.

Concomitant with the calls of these many vessels was the beginning of commerce with the outside world. Merchant ships brought goods to stores that were established to serve the needs of calling vessels and foreigners who were settling in the Islands.

As long as this tip of the Polynesian triangle was isolated from the rest of the world, Hawaiians were a healthy people. They had a good climate, all the fish they wanted to catch, and the food they cultivated on land. They had land sports and swimming, canoeing, and surfing. Communicable diseases such as venereal disease, tuberculosis, cholera, measles, and smallpox were unknown until explorers and adventurers brought them. These diseases took a heavy toll of a population that had no immunity.

The waning of the whaling industry coincided with the establishment of sugar-cane plantations—but where could the necessary labor be found? The native population had been severely reduced by disease; even so, Hawaiians did not take kindly to working in cane fields. The planters had to look elsewhere. Beginning in 1852, thousands of field workers came in successive migrations—Chinese, Portuguese, Japanese, Puerto Ricans, a few Spaniards and Russians, and finally Filipinos in the 1930's and 1940's.

These imported laborers were mostly young unmarried men. They lived in racially separated camps on the plantations. At the expiration of their contracts many settled in Honolulu and in the course of time on all the islands descendants were born of racially mixed unions.

THE COMING OF THE MISSIONARIES

The development of the Hawaiian Islands was greatly influenced by the missionaries sent out from Boston by the American Board of Commissioners for Foreign Missions. The first company arrived in 1820, the last of twelve companies in 1848. Their descendants have distinguished themselves in the professions, as land owners, and as entrepreneurs in industry and commerce. The first company was instructed:

You are to aim at nothing short of covering those Islands with fruitful fields and pleasant dwellings, and schools and churches; of raising up the whole people to an elevated state of Christian civilization . . . to obtain an adequate knowledge of the language of the people; to make them acquainted with letters; to give them the Bible with skill to read it.[4]

These missionaries, men and women, dedicated to the elevation of the natives of the Sandwich Islands, found upon their arrival that a very different caliber of foreigners had preceded them and had already sown seeds of social corruption with which they would have to battle. This was particularly evident in the immorality resulting from grogshops and saloons that lined the waterfront during the influx of traders and whalers. The next chapter tells of means taken by the missionaries to meet this social problem.

A Bit of Background 7

[1] Bryan, Edwin H., Jr. *Ancient Hawaiian Life* (Honolulu: Reprint from "Books about Hawaii," Honolulu Advertiser, 1950).

[2] Hawaii, Maui, Kahoolawe, Lanai, Molokai, Oahu, Niihau, and Kauai. All but Kahoolawe are inhabited.

[3] On March 12, 1959 President Dwight D. Eisenhower signed the bill which authorized the admission of Hawaii as the 50th state of the United States of America. If the people of Hawaii approve statehood at a plebiscite to be held June 27, 1959 the governor of Hawaii will so certify to the President of the United States who will issue a proclamation admitting Hawaii as a state.

[4] *Instructions of the Prudential Committee of the American Board of Commissioners for Foreign Missions to the Sandwich Islands Mission* (Lahainaluna: Press of the Mission Seminary, 1838).

LITERATURE REVIEWED (Chapter I)

Buck, Peter H. *Vikings of the Sunrise* (Philadelphia: J. B. Lippincott Co., 1938).

Kuykendall, Ralph S. *The Hawaiian Kingdom 1778–1854: Foundation and Transformation* (Honolulu: Honolulu Star-Bulletin, 1938).

———. *The Hawaiian Kingdom 1854–1874* (Honolulu: University of Hawaii Press, 1953).

Kuykendall, Ralph S., and Day, A. Grove. *Hawaii: A History from Polynesian Kingdom to American Commonwealth* (New York: Prentice-Hall, Inc., 1948).

II

Stranger's Friend Society

(Period included: 1852–1952)

In any newly opened country, means for combating social ills introduced by unscrupulous foreigners inevitably follow those established in older civilizations for meeting comparable problems. This is true also of services established to meet the needs of a growing or changing population. The missionaries sent to the Hawaiian Islands by the American Board of Commissioners for Foreign Missions were particularly concerned about the immorality resulting from grogshops and saloons along the water front. As a result of their efforts the American Seamen's Friend Society of New York appointed the Reverend John Diell to work in Honolulu.[1] He arrived with his wife in 1833.

SEAMEN'S BETHEL

With materials contributed by friendly shipowners and land granted by King Kamehameha III, the Seamen's Bethel was erected where King Street intersects what is still called Bethel Street.

Mr. Diell had been advised to build as near the beach as possible as "every square foot was covered with grass roofs of dwellings and grogshops." The building, long since gone, included a chapel, reading rooms, and Mr. Diell's study, open at all times for conferences with seamen. In addition to the large number of sailors in Honolulu, there were two hundred resident foreigners, exclusive of missionaries. Mr. Diell felt it his duty to minister to the resident foreigners as well as to the sailors. In 1837 he had established the Oahu Bethel Church, the first church for foreigners in Honolulu.[2] On his return voyage to America in 1841, Mr. Diell died of tuberculosis, perhaps contracted from those to whom he had ministered. He was

8

succeeded by the Reverend Samuel Chenery Damon, who arrived in Honolulu with his bride in 1842.[3]

Mr. Damon's report of 1851 reflects the rapid growth of the whaling industry—some 15,000 sailors, subjects of various nations, had come into port. By that time the United States, Great Britain, and France had established hospitals for their sick seamen but there were other nationals for whom no comparable provision had been made and among them were men who needed counsel, friendship, and admonition against intemperance; there were visits to be made to deserters and mutineers in prison, ministrations to the sick and dying, and letters to write. Chaplain Damon needed help.

STRANGER'S FRIEND SOCIETY—1852

Thus it was that, in 1852, the Stranger's Friend Society, still extant, took shape at a meeting in the home of the Mr. and Mrs. Damon in Chaplain Lane.[4] It is said to be the oldest charitable organization west of the Rocky Mountains. Fifty-two "ladies" signed the constitution which started them "on their mission of love to the sick and destitute and strangers within our gates." The following is from the *Friend,* July 1852:

> It affords us unfeigned pleasure to announce that the ladies of Honolulu have associated themselves into a society to aid the sick and destitute stranger. The necessity of such an association has long been felt. Repeatedly have instances occurred when aid has been cheerfully rendered but for the want of some efficient and responsible organization much good has been neglected which might easily have been accomplished. Those ladies of Honolulu have become interested in the enterprise whose benevolence and capability are a sure pledge that it will succeed. The term "stranger" will not be narrowed down to signify only a select few, but it is intended that charity shall spread wide her mantle. We have bespoke for the sick sailor a berth, and feel confident that his case will always be attended to whenever the foreign consuls in Honolulu do not make provision for him.
>
> We have heard it rumoured that soon the members of the Society will invite the gentlemen to a tea party for the purpose of commencing the Society's usefulness with a full treasury.

Today this language sounds quaint, but it is in keeping with an era when causes and reforms were motivating forces. Beneficiaries of the Stranger's Friend Society were spoken of as proteges, and, following the philosophy of that time, decisions were made according to the "worthiness" of the one seeking help. This was not always of a monetary nature. For example, in 1856, "the ladies met at the Sailors' Home [successor to the Seamen's Bethel] to assist in making up the bed linen for the rooms then ready for occupation . . . it was hard for anyone to get sewing done and bachelors, especially, were thankful to get the Society to do even their mending." The ladies were not to be taken advantage of, however. On one occasion "several young men hired a carriage which unfortunately they smashed, and having no money to pay damages they were incarcerated in the Fort [the prison in those days, situated at the foot of Fort Street]. They applied to the Stranger's Friend Society to get them out of durance vile by paying their fine, but had to be told that the Society was not founded to treat such wounds." [5]

Support

In its early years the support of the Stranger's Friend Society was by special contributions as well as membership dues. Today it is supported chiefly by the interest from the investments given or bequeathed by philanthropists of bygone years. In an old iron box, such as was commonly used for securities before the days of banks and trust companies, is the following letter written in longhand, dated February 28, 1881.

Mrs. S. C. Damon
President of the Stranger's Friend Society
Dear Madam:
    As we today open business in our new store, we feel that the most appropriate thing, is to write our first check in the new building, in favour of the society of which you are the head.
                                        Yours very truly
                                        LEWERS AND COOKE [6]

Headquarters

So far as is known the Stranger's Friend Society has never had an office or a salaried official. In keeping with the spirit of a bygone age and a much smaller population, meetings were held in the homes of members, usually the president of the society. In recent years meetings have been held in Diocesan House, St. Andrew's Cathedral Parish.

PURPOSES OF THE SOCIETY

The Stranger's Friend Society was not incorporated until 1891. Its purposes were: (1) to secure needed and proper aid for the destitute and suffering without regard to their nationality or religious belief; (2) to provide friendly visitors who shall render personal service, give suitable counsel, provide adequate and necessary relief in all cases of need brought to the notice of this society; and (3) to relieve poverty and distress, sickness and suffering by social and sanitary reforms, and by inculcating and encouraging ideas and habits of self-control and self-support.

The Stranger's Friend Society, as noted previously, was organized to counteract untoward social conditions brought about by the influx of traders and whalers mentioned in the previous chapter. The whaling industry had by now come to an end, but social and health needs continued.

"Sanitary reforms" were included in the incorporated purposes of 1891, notwithstanding the fact that the Board of Health had been in existence since 1850,[7] two years prior to the founding of the Stranger's Friend Society. The inclusion of sanitary reforms may have been motivated by the memory of smallpox epidemics during the 1850's and 1860's. This clause has never been eliminated from the charter of the society.

The Sick, A Dominant Interest

The Stranger's Friend Society was founded in a prescientific era, when only the poor or transients would go to a hospital when ill. The Queen's Hospital, the first general hospital in Hawaii, was not opened until 1860. It was natural, therefore, for the Stranger's Friend Society to become interested in the sick poor and the sick stranger.

This interest was strengthened by four endowed beds in The Queen's Hospital. In 1891 Mr. Charles R. Bishop[8] endowed a bed for $5,000 and in 1895 three more for a total of $18,000—the beds "to be always of superior quality in all respects, though plain and strong." They were first known as the Bishop Beds, later as the Stranger's Friend Society beds, Mr. Bishop having put them "at the disposal and under the control, subject to the rules of the Hospital or the President, for the time being, of the Stranger's Friend Society of Honolulu, so long as such Society shall exist." [9]

These four endowed beds and the allocation of patients to them represented something tangible about which the Stranger's Friend Society could function. This was particularly true when, in 1923, the Hospital Flower Society [10] established social service in The Queen's Hospital. It became routine for the Social Service Department to screen referrals for all endowed beds, including those of the Stranger's Friend Society.

The director of the Social Service Department at The Queen's Hospital furnished quarterly reports to the society. Concealing identity of patients by the use of initials, a succinct statement was given of each beneficiary, the nature of the illness, and reasons for granting an endowed bed or any other assistance. All endowed beds are in wards. Occasionally the Stranger's Friend Society would pay the difference between ward and private room rates when an attending physician thought that, for medical reasons, a private room was indicated. Also at the request of the Social Service Department, the society would pay for convalescent care.

However, the interest of the Stranger's Friend Society has gone beyond the allocation of patients to endowed beds and beyond The Queen's Hospital. The society will advance comparatively large sums of money, if convinced by a case history that this should be done. For instance, there was the case of a sensitive teen-age girl whose teeth needed straightening. Her parents, once fashionable and wealthy residents of a mainland city, had separated, dissipated their fortune, and broken up their home. The mother had sold her jewels and brought her daughter to Hawaii. Later the mother died, leaving her adolescent daughter without funds. It seemed important to the caseworker that the young girl's teeth be straightened, and this was done, the Stranger's Friend Society paying the $300 bill. Years later, after she had grown up and moved away from the Islands, she wrote the society a letter of deep appreciation.

For years the society has sent a monthly contribution of $25 to the Director of Social Service at The Queen's Hospital to be spent at the discretion of the director; it still makes a generous contribution each year toward Christmas cheer. There comes to mind the touching contentment in the face of an elderly English lady in reduced circumstances when given a

Kamehameha I, first monarch of the Hawaiian Islands, Birth C 1758; accession 1795; death May 8, 1819. (Bernice P. Bishop Museum photo.)

Liliuokalani, last monarch of the Hawaiian Islands. Birth September 2, 1838; accession January 29, 1891; deposed January 17, 1893; death November 11, 1917. Photo taken in 1891. (Robert E. Van Dyke Collection.)

Sanford Ballard Dole, president of Provincial Government January 17, 1893 to July 4, 1894; president of Republic of Hawaii July 4, 1894 to June 14, 1900; governor of Territory of Hawaii June 14, 1900 to November 23, 1903. Birth April 23, 1844; death June 9, 1926. Photo taken in 1900.

Above: Home of the Reverend Samuel Chenery Damon. An adobe house built by his predecessor, the Reverend John Diell, in 1833. No longer existent. (Hawaiian Evangelical Association photo.)
Below: Fort Street in 1856.

Honolulu Harbor—1882

City of Honolulu in the 1950's. (The Honolulu Advertiser photo.)

new black dress at Christmas. Her husband had not long since died and to her this outward symbol of mourning was an essential.

GENERAL COMMUNITY SERVICE

The Stranger's Friend Society does not put its entire emphasis on the sick. In an old ledger is a sheet entitled "persons assisted out of the country"; one of these was a blind man persuaded to return to California, "as he was encroaching on the newsboys." Sometimes Islanders were brought back. One of these was a woman deserted on the mainland by her husband. The Stranger's Friend Society not only paid the return passage of this mother and her child, but also assumed the cost of her training as a teacher. When she was able to do so she refunded the money spent in her behalf by the society.

For many decades the Stranger's Friend Society was the only social agency in Hawaii; it thus helped many who were not strangers. Even today well-established agencies occasionally request supplementary aid from the society.

In the last quarter century the Stranger's Friend Society has widened its program to include community projects. In the 1920's it cooperated with the Associated Charities and the Department of Public Instruction in a nutritional experiment by paying the cost of thousands of bottles of milk sent to public schools, organizations, and families. It helped the Medical Social Service Association in the early years of its development by paying the salary of an assistant and has also contributed toward the training of medical social workers. With a contribution of $500 it helped to establish, in 1938, the Hawaii Medical Service Association. It also gave $1,000 toward the founding of the Maunalani Hospital and Convalescent Home, opened in 1950.

In 1945 the charter was renewed with no amendments to the original three purposes, but with a fourth added, viz., "to engage in such other charitable or benevolent activities as may from time to time be considered advisable." [11]

THE FUTURE

A hundred years have gone by since "the ladies of Honolulu united on a mission of love to the sick and destitute strangers within our gates." Long since have the grass-covered huts and

grogshops on the waterfront given place to substantial buildings, and long since have we had a Department of Health
alert against the introduction of infectious diseases. Over the
years, too, many private and governmental social agencies have
been established in Hawaii to aid the sick and destitute, including the stranger. As accredited organizations have come
into being the need has diminished for the Stranger's Friend
Society as originally established.

Marking the hundredth anniversary of the Stranger's Friend
Society in 1952, a committee of three members was appointed
by its president to study the question as to whether or not the
society had served its day and should remain in being. To
date the question remains unanswered. The roots of an association so long established grow deep.

¹ Ethel M. Damon, "The Seamen's Bethel at Honolulu," *The Friend,* June
1933, p. 124.
² *Ibid.,* p. 127.
³ *Ibid.*
⁴ *Ibid.,* p. 128.
⁵ Minutes of the Society.
⁶ A mercantile establishment founded in 1852 by Christopher H. Lewers, a
cabinetmaker, born in Dublin, Ireland. The firm is now one of Honolulu's
largest retailers of building materials.
⁷ Ruth Ackland, *A Century of Public Health in Hawaii,* Department of
Health, Territory of Hawaii, August 1949, p. 2.
⁸ Mr. Bishop, whose wife Bernice Pauahi was a direct descendant of Kamehameha I, was one of the founders of the Bank of Bishop Company, now known
as the Bishop National Bank at Honolulu.
⁹ *Extracts from Minutes of The Queen's Hospital,* March 7, 1891, August 10,
1889; extracts from a letter from George W. Smith, president, The Queen's
Hospital, to Mrs. E. W. Jordan, president, Stranger's Friend Society, Nov. 8,
1916.
¹⁰ Subsequently the Medical Social Service Association of Hawaii.
¹¹ Stranger's Friend Society, Treasurer's Office, Territory of Hawaii; renewed
charter in 1945.

III

Hawaiian Humane Society[1]
(Period included: 1883–1935)

The *Hawaiian Gazette* of July 25, 1883,[2] announced that on July 23 a number of representative people in the Hawaiian Kingdom, including "a generous sprinkling of the fair sex," met in the YMCA[3] to discuss the formation of a humane society, patterned after the American Society for the Prevention of Cruelty to Dumb Beasts. The group decided that its activities would also include the protection of children. Officers were elected, with the Honorable J. S. Walker as president. The following month it was reported that 350 people had joined the Hawaiian Humane Society and that a constitution and by-laws had been adopted. No further mention of the group is found until 1894, when Helen Kinau Wilder, whose love for animals stemmed from early childhood, issued through the newspapers a rousing call to a meeting for the organization of the Humane Society. It was reported that "the hall was crowded with the best people eager and ready to enter upon work."

The First Policewoman

But Helen Wilder found "the best people" were not sufficiently aroused, due, she thought, to the members' disinclination to offend their neighbors or to appear in court. For two years the Society remained more or less dormant. Then, when Helen Wilder was granted power to arrest, it sprang to renewed life. As president of the Hawaiian Humane Society, she was commissioned in 1897 by the Marshall of the Republic[4] as a special police constable, thus becoming the first policewoman in the Hawaiian Islands. We know from the few historical facts to be found, and from those who remember her, that animals, especially horses, were Helen Wilder's principal concern, and

15

that she was not loath to exert her police authority in their behalf.

Support

In the early decades of the Humane Society, support came easily. Members included persons of leisure and means. Sizable contributions and bequests were made by interested persons, and at various times the society received appropriations from the City and County of Honolulu. Bazaars and sales of various sorts brought in money for special needs. The society was a charter member of the United Welfare Fund,[5] but support from this organization was withdrawn in 1935 when children were excluded from the Society's program.

Administration

The Hawaiian Humane Society was governed by a mixed board of men and women. Though for many years its staff consisted of one woman, known as the agent, members of the organization gave many hours in voluntary service to children and animals, according to their interest.

Headquarters

In its initial years the Humane Society had no official headquarters. Honolulu was a comparatively small community in those days; this permitted the agent to function from her home. Later, after the Associated Charities was founded,[6] the two organizations had offices in the same building.

ANIMALS OR CHILDREN?

Among the members of the Humane Society there were sharp divergences of interest concerning animals and children. In 1908, for example, the discussion waxed hot as to the appropriateness of bracketing children with dogs and horses. Some members were opposed; others declared that unless children were included they would withdraw from the Society. The latter won, and both animals and children were equally the concern of the Society for many years.

Miss Wilder resigned in 1908. In addition to her regular duties she had initiated "Humane Week," with its emphasis on kindly treatment of animals and had edited and published the *Humane Educator*. She was succeeded by Miss Rose Davison, the first paid agent of the society.

Miss Davison also was commissioned a special police officer, and her chief interest, like that of her predecessor, seems to have been animals. Those who knew her remember vividly the tall, tailored Rose Davison as she drove about in her buggy, or rode her horse, inspecting stables and barns, taking horses and mules out of shafts, compelling owners to drop checkreins or to lighten loads on hills. She displayed her police badge at any sign of resistance to her orders. Miss Davison died in 1913 and was succeeded by Miss Lucy K. Ward, who previously worked as a volunteer for the Society.

Miss Ward also acquired a reputation for getting things done. She would respond to a call in behalf of a child or an animal, be it ever so late or far away. Miss Ward also was commissioned a special police officer. Police commissions were not restricted to the employed agents of the organization. According to the report of the Hawaiian Humane Society for 1914–15, twenty-five or more members were issued badges as legally authorized humane officers.

Though the Hawaiian Humane Society was established quite as much for the protection of animals as of children, the emphasis in the succeeding pages will be on children.

The chief concern of one board member was for little Japanese girls playing in the streets with younger brothers or sisters strapped to their backs, a custom in Japanese families of that time. This director of the Humane Society would have her coachman stop the carriage to pick up little girls and take them to their homes. Here she would talk, in pidgin English to their mothers, explaining the possible bad results to young backs allowed to carry such heavy burdens, and to the babies' legs, which would become bowed by the position in which the babies were carried. It is easy to imagine the feelings of these overworked mothers as they were admonished by one who had no such problem.

SOCIAL ACTION

As stated above, the Hawaiian Humane Society and the Associated Charities shared headquarters after 1899. It became the custom for the Associated Charities, and its successors in name, to refer to Miss Ward cases needing court action. Her

services were sought also by the Police Department and the
Juvenile Court, as well as by nongovernmental organizations.
All this helped to stimulate an interest in the need for adequate laws for the protection of children: "laws that would
prevent little girls' selling newspapers before the dawn and
in the evening"; statutes that would prevent the employment
of boys as helpers on ice wagons, "starting at 4 or 5 A.M. and
not returning until 11 or 12, [the boys] being in wet clothes
for six, seven, or eight hours." In one such group four cases
of tuberculosis were found.

Honolulu was still in the preprofessional era of social work.
What was lacking in technique was made up by the use of
authority in getting a question settled—at least to outward
appearances. The Humane Society reported as an achievement
twelve enforced marriages during 1914–15.

A story told in those years concerned an unmarried girl
expecting a baby, in the days when it was of prime importance
"to give the baby a name," even if this entailed an unsuitable
marriage. This girl's mother was so distressed because of the
threatened family disgrace that she sought the help of the
Humane Society to force the young man to marry her daughter.
Although the girl's mother took ill and died, the marriage took
place—beside her coffin.

Nothing daunted the dedicated women in the early decades
of this century. In their annual report for 1920 we learn that
three directors of the Hawaiian Humane Society were paying
for the upkeep (in a private home) of a clinic in which children were treated for venereal disease. The Children's Hospital
has now long had a communicable disease ward to which children with venereal disease can be admitted. Both The Queen's
and St. Francis hospitals are similarly equipped.

INCORPORATION AND FUNCTIONS

The early eleemosynary institutions in Hawaii were not incorporated until years after their organization. The Hawaiian
Humane Society did not take this step until 1920. The purposes of the society relating to children as set forth in their
by-laws included:

Provisions to effect means for the prevention of cruelty to children
throughout the Territory of Hawaii, to provide temporary aid and/or
permanent homes for vagrant, destitute and exposed children and

to provide for such children any other and further relief as may be advisable, requisite, or necessary to rescue them from moral ruin. To secure the enactment of adequate legislation for the prevention of cruelty to children . . . and the better enforcement of the present laws relating to such subjects. To encourage and promote investigation and research relating to the subject of the humane treatment of children.

Between 1920 and 1923, branches of the Hawaiian Humane Society were established on the islands of Hawaii, Kauai, and Maui. In 1929 the by-laws were revised and simplified to "provide effective means for the prevention of cruelty to children throughout the Territory of Hawaii."

In 1923, when the Shriners [7] became interested in establishing in Hawaii services for crippled children, Mrs. Wade Warren Thayer, a member of the Humane Society, took responsibility for locating crippled children throughout the Territory —150 of them.

NEED FOR COMMUNITY ORGANIZATION

As the city grew so did social problems and, with them, confusion as to agency function. Miss Ward was accepting referrals that were neither animals nor children. Not infrequently she was asked by court or agency to help in adult cases, particularly those of Hawaiians. She herself was part-Hawaiian and spoke the language fluently. Once, in response to a call, she rowed over to Sand Island to see an aged Hawaiian couple. The man had been King Kalakaua's coachman and the woman a servant of his queen, Kapiolani. It was reported that this man was an alcoholic and was neglecting his wife, who was blind. Miss Ward brought them back to the Old Plantation (the Ward family home) where they were given a cottage in the grounds and were supported with the aid of the Social Service Bureau, successor to the Associated Charities.

In 1926 Lucy Ward tendered her resignation. This news was received with consternation, particularly among the Hawaiians. A petition signed by 500 people, chiefly Hawaiians, was presented to the agency by Mayor Charles N. Arnold and Mrs. Julia K. Smyth.[8]

At that time Mrs. J. Platt Cooke, president of the Humane Society, spoke emphatically about its prodigious growth, the heavy load Miss Ward was carrying (in 1926 the caseload for

adults and children was 6,609 as against 207 in 1915), and the
need for reorganization. Pressure from concerned people and
suggestions for reorganization influenced Lucy Ward to continue in office seven years longer. In 1933 she resigned [9] and
Mrs. Clorinda Lucas became executive officer of the Humane
Society.

In her first report Mrs. Lucas drew attention to the need of
differentiation in agency function and the avoidance of duplication; also the need of referring to other agencies cases more
properly belonging to them. For example, the Humane Society
spent several years getting a law enacted in 1933 [10] command-
ing children, to the extent of their financial ability, to support
their aged parents who were in need.

In the same year (1933) forty-one bastardy cases were referred to the Humane Society. Mrs. Lucas considered these
the responsibility of the Court of Domestic Relations. "Just
because it had grown that way" was no reason why confusion
should continue.

One other significant thing in Mrs. Lucas's report of 1933
was the large percentage of Hawaiians and part-Hawaiians (55
per cent of the caseload) who applied for service. This is
quite understandable; they went where they could express
themselves in their own language, if necessary, and to their
own people. Undoubtedly this was one reason why the Society
had come to assume activities that concerned neither children
nor animals.

During her tenure Mrs. Lucas had several assistants, one
of whom was paid by the Police Department and all of whom
carried police badges. It is no longer the custom for social
workers to be so armed. The time came when a knowledge of
the Hawaiian language was not a prime factor, though it is
still desirable, in helping Hawaiians. What was more important was a growing awareness of professional casework and the
decentralization of functions.

DELETION OF CHILD WELFARE FUNCTIONS (1935)

Chapter IX ("Children's Service Association") details the
action taken to reduce the growing confusion among social
agencies. Suffice it to say here that in January and February,
1935, a study was made of children's organizations in Honolulu

by the Child Welfare League of America, Inc., under the direction of Mr. C. C. Carstens, its executive director.
This analysis proved that the Humane Society was dealing
with many forms of social work that should ordinarily be the
function of the Social Service Bureau, the Court of Domestic
Relations, or the Juvenile Court. Mr. Carstens realized how
tradition and knowledge of laws concerning children had given
the society prestige. He therefore recommended the establishment of a Children's Service Association and in it a Department
of Child Protection to which would be referred complaints
regarding cruelty and abuse of children. On September 1,
1935, the Hawaiian Humane Society, approving the recommendation of the Child Welfare League of America, Inc., transferred its children's work to the newly-organized Children's
Service Association and from that time devoted its attention
solely to animals.

Recognizing the bond between children and animals, the
Humane Society provides talks and movies for children and
encourages them to visit the well-kept kennels in the grounds
of the Humane Society on Waialae Avenue, or the bird sanc-
tuary which was established in 1944 in the adjacent grounds.

[1] Information not otherwise documented was obtained from the records of
the Hawaiian Humane Society.

[2] "The Hawaiian Humane Society," *Hawaiian Gazette*, July 25, 1883, p. 3,
col. 4; Public Archives of Hawaii.

[3] The Young Men's Christian Association in Honolulu was organized at a
meeting of philanthropic and civic-minded friends in 1869 at the home of
Mr. Peter Cushman Jones. For some thirteen years the Association functioned
in rooms leased in the headquarters, respectively, of the Sailors Home and the
Lyceum. In 1882 the cornerstone of the YMCA's first building was laid at the
southwest corner of Hotel and Alakea streets. In 1910 the Y moved across
the street to its newly erected and larger building at the northwest corner of
the same streets. In 1944 the Association sold this building and moved to the
Nuuanu Branch of the YMCA (established in 1917) on upper Fort Street.
Headquarters remained there until 1951, when the new Central Branch of the
Young Men's Christian Association was opened at 401 Atkinson Drive. In
addition to the Central Branch this building is the headquarters for all branches
of the YMCA in the Metropolitan area.

[4] The Republic of Hawaii (1894–98) followed the overthrow of the monarchy
and the end of the Provisional Government. Hawaii was annexed to the United
States in 1898.

[5] The United Welfare Fund was organized in 1919 by the Honolulu Chamber
of Commerce for the purpose of bringing all private money-raising drives into
one campaign in an endeavor to save time, effort, and expense. The Fund was
incorporated in 1938. In 1943 it changed its name to the current one of

Honolulu Community Chest. (Information obtained at the office of the Honolulu Community Chest.)

[6] In 1899. See chapter V.

[7] A Masonic order founded in the early 1920's originally for social programs. It became interested in helping crippled children.

[8] Mother of Mabel L. Smyth, who was among the earliest Island-born women to be trained as public health nurses. The Mabel L. Smyth Memorial Building is dedicated to her memory.

[9] Lucy K. Ward died March 20, 1954.

[10] *T.H. Session Laws* (1933), Act 66, p. 62.

IV

Kindergarten and Children's Aid Association[1]
(Period included: 1892-1951)

There remain in Honolulu a few historic landmarks that have not been obliterated in the name of progress; structures that, through their associations with the past, have acquired over the years a mellowness and serenity. One such building stands at the head of Mission Lane in close proximity to Kawaiahao Church, a companion of similar historic interest. On a sign at its entrance are painted these words:

OFFICE
KINDERGARTEN AND CHILDREN'S AID
ASSOCIATION. 880 MISSION LANE.
ADOBE SCHOOL HOUSE ERECTED 1835.
VISITORS WELCOME

Built over a century ago for beginners in education, it seems fitting that this adobe house should still be the headquarters of beginners. In the early days, the majority of the pupils were adult Hawaiians, whereas today they are children of varied ancestry. The property now belongs to the Kawaiahao Church, which rents it to the Kindergarten and Children's Aid Association for one dollar a year. The activities of The Association, particularly in its early years, were not limited to kindergartens, but included child welfare in general.

Kindergarten teaching was introduced into the United States from Germany in 1848.[2] By 1891 it was well established in California[3] and was therefore undoubtedly known to philanthropic persons of Honolulu familiar with that state.

The first kindergarten in Hawaii was started for Chinese children in 1892 by Francis W. Damon, son of the Reverend Samuel Chenery Damon. This minister's son, though not

23

ordained, had a lively interest in missions, particularly the
Chinese Mission Church on Fort Street, long since gone. He
may have got his introduction to kindergartens while serving as chargé d'affaires in Germany in 1878.[4] His concern for
Chinese children may have been inspired by his marriage to
the daughter of the Reverend and Mrs. Andrew Happer, missionaries in Canton, China.

Although Mr. Damon had taken the lead in founding kindergartens in the Islands by opening the first one, a similar interest
was developing in the Woman's Board of Missions of the Pacific,
in Honolulu. In 1894 the Board added a Kindergarten Department to the organization.[5] This group had general supervision over kindergartens that had been, or were being, established. A Portuguese kindergarten was opened on Miller Street
in 1893 by the Reverend Antonio V. Soares. In the same year,
separate kindergartens were established for Hawaiians, Japanese, and "foreign" children (mainly Caucasian), who did not
belong to the other racial groups. In 1897 the first plantation
kindergarten was opened at Ewa Plantation.

Incorporation

In 1895 the Kindergarten Department of the Woman's Board
of Missions was incorporated under the name of Free Kindergarten and Children's Aid Association of the Hawaiian Islands.[6]
Its object was "the care and maintenance of existing Free
Kindergarten Schools,[7] the establishment and care of such other
Kindergartens as said Association shall deem necessary throughout the Hawaiian Islands . . . and for such aid and assistance
to children as may be deemed necessary and proper from time
to time." [8]

The incorporators were women well known for their cause-
inspired efforts. One of the best known was Mrs. Harriet Castle
Coleman. Through Mrs. Coleman's interest the Castle family
contributed largely to the development of kindergartens.

Support

Obtaining support was apparently not a difficult matter.
Several kindergartens were founded by members or friends
of the Association as memorials to children who had died.
Generous contributions were given for specific purposes, or
came as bequests from estates of interested persons. In addition, there were membership dues and numerous fund-raising

projects for special programs. The Free Kindergarten and Children's Aid Association was a charter member of the United Welfare Fund founded in 1919.

Administration

The Kindergarten and Children's Aid Association has always been directed by a board made up of women; for many years these women were closely associated with the missionaries. The first superintendent of kindergartens was a trained worker, Miss Hannah Eastman, who came from California in 1894 to superintend kindergartens and to conduct a training school.[9] The value of a training school, as expressed by a board member, was to help "waifs" and to give Hawaiian girls "an opportunity for community service and also preparation for happy motherhood." Miss Eastman was succeeded in 1896 [10] by Miss Frances Lawrence, who came from the mainland the same year and who served until 1935.[11]

Miss Lawrence was also a trained kindergartner, but her training was incidental compared to her worth as a person, with exceptional qualifications for the profession of her choice. She was a born leader with a wide, kindly vision. No important movement concerning children of her day was without the participation or the leadership of Frances Lawrence.

Headquarters

The first headquarters of the early kindergartens was in Queen Emma Hall, formerly Rooke House (no longer extant), at the corner of Nuuanu Avenue and Beretania Street.[12]

In the beginning, children were grouped according to racial ancestry, the Hawaiians and Japanese in separate rooms on the first floor and the "foreign" children on the second floor. In those years, when English was not commonly spoken by the immigrant population, grouping children according to racial background made it easier to handle them and to find assistants who could understand them. Segregation, too, resulted from the fact that migrants to a new country tend in the earlier years to congregate in particular areas with those of the same ancestry and with whom they share common mores and speech. In Honolulu the Chinese lived in what came to be known as Chinatown; the Portuguese built their homes at the foot of Punchbowl; and others settled as racial groups in various neighborhoods.

During the plague epidemic of 1900 every house in Honolulu in which the disease occurred had to be burned. One day the fire in Chinatown got beyond control and spread, destroying many of the buildings in the neighborhood of Queen Emma Hall, forcing the Association to find temporary quarters elsewhere. For a time they occupied rooms in the Old Damon Home in Chaplain Lane.

In 1924 the association moved to its permanent home in the adobe house in Mission Lane,[13] mentioned above. In the meantime, kindergartens had been opened in different, more or less congested, sections of the city. Racial segregation was no longer a policy of the association, but for a long time the race of most children attending any kindergarten was the same as the predominant race of its neighborhood. Teachers or assistants were appointed on a racial basis—Chinese, Japanese, Portuguese, and Hawaiian. With progress in acculturation there is no longer need for such differentiation.

RELATED FUNCTIONS

Child Health

In the early years of the Free Kindergarten and Children's Aid Association, there was a growing interest in the health of children. Children were going to school with running noses and sores; many were hungry and often dirty; many needed medical attention. Mrs. Ulrich Thompson, a trained nurse, is accredited as being the first visiting nurse in Hawaii. For ten years, beginning in 1897, Mrs. Thompson visited kindergartens and called on mothers, instructing them "in home nursing, cleanliness and diet," the Oriental diet of that era consisting chiefly of polished rice.

The association was a participating agency in the Nutritional Institute (discussed in the following chapter) conducted in 1922 to combat widespread malnutrition. Largely as a result of the institute, the association developed an intensive nutritional program under the supervision, for some twelve years, of Mrs. Nellie Russell. The Junior League paid Mrs. Russell's salary and supplied volunteers to assist in weighing and measuring the children.

Since tooth decay was prevalent among its charges, the Free Kindergarten and Children's Aid Association opened a dental clinic at headquarters in Mission Lane in 1924. A dental hygienist was employed to clean the children's teeth and chart cavities. At first a number of dentists volunteered their services. The work increased to such an extent, however, that the Association had to employ a part-time dentist who visited the kindergartens in turn with a portable chair. World War II, with its demands on trained personnel, put an end to the association's dental program.

A Children's Home

Another early concern of the association was the need of a home for dependent children. In 1899 the Castle family, having decided to convert into an orphanage their old homestead on King Street (no longer in existence), asked the association to assume the responsibility of management. It was stipulated by the board that "Anglo-Saxons are to be given preference at all times, and for the present, at least, Asiatics are not to be considered." This may seem a strange attitude for a community which today prides itself on racial harmony, but that was in 1899. Racial harmony and mutual respect grow slowly. They are still growing.

With the decision of the Castle family to convert their old homestead on King Street into an orphanage, Mary (Mrs. S. N.) Castle, the widowed mother of the family, moved into a new and spacious residence in upper Manoa Valley. After her death the Samuel N. and Mary Castle Foundation offered it to the Association. From 1908 to 1923 the Castle Home, high in Manoa Valley, sheltered up to thirty children. However, it proved too expensive a project; with arrangements made for transferring the children elsewhere, the Castle Home reverted to the Samuel N. and Mary Castle Foundation in 1923 and was subsequently sold. The association did not establish another boarding institution, but takes credit for the passage in 1913 of an act providing for the maintenance of a shelter home (later known as the Detention Home) for children awaiting final disposition of their cases in the Juvenile Court.[14]

By this time the association had spread its activities to "include juvenile delinquency, child labor laws and schools or homes for the mentally and physically unfit." They also introduced supervised play into Honolulu. It was largely due to their success as pioneers in this movement that the Board of Supervisors of the City and County of Honolulu assumed full responsibility (1922) for the management of playgrounds.[15]

Castle Kindergarten

To avoid confusion a digression is made here regarding an independent kindergarten. In 1900 the Castle family founded the Henry and Dorothy Memorial, generally known as the Castle Kindergarten, in memory of Henry Castle and his four-year old daughter, who were drowned at sea. It also was a free kindergarten but, though a friendly relationship was maintained with the older organization, the Castle Kindergarten had its own board of directors and was governed as a separate entity. Because it could afford better equipment, it attracted the children of a growing merchant class and gained the reputation of being "swank."

COMMUNITY ORGANIZATION

In the last chapter attention was drawn to the confusion and overlapping of function in Honolulu when programs and social agencies were established without adequate over-all organization. An awareness of this problem led to the establishment of the United Welfare Fund in 1919 and of the Honolulu Council of Social Agencies in 1927.[16] The concepts of these agencies are based on suitability of program, avoidance of duplication, and the need for co-ordination.

When these concepts were applied to kindergartens in 1940, the Castle Kindergarten mentioned above was dissolved and the trustees of the Samuel N. and Mary Castle Foundation voted $100,000 toward the building of a kindergarten-nursery school to be affiliated with Teachers' College, University of Hawaii.[17]

By 1942 the Free Kindergarten and Children's Aid Association had worked out, with allied agencies, a co-ordinated program, whereby they are drawing as needed upon the University of Hawaii Extension Service for help in teaching mothers what, and how, to cook; upon the Bureaus of Nutrition, Maternal and Child Health, and Mental Hygiene in the Department of Health; and the Strong-Carter Dental Clinic. They also make referrals to the Child and Family Service and to the Department of Public Welfare.

WORLD WAR II

Following the Pearl Harbor attack on December 7, 1941, private and public schools were closed for eight weeks and their classrooms and buildings were converted to war purposes. Daily, at the headquarters of the Free Kindergarten and Children's Aid Association in Mission Lane, the staff met to roll bandages.

The superintendent, Miss Mary Musgrove, who had only recently come to Hawaii, has spoken of the impression she received from being with women of all nationalities, including that of the enemy, rolling bandages and singing Hawaiian songs as they rolled. It was a hectic time for children, though, and she was glad, she said, when the schools were reopened and they could feel the security of a familiar environment in an unsettled world.

DAY CARE CENTERS

High wages, along with patriotic appeals, enticed so many mothers into war work, with consequent neglect of their children, that the association, in addition to its kindergarten activities, opened day care centers in several kindergartens. Little children were brought daily to be tended during the hours their mothers were at work. Day care centers have become an established function of the Kindergarten and Children's Aid Association. Although primarily they are for children of working mothers, the association will accept children for other sufficient reasons; for example, if the mother is ill and the father is working, or if a child lives in a neighborhood where there are no playmates and he needs to be one of a group.

As the general economic level in Hawaii rose and parents became more cognizant of benefits derived from kindergartens, they were charged accordingly, so in 1949 the word "free" was deleted from the association's name. If a request is made by a social agency, however, the small monthly fee is reduced or eliminated.

KINDERGARTENS INTRODUCED INTO THE PUBLIC SCHOOLS

The history of kindergartens in Hawaii is the story of what was accomplished by women of a preprofessional era in child welfare. One who is still remembered as an example of indefatigable perseverance for a cause is Mrs. Francis Mills Swanzy. Mrs. Swanzy was president of the Free Kindergarten and Children's Aid Association from 1915 to 1934. Her chief aim was the establishment of kindergartens in the public schools. She had the security of inherited position and wealth, but any-

one of less courage and will would have given up—four legislative sessions, one after another, refused to enact a law which
would provide for public kindergartens. Mrs. Swanzy and her
associates in the Kindergarten Association presented their cause
over and over again, and thought they had finally won their
battle. The legislature in 1919 provided funds for one public
school kindergarten on each of the major islands, but the experiment was allowed to die after one year's trial.[18]

In 1920 a Federal survey was made of the territorial school
system. The surveyors visited and gave the Free Kindergarten
and Children's Aid Association a high rating, but their recommendation that kindergartens be included in public schools
fell on deaf ears in the legislature.

Mrs. Swanzy continued to hammer away, but it required
a long, slow process of education before both legislators and
the general public accepted the fact that children with a
kindergarten background show a distinct advantage in ad-
justing to the first grade. Patience and determination finally
obtained the enactment of a law in 1943 for the establishment
of kindergartens in public schools.[19] The first twelve proved
so successful that each legislative session since 1943 has added
kindergarten classes. In January 1951 there were 239 located
in public schools throughout the territory. Attendance is not
compulsory, nor are children under five years admitted.

The association still has some kindergartens which will admit children under five years of age, but its program today is
chiefly a combination of kindergarten and day care centers in
various parts of Honolulu, for mothers who work outside the
home. In 1951 the association was conducting five combined
kindergartens and day care centers and one solely for day care.
Minimum age for acceptance is two and one-half years.

In bringing this chapter to a close, one is reminded of a
service rendered by the early kindergartens to the debutantes
of that day. In that era it was the exception, rather than the
rule, for island girls to go to college, and unless they needed
money they did not take jobs. It was a period, too, when
domestic help was both plentiful and cheap, and girls of the
leisure class had little responsibility in the way of household
duties. Until they were married, girls graced their parents'
homes, and drove their mothers by horse and carriage to market
or to make formal calls. They gave parties—riding, swimming,

tennis, and dancing. Taking their sewing, embroidery, or crocheting, the young ladies of Honolulu would spend an afternoon or day with one another. They had picnics, card parties, and tea parties.

Girls of that time, brought up with a sense of *noblesse oblige*, also gave many hours in volunteer service to church or community. This brought them under the dynamic influence of Frances Lawrence, who saw in them potential kindergartners. Some became identified with the association as volunteers; others took the training course leading to salaried positions, beginning at five dollars a month. Some were led to an even greater responsibility such as the direction of a kindergarten. A number of the girls later became valuable board members of the Kindergarten and Children's Aid Association.

The emphasis here on the Kindergarten and Children's Aid Association to the exclusion of the many others established throughout the territory by private schools and churches derives from the fact that the pioneer organization of them all was also a pioneer in the more general field of child welfare.

---

[1] In writing this chapter the author has drawn upon her personal knowledge of the agency, has conferred with those still closely associated with it, and has consulted *A History of the Free Kindergarten and Children's Aid Association of the Hawaiian Islands 1890–1945*, by Charlotte P. Dodge.

[2] Charlotte P. Dodge, *op. cit.*, p. 3.

[3] *Ibid.*

[4] Diplomatic Correspondence, *Special Missions 1877–1900*. Archives of Hawaii.

[5] Dodge, *op. cit.*, p. 51

[6] *Ibid.*, p. 61

[7] In 1949 the word "Free" was deleted.

[8] Dodge, *op. cit.*, p. 62.

[9] *Ibid.*, p. 25.

[10] *Ibid.*, p. 25.

[11] *Ibid.*, p. 56.

[12] Dr. and Mrs. T. C. B. Rooke had been foster parents of Queen Emma.

[13] Dodge, *op. cit.*, p. 54.

[14] *T.H. Session Laws* (1913), Act 68, p. 82.

[15] Dodge, *op. cit.*, p. 37.

[16] Organized in 1927 "to improve Honolulu social work by means of more intelligent teamwork, as the Chamber of Commerce does in the business field." (Information obtained at the office of the Honolulu Council of Social Agencies.)

[17] Benjamin O. Wist. "A Century of Public Education in Hawaii 1840–1940," *Hawaii Educational Review* (Honolulu Star-Bulletin, 1940), p. 170; copy in DPI Library.

[18] *Ibid.*

[19] *T.H. Session Laws* (1943), Act 220, p. 34.

V

Child and Family Service[1]
(Period included: 1899–1950)

The Child and Family Service originated with the founding, in 1899, of its progenitor, the Associated Charities of Hawaii. There was a growing concern in Honolulu about the problem of beggary. Beggars, generally deserting sailors or "black sheep" whose families in home countries had sent them abroad to get rid of them, were making the rounds of various national-group benevolent societies and churches in Honolulu. Relief was duplicated and indiscriminate. Some beggars were getting too much, some too little, and others nothing at all.

This picture was but an echo of similar problems in America and, before that, in Great Britain. In both countries private citizens became interested in a charity organization movement as a means for combating the problem of beggary. Among those in America was Mrs. Lydia P. Williams of Minneapolis. In 1899 Mrs. Williams came on a visit to Honolulu. On March 27 of that year she addressed a representative group of local residents on "the old and the new" in philanthropy: the old was unco-ordinated and indiscriminate giving; the new was giving in accordance with the principles of organized charity.[2]

Mrs. Williams traced the history of philanthropy. This included the first Charity Organization Society, established in London (1869) and the guidance given to the movement by Charles Stewart Loch,[3] as well as the founding of similar societies in America—the first on a city-wide basis being in Buffalo (1877).[4]

Now Mrs. Williams was advising Honolulu organizations to do likewise. She cited three characteristics of organized charity: registration, investigation, and co-operation. She predicted that the new philosophy, or organized charity, would reduce alms-
32

giving by the application of the work test. The belief was general in that day that if a man would work he need not beg.

ASSOCIATED CHARITIES OF HAWAII (1899)

Mrs. Williams' address was the incentive for the "new" in Honolulu. Composed of two members from each of the organizations wishing to affiliate (and wholly or partially engaged in charitable work), the Associated Charities of Hawaii began to function in August 1899. The affiliating members included benevolent societies of foreign groups—British, German, Portuguese, and others—which were established when Hawaii was a kingdom. Besides these national-group organizations there were various churches in the community and the Stranger's Friend Society, all dispensing relief in some form. The Associated Charities was not to displace, but rather to co-ordinate the activities of all these organizations.[5]

Support

At first, considerable support came from affiliated benevolent societies. They depended upon the Associated Charities to make investigations for the purpose of determining the worthiness of persons applying for help. The appropriate society was expected to pay for such aid as was recommended, either temporarily or continuously. If a constituent agency rejected a referral considered "worthy" by the Associated Charities, the latter would assume the obligation, payable out of specially contributed funds at its disposal. If an applicant was a single man, able to work, he was not referred to an affiliate, but employment was found for him if possible; he then had "the choice of working or starving."

Support of the Associated Charities of Hawaii—under various names in succeeding years—was also by contributions from members, from bequests, and by appropriations for specific services from the territorial and county governments. In 1919 it became a charter member of the United Welfare Fund, now the Honolulu Community Chest.

Administration

The first president of the Associated Charities of Hawaii was Governor Sanford B. Dole,[6] who was president for four-

teen years. Sanford Dole is remembered as one who guided
the political crises through the overthrow of the monarchy in
1893, to annexation of the Hawaiian Islands to the United
States in 1898, and the establishment of the territorial government in 1900.[7]

The first manager of the Associated Charities, at an annual
salary of $950, was Mrs. E. F. Berger, who left the Kame-
hameha Girls' School in 1899 to assume the new post. Upon
her appointment she went to the mainland to acquaint herself
with agencies similar to the one she was going to manage in
Honolulu. In 1907 Mrs. Berger resigned from the Associated
Charities to return to the mainland, being succeeded by Mrs.
Alice C. Jordan, the only local resident throughout its long history to hold that position. In her qualifications as manager it
was noted that Mrs. Jordan, like Mrs. Berger, sympathized with
the poor and suffering but "never let her sympathy control
her judgment."

Headquarters

The Associated Charities had its headquarters in several
downtown places prior to 1915, then moved to the Bungalow
(no longer existing) in the Palace grounds. This building had
served as the residence of King Kalakaua and his queen, Kapiolani, until the completion of Iolani Palace in 1882. In 1919
the Associated Charities and the Hawaiian Humane Society,
which had had offices in the same building since their beginnings, rented offices at 1134 Miller Street. Later the Associated
Charities bought this property. As their activities expanded,
larger quarters were needed, so in 1933 they purchased the
property at the corner of Miller and Beretania streets, where
the Child and Family Service now has its offices. (In 1957 the
territorial government acquired this property for a proposed
civic center. In December 1958 the Child and Family Service
moved to a building they have leased in the grounds of the
Kauikeolani Children's Hospital.)

Objects of Associated Charities

In the early charity organization movement, in the Hawaiian
Islands as well as elsewhere, the general belief was that the
cause of poverty was inherent in the individual seeking relief.
To obtain it, he had to be "worthy," a judgment then based
largely on the subjective feelings of the dispensers of relief.

These persons were often patronizing, authoritative, and even punitive.

This attitude was reflected in the objects of the Associated Charities of Hawaii in its first by-laws (1900). They were to secure the concurrent and harmonious action of the different charitable and benevolent societies of Hawaii, in order to (1) prevent children from growing up as paupers; (2) encourage thrift, self dependence, and industry, through friendly intercourse, advice, and sympathy, and to help the poor to help themselves; (3) raise the needy above the need of relief, and prevent begging and imposition.

To accomplish these objects the policy was to (1) provide that the case of every applicant for relief should be thoroughly investigated; (2) place the results of each investigation at the disposal of the charitable societies and agencies organized here; (3) provide employment if possible; and (4) make relief conditional upon good conduct and progress.

Its basic principles were stated as follows: [8]

Every department of its work shall be completely severed from all questions of religious belief, politics, and race;
The Society, as far as possible, shall not dispense alms in money, but assistance in the way of employment, food, clothing, and medical attendance, which shall be furnished by orders on dealers or otherwise;
It shall be the duty of the manager to keep a full registry of all applicants for charitable aid or employment, and to investigate all such applications, and to keep a record of the aid given them; also memoranda of information obtainable regarding them.

In the first annual report of the Associated Charities, while the severity of the existing law of jail sentences and chain gangs for vagrants was deprecated, the need was expressed for a special statute whereby "these gentlemen of leisure would be confined for a term and compelled to work."

Aside from those considered professional beggars, there were, of course, genuine cases in need of help. "For them, we listen, counsel, plan, clothe, cut and sew, distribute, diagnose, prescribe, furnish and discipline, meet with the heads of the affiliating societies to discuss matters, and we receive material, ready-to-wear clothing, books and periodicals, furniture and help of all kinds." Food and other material aid as needed were furnished by orders on dealers rather than by cash.

With the conviction that if people would work they need not starve, job finding was an important function of the Associated Charities of Hawaii in its early days. For women it was washing, general housework, nursing, and embroidery. This last, done exquisitely, was an art introduced by Portuguese immigrants, and in great demand by brides of that day.

A considerable portion of the agency's clientele at one time were immigrant contract plantation laborers who, dissatisfied with their new environment, drifted into Honolulu. They were given any necessary temporary aid, but were urged, sometimes with the help of police and planters or by withholding assistance, to return to the plantations. There were occasions when, if one member was ill, the whole family would accompany him to town and remain until he had recovered, being supported in the meantime by the Associated Charities.

Agency Staff

In the early years of organized philanthropy, professionally educated personnel were unknown. The manager of the Associated Charities may have been a salaried person but generally the workers were volunteers or "Friendly Visitors," usually women possessing social and economic advantages. In keeping with the philosophy of their day they thought that to solve the problem of pauperism "a friend, not alms," was needed.

In the report of the Associated Charities of Hawaii for 1908, we learn that eleven Friendly Visitors were assigned to certain localities "to visit among the needy and through sympathy and kindly direction seek not so much to relieve temporary need as to encourage any effort toward better living." At least one of these good Samaritans believed in action as well as words; through her efforts arrangements were made with a dentist for alleviation of the acute suffering of one of her charges. It was also noted that a Friendly Visitor bought a phonograph in order that shut-ins might have music. Another collected funds to buy a wheel chair for those in need of outings.

EXPANDING SERVICES

Approaching its second decade, the Associated Charities was accepting social problems incidental to a growing population and in an era when community planning was still unknown. As Honolulu grew [9] so did social problems increase, and this agency was looked upon as the legitimate place for referral. Over the years a wide assortment of services was undertaken by the Associated Charities of Hawaii.

Confidential Exchange

Though the eradication of beggary was a primary reason for organizing charity in Honolulu, it took years for the community to recognize the advantages of referring to the Associated Charities persons soliciting help. Mrs. Jordan, the manager, drew attention to the fact that, because the records of the agency were not being consulted, duplication of aid existed and some families were getting more than others. It was not uncommon for the more wily beggar to get meals handed out from private homes, or clothes, which he sold at profit; and to obtain help from benevolent societies and the Associated Charities to boot. Mrs. Jordan reported that several tried the scheme of begging money "to bury a dead relative." She met such requests with the assurance of help, but told the applicant first to ask the undertaker to get in touch with her! She would hear no more on that score.

The difficulty of bringing beggary in Honolulu under control lay as much with givers as with beggars. Undoubtedly some of the former were motivated by religious convictions or by the ego satisfaction they got from giving. Some gave because they felt the Associated Charities was cold or indifferent; others took the line of least resistance and gave to rid themselves of importunate tramps.

A story is told of a personable young Englishman who, after having exhausted the interest of the British Benevolent Society, was admitted with an infected foot to The Queen's Hospital on free service. A week or two after discharge he was readmitted for the same cause. He kept up this procedure until the suspicion was confirmed that he was purposely infecting his foot to get free board and lodging. Between times he had gone from place to place with such a plausible story that he invariably won assistance.

When the young man had worn out Honolulu's charity, he went to Hilo, masquerading as a Roman Catholic priest. As soon as this disguise was discovered he fled the island of Hawaii and returned to Oahu. His next appeal was to an Episcopal minister in Honolulu, who unsuspectingly gave him aid. One morning, upon entering his office, the minister found his desk rifled and ten dollars missing. Gone also was the uniform he wore when officiating as chaplain in the National Guard. That same day the police found the impostor wearing this uniform, in a drunken stupor by a roadside. By then he had become so notorious in the community that no one would sponsor him, so he was put in jail pending arrangements by the British Benevolent Society to send him back to Vancouver from whence he had come.

The problem of indiscriminate charity and duplication of services grew so serious that a registration system was finally established in 1913. In 1914 it became known as the Confidential Exchange.[10] For a time it continued as an activity of the Associated Charities but it has long since been transferred to the Honolulu Council of Social Agencies.

Concerning Children

Referrals to the Associated Charities also included children, and one of its most active programs in this regard was foster care. Apparently, upon nothing more than appeals from parents, offspring would be placed in boarding institutions. This seems to have been particularly true of the large Portuguese families of that generation.

Although realizing that such children did not belong in orphanages, the Associated Charities in 1905 filled the Salvation Army Rescue Home [11] in Honolulu with them, as well as the Kona Orphanage on Hawaii (no longer extant). The agency's report cited the need for a home in Honolulu for children whose parents requested placement. Children were disposed of that easily. In commenting upon this problem the agency bore witness to the innate fondness of Hawaiians for children. A Hawaiian could always find room for one more, irrespective of race, but it was quite the opposite with some other cultural groups, even in taking a child of their own racial ancestry.

In 1908 there was real concern on the part of the Associated Charities because, "due to poverty, mothers actually had to feed their babies on condensed milk!" The manager had been informed by "an eminent medical authority that a large percentage of bone disease and rheumatism was caused by bringing up children on condensed milk." Since at that time the

Associated Charities was receiving from a local firm a monthly allowance of $25, the agency decided to use it in providing fresh milk for poor children.

Treating Symptoms

The Associated Charities' annual report for 1909 listed the causes of destitution and suffering as the "same old pathetic ones; old age, insufficient earnings, desertion, crime, sickness, injury, death." It also stressed the unwholesomeness of tenements. Looking toward the future the organization named three major problems for consideration—tenement house improvement, the need of a detention home, and the prevalence of tuberculosis.

At the annual meeting in 1909 the president, Judge Dole, expressed concern that charities everywhere were treating symptoms of pauperism with little thought of eradicating causes. He had a conception, far beyond his time, of governmental responsibility in this regard. The following, quoted from his report, is a classic of prophetic vision:

> The eradication of pauperism is impracticable through the work of private societies and cannot be accomplished until governments become alive to its importance as a national question deeply affecting their own strength and prestige. In other words, until pauperism is taken up on other grounds than philanthropy or charity, there seems little hope for its final suppression, and it is only when governments shall recognize it as a menace to national prosperity and act upon such recognition that it can be successfully dealt with.[12]

Medical Care

Any charitable family organization must be concerned about the provision of medical care for its charges. The government operated a part-time clinic prior to 1904 when the Free Dispensary was opened in a building adjacent to the Board of Health; apparently the Associated Charities was interested in this venture for it is reported that the Free Dispensary was maintained "by private charity" until 1905, when the government assumed full financial responsibility.

Serving at the Free Dispensary was only a part-time job for the attending physician. He had a private practice, and in addition, as boarding physician for the Board of Health, he inspected incoming vessels for diseases quarantinable under the law.[13] The Associated Charities' annual report for 1913 pointed out that the hour for examining patients—8 to 9 A.M.—was too early for agency clients and that, furthermore, the doctor was sometimes required to be on shipboard at that hour.

In 1915, under an agreement with the city and county, the dispensary was transferred from the Board of Health to Palama Settlement,[14] where it remained until 1947, when outpatient departments were opened in St. Francis and The Queen's hospitals.

As for the poor who needed full-time hospital care, it was offered free at The Queen's Hospital, founded originally "for the relief of indigent sick and disabled people."[15] Besides governmental subsidy The Queen's Hospital had a number of endowed beds, and if necessary the Associated Charities could call upon its affiliated organizations for financial help.

Domiciliary Homes

Within two years of its establishment the Associated Charities drew attention to "the need of a home for aged foreigners who were not invalids." By 1907 the majority of recurrent cases were "old, feeble, white men and women."[16]

The organization had no problem in this regard for Hawaiians. Aged Hawaiians were provided for by King Lunalilo, who died in 1874, leaving his property to establish a home for "poor destitute people of Hawaiian blood or extraction, giving preference to old people."[17] Lunalilo Home was built on the slopes of Makiki and opened in March, 1883. In 1928 the Home was relocated at its present site at Koko Head.[18]

The report of the Associated Charities in 1907 may have helped to motivate the King's Daughters' Circle of Honolulu to open a home in 1910 in an old family residence on Makiki Street for "indigent Anglo-Saxons." Its capacity was limited, so the King's Daughters raised funds, bought its present site on Waialae Avenue, and in 1916 built a comfortable home with provisions for expansion. An annex constructed in 1957 raised the capacity of the home to about forty.

At first the Circle accepted for domiciliary care both men and women, single or married; then they adopted a policy eliminating single men but admitting aged couples "who didn't want to be separated." For many years, however, the policy has been to accept only aged women. This trend was undoubtedly influenced by the establishment on Maui (1911) of the Fred Baldwin Memorial Home for aged Caucasian men.

Although the *raison d'etre* of the King's Daughters' Home was to supply a needed haven for poor, elderly Anglo-Saxons, the time came when women of independent means had as great a need for domiciliary care. This led to an arrangement in later years whereby Caucasian women irrespective of income might become residents. All are treated alike and have individual rooms and equal freedom in the Home.[19]

Additional Staff

For fourteen years the office staff of the Associated Charities consisted of only one woman, Mrs. Jordan, as manager. She kept office hours from 9 A.M. to noon, and driving her horse and phaeton she made social investigations and home visits in the afternoon. (At one time she had an allowance of $10 a month to feed her horse; today it is common for social workers using personal cars for professional duties to receive a mileage allowance to feed their cars.) It became apparent that an additional worker was needed, and that the office should be open all day. Both these improvements were effected in 1913.

A problem at the time was the serious amount of unemployment, both in the territory and on the mainland, throwing an extra load on the Associated Charities. The board minutes of May 18, 1914, note the reduction of food orders from $1.13 to $.87 and the recommendation "to gradually eliminate the present practice of furnishing aid in a permanent way and to look forward to furnishing food not more than one or two days and other assistance as briefly as practicable." As finding jobs had been one of its original functions, it opened a Central Labor Exchange in 1913. This. however, nearly swamped the agency, jeopardizing other services, so in 1914 the Exchange was closed.

REORGANIZATION OF ASSOCIATED CHARITIES OF HAWAII (1914)

In the second decade of the Associated Charities memberships had so dwindled as to threaten its support. In January 1914 George R. Carter,[20] in a letter to the organization, stated that out of some eighty agencies in Honolulu only eighteen were affiliated with the Associated Charities—only four more than in the first year of organization, fifteen years earlier! Mr.

Carter advised that if the agency wanted to hold the confidence of the community, it should send for "an expert trained social organizer" to reorganize the Associated Charities of Hawaii on an efficient and economical basis. This led to correspondence with the American Association for Organizing Charity. In October 1914 its associate secretary, Miss Margaret Bergen, arrived in Honolulu to take on the assignment of reorganization.

Margaret Bergen

Miss Bergen (1861–1938) was one of three pioneers who furthered social welfare in widely scattered areas—Sir Charles Stewart Loch, in England; Mary E. Richmond, in America; and Margaret Bergen, in Hawaii.

Like her two colleagues,[21] Miss Bergen was a product of an era when deep interest in a cause, and zeal and enthusiasm to carry through, established some of the greatest movements in the history of social welfare. In a conversation I once had with her, she said that religious conviction took her into social work. This was a common motivation of that age, making for a sense of purpose over and above any personal gain.

In her youth there were no professional schools of social work but Margaret Bergen was essentially a student. She read widely in her own and allied fields, both in America and in Great Britain, supplementing these studies with experience in such famous places as Toynbee Hall in London, the forerunner of all settlement houses, and later at Hull House in Chicago. She also had administrative experience in Chicago's Associated Charities.

At the first meeting of the Associated Charities which Miss Bergen attended in Honolulu she spoke of a general trend toward state aid in behalf of voluntary organizations, and expressed the thought that the basic principles of social work, which she had studied in London and which were being applied in various places on the mainland, would, with some modification, be applicable to Honolulu. Thus common movements underlay the organization of charities, no matter where they were practiced.

Social Casework

In those years casework as a technique was very much in its infancy. As described by Miss Bergen, it consisted of investigations ("a careful and sympathetic inquiry into all causes of distress and all the resources for relieving the distress within the circle of a man's own exertions, relatives, or friends"), central registration, co-operation of agencies, and rehabilitation.

In her final report, June 7, 1915, Miss Bergen commented on the strengthened rapport achieved in Honolulu between co-operating agencies. An increasing number of requests for investigations were coming to the Associated Charities, while other organizations were increasingly accepting families referred to them by the agency for assistance. Her leadership was evident.

Miss Bergen stressed the point that a sequel to casework is the discovery of new needs and consequent extension of services. There was no doubt in her mind of the immediacy of the need for a service in behalf of aged Chinese, known to the Associated Charities, who were living in substandard conditions in "society houses."

Chinese Societies

A few Chinese had settled in the Sandwich Islands prior to 1852 but in that year some 200 coolies were brought here as contract laborers in the development of the sugar industry. Their contracts were for five years and they were to receive food, clothing, shelter, and three dollars a month in addition to the cost of transportation from China.[22] In succeeding years thousands more Chinese were brought to the islands.

Immigrant groups anywhere usually react to the strangeness of a new land by establishing organizations for mutual protection and to keep alive the traditions of the homeland. Chinese immigrants to Hawaii organized such associations and societies and named them according to family clans, similarity of dialect, or according to occupations or trades. Generally the purposes were to assist and protect new arrivals (there was no Chinese consular representative in Hawaii), and to settle disputes, maintain Old World traditions and customs, and provide respectable funerals for their members.

Many of the early immigrants did not return to China upon completion of their contracts, but remained in Hawaii to seek an independent livelihood. They gave leadership to the development of Chinese Societies and in the process acquired property for headquarters and revenue. Most of the holdings are in Honolulu, west of Nuuanu Street, a section long since

known as Chinatown. The estimated realty wealth of the
Chinese societies in the Territory in 1952 was $2,000,000.[23]

As membership is in accordance with the rules governing
clans and names, men of all levels of wealth and social status,
from the poorest to the most affluent, are included in the Chinese societies. Women are excluded, for in China, as in many
other countries, most women have been traditionally considered
of little account.

In the early decades of Hawaii's sugar industry, if laborers
grew too old to work they were turned off the plantations to
fend for themselves. Among them were numbers of Chinese
who came to the Islands originally as contract laborers and
who remained on the plantations as long as they were able
to work. The societies to which they belonged gave them
shelter in their old age, but for food and clothing they had
to beg. Shopkeepers in Chinatown would dip from bags,
open for display, a measure of rice for these passing beggars.
Chinese restaurants gave them leftovers and allowed them
to forage in the garbage. That is all changed now, and to Miss
Bergen goes the credit for initiating the change.

There are still Chinese society houses on all the islands and
in rural Oahu as well as in Honolulu (some sixty of them in
1951, but over the past hundred years, social and industrial
evolution, together with the process of acculturation, has
changed the complexion of Chinese societies. Hawaii has now
a Chinese Consulate, a Chinese Chamber of Commerce, and
social security for the needy, irrespective of racial background.

But traditional roots grow deep and are particularly tenacious when nurtured by such collective financial security as
has been attained by the Chinese societies in Hawaii. Most
of the societies have lodgings in close proximity to the main
buildings. These lodgings are still occupied by poor, aged
members who share sleeping quarters and do their cooking
on individual oil or wood stoves, in detached sheds that are
more or less disreputable shacks. Aside from dwellings for their
indigent aged, the principal function of Chinese societies today
is a social one, as gathering points of ancestral clans in celebrating traditional Chinese festivals.

WIDENING HORIZONS

An important result of Miss Bergen's reorganization was the
incorporation of the Associated Charities of Hawaii in 1915.

Young Men's Christian Association, 1882, corner of Hotel and Alakea Streets. Many of the early eleemosynary organizations had their inceptions in this building.

Young Men's Christian Association, Central Branch, Atkinson Drive. Opened in 1951.

Mission School House erected in 1835. The building still stands at the corner of Kawaiahao Street and Mission Lane.

The Bungalow. Residence of King Kalakaua and Queen Kapiolani prior to the completion of Iolani Palace in 1882.

Entrance to Kung Tong Society. Photo taken in the 1950's.

Wood Stove still used by the inhabitants of shelters in the Chinese societies.

Palolo Chinese Home. Margaret Bergen Dispensary; a dormitory to the right.

Residents sitting on the veranda of a dormitory at Palolo Chinese Home.

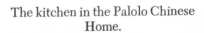
The kitchen in the Palolo Chinese Home.

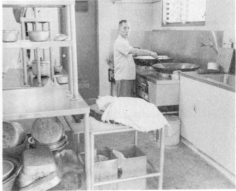

Above: Lunalilo Home for aged Hawaiians. Photograph taken in 1950's.

Right: Residents of Lunalilo Home.

Below: Washington Place. Once the home of Queen Liliuokalani, now the official residence of successive governors of Hawaii. Photo taken about 1918. (Bernice P. Bishop Museum photo.)

The original purposes adopted in 1900 remained the same, with two additions: to find the causes and remedies for conditions requiring charitable aid or relief, and to suggest legislation. There were also two modifications in policy: good conduct was now no longer a requirement for granting relief, nor was there any stipulation as to the form—in cash or in kind—that relief should take. A greater understanding of human nature is apparent.

At the completion of her assignment in 1915, Miss Bergen left Honolulu but in 1920 returned as manager of the Associated Charities. During the five-year interim Miss Lena Waters acted as manager of the association.

In 1917 America entered the first world war, and though Hawaii was not in a combat zone, it buzzed with activities in connection with sending men and women overseas. Miss Waters initiated the Home Service of the Hawaii Chapter of the American Red Cross.

In addition to its war services the Associated Charities set itself to carry out Miss Bergen's recommendations, including those concerned with the aged Chinese men living in substandard conditions in society houses. The first step was the appointment of a special committee headed by the Chinese Consul, and the addition to the Associated Charities staff of a Chinese worker, Mrs. E. E. Goo.

In a recent letter, Miss Waters gives a vivid picture of how Mrs. Goo treated her old men. At that time the Charities occupied the Bungalow in the Palace grounds, and every Saturday morning the old men, sitting in a circle on the Palace lawn, would meet with Mrs. Goo. After she had talked to them in their own language, each old man would receive his week's supply of rice. (In those days it was common practice for social workers to talk *at* a client, rarely to hear what *he* had to say.) Mrs. Goo is still remembered as a very efficient and kindly young woman, one of the earliest, if not the first, of Chinese social workers in Honolulu.

Palolo Chinese Home

Before Miss Bergen's return to Honolulu in 1920 the Associated Charities had raised $10,000 to purchase the former Gospel Mission Home—fifteen acres and six buildings—in Palolo Valley. This was put in order and was opened in 1920 as the Palolo Chinese Home. It was administered by the Associated Charities or its successors until 1941, when, in accordance with the recommendation of the Honolulu Plan, it became an autonomous agency under its own board of directors, the majority of whom now are of Chinese ancestry. Its capacity at first was 20. In 1951 it was caring for 100; but today (quoting the manager, Mr. Rene C. K. Hu), "if beds are put close together we could take about one hundred and forty."

The Palolo Chinese Home was founded for indigent Chinese men. The need, however, has become so acute for domiciliary care of the aged, irrespective of income (true of the population in general), that the Home is now admitting Chinese men of sixty-five years or over who are able to pay all or part of their expenses. The Home is otherwise supported partly by the Department of Public Welfare under its Old Age Assistance program and partly by the Honolulu Community Chest.

During a tour conducted by Mr. Hu—of the society houses in Chinatown and of the Home in Palolo Valley—I noticed the name, Margaret Bergen, over the entrance to the Home dispensary. And in the kitchen an old man, who in his younger days may have been a butcher or a cook, was using an electric saw to cut fresh sides of mutton in preparation for the day's dinner. Quite different were the bygone years, when bent, elderly men, some blind, all shabbily dressed, hobbled along with sticks, carrying bags and pausing here and there for a kindly shopowner's measure of rice or some restaurant's leftovers.

Not all aged Chinese men will go to the Palolo Chinese Home; some prefer the independence of society houses but they no longer live in them as beggars. As in the Home, so in the societies, those who are indigent receive monthly allowances from the Department of Public Welfare.

Boards of Child Welfare

Judge Dole's and Miss Bergen's words bore fruit when, in 1919, a territorial law created boards of child welfare,[24] whose program was popularly known as "Mothers' Pensions." The respective counties were mandated by the legislature to appropriate funds to their boards of child welfare to be used toward the support of needy mothers in certain circumstances. The boards were composed of unsalaried members appointed by the governor. On Oahu the Board of Child Welfare had the

Associated Charities conduct the investigations and supervise the families who were granted Mothers' Pensions.

In 1921 this law was amended to include Pregnant women and indigent children orphaned of one or both parents or who, for other specified reasons, needed support. The amendment also authorized the respective counties to employ "a trained social worker or nurse whose duty it shall be to assist the Board in all matters pertaining to the administration of the Act and to instruct, counsel, and aid all persons who make application." [25] The amendment was brought about largely by the program of the visiting housekeeper, Miss Ruth Frick, who joined the Associated Charities in 1919, to work primarily with families in their homes.

Not only was Miss Frick to teach mothers what to buy but she was to teach them also how to prepare food nutritiously as well as economically. Her function included providing clothing, of a kind to "preserve and encourage a feeling of self respect." She was also to be concerned not only about cleanliness of the home, but also that there be sufficient space to insure privacy for each individual—a tall order, and standards by no means yet common. Again, a deeper content was emerging in social service.

Undoubtedly this emphasis on child welfare, and the conditions it revealed, increased an anxiety in the community about the prevalence of malnutrition, particularly among school children. Related to it was the high incidence of tuberculosis. The Hawaiian Humane Society, the Free Kindergarten and Children's Aid Association, the Board of Health, and several public schools were concerned about the problem.

Taking advantage of the interest regarding the prevalence of malnutrition, Miss Bergen, upon her return to Honolulu in 1920, added a worker to the Household Economics Department of the Associated Charities to make a study of 100 school children in the Pohukaina and Kalihiwaena Schools. Every child in this group was 14 per cent or more underweight. Therefore each one was given, at midmorning, a half pint of whole milk and percentages of gain or loss were charted. The daily charge of five cents for milk was paid by the Central Committee on Child Welfare for those children whose parents could not afford it. The workers spent the mornings at the schools and in the afternoons they visited homes of the under-

nourished children to explain to the mothers the meaning of the
nutrition classes and to win their co-operation. There was no
doubt of the latter. Following the home visits of the nutrition-
ists, there was a dramatic improvement. The investigators
went on to weigh and measure 15,296 children in twenty public
schools and reported 5,593, or 36.9 per cent, to be 7 per cent
or more underweight.

A Nutritional Institute

Armed with facts, the interest of the community, and the
encouragement of a sympathetic board, Miss Bergen set plans
in motion which brought Dr. William R. P. Emerson, associate
with the Nutrition Clinics for Delicate Children in Boston,
Massachusetts, to Hawaii to conduct an institute for field workers. To this institute, December 6 to 20, 1922, came nurses,
teachers, social workers, and others from all over the territory.[26] One important result of this institute was a legislative
appropriation for the establishment of a nutrition division
within the Department of Public Instruction. The Social Service Bureau co-operated with these teachers by increasing food
allowances for families under their care whose children were
underweight.

Not only the public schools followed Dr. Emerson's Institute
with nutrition programs. Similar projects were undertaken in
Punahou School, the Free Kindergarten and Children's Aid
Association, and other institutions.

SOCIAL SERVICE BUREAU (1921)

In 1921 the Associated Charities of Hawaii became the
Social Service Bureau. The word "charity" had been eliminated
from the titles of such organizations in Great Britain, mainland
America, and Hawaii, only in reverse order.

The Charity Organization Society of London, established in
1869 and the first of them all, did not change its name to
Family Welfare Association until 1946; [27] in America the majority of members of the Family Service Association of America
still had titles including the word charity when, in 1921,
Hawaii had discarded it.[28]

The change of titles got rid of the word "charity," which
in the earliest days of the charity organization movement was
largely associated with depravity; the word also had, and still

has, a connotation of failure—were one successful, many think, one would not need "charity." Social workers, however, come into contact with persons who, through unavoidable circumstances, are forced to apply for help, but to whom the very idea of "charity" is repellent because of its implication of failure or degradation. Among other reasons for discarding old titles was the need of new ones to designate casework services not necessarily limited to economic dependency.

The original name of this first family service organization in the Islands—Associated Charities of Hawaii—was changed over the years, in keeping with expanding programs, several of which were assumed later by the territorial and county governments. The two mentioned above were on the territorial level—boards of child welfare and school nutritional programs. A third was conceived by the Social Service Bureau—the visiting schoolteacher. The program on the County level is described under Social Legislation and Financial Investigator.

Visiting Schoolteacher

In 1925 the Social Service Bureau assigned Miss Nell Findley, a member of its staff and subsequently its manager, as visiting teacher to the Pohukaina School. She was to act as a liaison caseworker between school and home for those children manifesting untoward behavior. There being no reference to this assignment in subsequent reports, it is assumed that it was discontinued.

In 1931–32 the Department of Public Instruction recruited from the mainland two visiting schoolteachers for home liaison, one each for the Kawananakoa Experimental School and the McKinley High School. These positions were subsequently eliminated because of retrenchment due to the general economic depression.

FAMILY CONSULTATION SERVICE (1939)

In 1939 the Social Service Bureau became the Family Consultation Service. Although the Department of Public Instruction found it necessary to drop the visiting schoolteacher program, the Family Consultation Service, unwilling to allow the plan to die, assigned in 1939 a staff member to the Royal School. In 1941 she resigned and again there was a hiatus, but not for long.

In response to a request for help on adjustment problems of pupils, made by principals of elementary schools to the Honolulu Council of Social Agencies, a school and social agencies co-ordinating committee was organized. By February 1942, its School Referral Plan was under way. Miss Belle Shalit (now Mrs. Clayton Chamberlin), especially qualified by training and experience on the mainland, was engaged by what had now become the Child and Family Service to initiate the plan. She did this as a consultant and co-ordinator between the elementary schools and social agencies in Honolulu. According to the type of social or psychological problem referred to her by a teacher, she selected the suitable agency to help each child. By 1943 the seed sown eighteen years before by the Social Service Bureau had become a sturdy plant. By legislative enactment, a division of Pupil Guidance was established in that year within the Department of Public Instruction.[29]

Social Legislation—City and County

When social service first began to function in The Queen's Hospital (1923), the majority of referrals concerned patients in the lower income brackets. This meant consultation with the City and County Physician, Dr. A. K. Hanchett, regarding those patients unable to meet the cost of medical care. It also meant drawing to Dr. Hanchett's attention the exploitation of county funds by some patients admitted to The Queen's Hospital on county service. One was a man who had been hospitalized for weeks on City and County Service who, dying, left an estate of two hundred thousand dollars. Dr. Hanchett saw the necessity of financial investigations.

Financial Investigator

By now the Social Service Bureau was so well established in the community that it was requested in 1926 by the Board of Supervisors, through Dr. Hanchett, to add a financial investigator to its staff, the expenses to be borne by the City and County of Honolulu.

Mrs. Kathleen McDuffie, a registered nurse, was appointed to this position. Her function included investigations for free burials as well as of patients applying for free hospital care. In 1931, this City and County Service was disassociated from the Social Service Bureau to become a section of the newly established City and County Health Unit in the annex on Miller Street, adjoining The Queen's Hospital. (Transferred in 1958 to Maluhia Hospital.)

Continuing Agency Functions

The preceding several pages have emphasized the opportunity a private social agency has in developing services that lead to social legislation. Following are mentioned several programs activated and continued as voluntary services by the Associated Charities and its descendants in name.

Child Placement Committee

In the 1920's there was a good deal of criticism in the community about the lack of definite standards for admission to the children's homes which were supported by the general public through the United Welfare Fund.

Under the leadership of the Social Service Bureau, therefore, the Child Placement Committee was organized in 1926 with headquarters at the bureau. The committee consisted of one representative each from the Social Service Bureau, the United Welfare Fund, and the four children's homes—Kalihi Orphanage,[30] Salvation Army Boys' and Girls' Homes, and the Susannah Wesley Home. It was found that because of the lack of uniform and adequate admission policies, there were some children not in need of institutional care filling spaces really needed by others.

The Child Placement Committee shared the opinion, prevalent at that time, that foster homes were better than institutions for the rearing of children. There was a time when well-conducted institutions under kindly administrators were considered superior to poor and indifferently kept foster homes; then followed a swing to the concept that the poorest home is better than the best institution.

At one time illegitimate babies were taken from their natural mothers; then in 1926 the Social Service Bureau, caring for twenty unmarried mothers, encouraged every one to keep her baby. Today we know there are no categorical solutions to these problems. All factors must be taken into consideration on an individual basis. For some children, a high-standard institution is advisable; for others, a good foster home is preferable; some unmarried mothers should be encouraged to keep their offsping, others should not. Whatever the decision, the well-being of the child is the chief consideration.

In 1928 Miss Bergen resigned as manager of the Social Service Bureau. The years in which she held this position had been a period of real growth, both for the agency and the community at large. For five years following her resignation she gave lectures in social work at the University of Hawaii. In 1934 the university conferred upon her an honorary M.A. degree "for distinguished services in the humanitarian field." Miss Bergen died and was buried in Honolulu in 1938. Miss Nell Findley, who had been Miss Bergen's assistant for several years, succeeded her.

Children's Bureau

One morning in 1929 the attention of Mr. J. R. Galt, president of the Social Service Bureau, was drawn to a picture in The *Honolulu Advertiser* of three neglected and homeless children. This was of such concern to Mr. Galt that a Children's Bureau was established within the Social Service Bureau. It included the head workers of childrens' institutions and the executive of the United Welfare Fund. The function of the Children's Bureau was placement of children outside their own homes.

With a Child Placement Committee having been established only three years before, the Children's Bureau seems today a duplicate program, especially as its reports and recommendations were subject to the approval of the Child Placement Committee, but in that era community organization was still very much in its infancy.

In 1929 the Child Placement Committee reported that of all children who had to be removed from their homes, the cause in 40 per cent of the cases was tuberculosis. Desertion, immorality, and death of parents were also reasons for placing children in public or private institutions or in boarding homes. These continue to be the major reasons for providing care outside their homes for scores of children.

SURVEY BY CHILD WELFARE LEAGUE OF AMERICA (1935)

Academic education in social work, particularly in its early years, accentuated specialization in social welfare, tending to multiply agencies on a functional basis. The Liliuokalani Trust, an autonomous agency, was founded in 1935 for "orphan and other destitute children" (chapter VIII).

For years the activities of two local organizations, the Hawaiian Humane Society and the Associated Charities and its descendants, included child welfare; with the establishment of a third organization in this field the need of a survey to avoid confusion and overlapping of functions became apparent. To this end a request was made by the Honolulu Council of Social Agencies and the United Welfare Fund to the Child Welfare League of America. Its executive director, Mr. C. C. Carstens, responded by coming to Honolulu in 1935. The result of Mr. Carstens' analysis was the establishment of the Children's Service Association (chapter IX), a composite of the Children's Bureau of the Social Service Bureau, the Children's portion of the Hawaiian Humane Society, and the Child Welfare Services of the Liliuokalani Trust.

The Children's Service Association began to function in September 1935. In early 1941 it closed its doors, but the years between were some of the most significant in the social service annals of the territory.

THE GREAT DEPRESSION

The most challenging years faced by the Social Service Bureau were those of its fourth decade, 1929–39. On the mainland an economic crisis caused mass unemployment and brought on a depression that swept the entire country and included Hawaii. The following significant quotation is from the 1929 report of the Social Service Bureau:

In contrast to such disabilities as illness, widowhood, old age, and personality problems, which are inherent in the physical, mental or social status of the individuals concerned, unemployment is a matter dependent upon industrial conditions and policies wholly beyond the control either of the individuals affected or of a case-working agency. What to do about destitute families of able-bodied men out of work is a puzzling problem and an increasingly expensive one. Thus far food has been supplied as sparingly as possible to prevent starvation and every effort has been made to find work. In about one-third of the cases some employment has been found, but usually of a temporary nature, not lasting more than a few days or weeks, so the time involved in locating it has been out of all proportion to the results obtained. As the year closes this situation is the most acute problem faced by the Social Service Bureau.

The depression became so severe that in 1930 the Board of Child Welfare advocated that, provided suitable employment was available, children of fourteen years be taken out of school to help in the support of their families applying for relief. In 1931, due to unemployment, 1,492 families were registered with the Social Service Bureau. By 1932, the registration reached 3,274, an increase of 119 per cent. The enforced reduction of relief payments was undoubtedly a factor when, in 1933, out of 301 children of client families, 112 were reported as tuberculosis contacts.

During 1931-32, when the pineapple industry was at a very low ebb and thousands were thrown out of employment, the Hawaiian Sugar Planters' Association and the Social Service Bureau co-operated in a relief program, the former paying the costs of opening a special office and the latter supplying the professional services, which included job finding, relief, and repatriation. The HSPA paid passage back to their homeland for 1,748 Filipinos.

Social Legislation

There was also an increasing number of the aged seeking help every year. In 1932 the Social Service Bureau reported over 50 per cent of its relief budget going to this group and raised the question of the Territorial government's responsibility in this regard. In 1933 the Old Age Pension Law was enacted.[31] Its benefits were restricted to United States citizens. Since the majority of the territory's population were alien Orientals, the elderly among these remained the responsibility of private charity.

In 1933 the Governor's Unemployment Relief Commission was established, the Social Service Bureau acting in an advisory capacity by assisting families in planning budgets on reduced incomes. The commission also opened a bread station in conjunction with the Salvation Army and under the supervision of the bureau's home economist.

In the meantime the federal government had established several temporary emergency programs, one of which was the

Federal Emergency Relief Administration. Through its Honolulu office the Social Service Bureau received, in 1934, $91,-240.07 for direct relief.

BOARD OF PUBLIC WELFARE AND COUNTY PUBLIC WELFARE
COMMISSIONS (1937)

In reviewing the history of the Child and Family Service far back to Associated Charities days, one feels the inevitability of Public Welfare; again Hawaii follows trends from further afield.

In 1935 the Federal Social Security Law was enacted. It stipulated that support was based upon need, not citizenship, but the territory, in order to participate in this federal program, had to enact a corresponding statute in public welfare. The territorial legislature had already adjourned and as it convenes biennially it was not until 1937 that the legislature established the Board of Public Welfare and County Public Welfare Commissions,[32] known since 1941 as the Department of Public Welfare.

This was a period in Hawaii, no less than on the Mainland, when there was much anxiety among workers in private agencies about the survival of voluntary organizations, in the face of increasing governmental direction in social welfare. As the Social Service Bureau expressed it, it meant looking at itself "in sharper focus." Voluntary organizations everywhere were taking stock; realizing in the process that no longer was their clientele composed exclusively of the chronically indigent—the "charity cases"—begging for food, shelter, and clothing. Their caseload now included the educated and the intellectual, the professional person and the skilled artisan, forced by the depression into want. It was not easy for these people to beg, nor easy for the social workers of that day to deal adequately with their problems. The Social Service Bureau was forced to the realization, of all casework agencies, that human beings, irrespective of economic status, have social and psychological problems that can be resolved by casework, provided the practitioner is professionally competent. Sharpening their focus meant to the Social Service Bureau, therefore, an academically prepared staff in the social sciences, and experience with a widened clientele that included persons of independent means.

In 1931 the bureau employed its first graduate from a school of social work. The time was to come when all their workers were required to have this basic qualification.

A concomitant to professional qualification is an awareness of the dignity and worth of the individual. There was concrete evidence of this in the Social Service Bureau when, in 1933, it substituted cash for food orders so that clients might shop where and as they wished. In approved social agencies, the old custom of issuing food orders in lieu of cash is today as obsolete as the word "pauper."

Mention has already been made of the effects of the depression on Hawaii and the increasing load this imposed on the Social Service Bureau. The load also became too heavy for the Children's Service Association. Both agencies therefore began to transfer their indigent cases to the newly established Board of Public Welfare. It took considerable time, however, for the latter to get its machinery in working order.

In the beginning the Board of Public Welfare was wary of overspending its budget. To know which referrals to accept and which to reject required experience and the establishing of policies. Private agencies were expected to assume responsibility for the rejections, and sometimes these cases fell between the two jurisdictions. "Closed Intake" became a common expression and workers in all social organizations grew short-tempered as they shopped around trying to discover what case belonged where. The problem was accentuated by staff turnover—personnel leaving private agencies to return to the mainland or to accept positions with Public Welfare.

In 1939 Miss Findley resigned from the Social Service Bureau and was succeeded by several others in turn. In that year the bureau changed its name to the Family Consultation Service.

THE HONOLULU PLAN (1940)

In the confusion of that period the Honolulu Council of Social Agencies and the United Welfare Fund decided that the time had come for another analysis with recommendations by qualified specialists concerning Hawaii's mounting perplexities in social casework. In response to a request from these two organizations, the Community Chests and Councils, Inc., New York, sent to Honolulu in early 1940 a staff of eight men and women, representing family and child welfare, recreation, and group work. The staff remained in the Islands four months, analyzing both governmental and voluntary agencies. It was their responsibility to submit a plan that would have "focus, unity, and co-ordination." They named their report "The Honolulu Plan." [33]

The Honolulu Plan includes a detailed analysis of public and private organizations and many recommendations regarding specific services, but it suffices here to say that the visiting analysts found a propensity in casework agencies, public and private, to treat members of a family as separate entities rather than as parts of a whole. They felt that this militated against prevention, because it left out of account foci of social infection leading to more serious breakdowns.

There was no doubt whatever in the minds of the survey group that Honolulu needed a private family casework agency. To this end they recommended a new organization in which would be merged the Family Consultation Service, the Children's Service Association, and the Columbus Welfare Association. The last named [34] was a Roman Catholic organization established during the World War I.

CHILD AND FAMILY SERVICE (1941)

In accordance with this advice, the Family Consultation Service and the Children's Service Association combined in 1941 to form the present Child and Family Service. Though provisions had been made for Roman Catholic representation in the administration of the new organization, the Columbus Welfare Association did not merge, as recommended, with the other two casework agencies.

In January 1941 the Child and Family Service was incorporated for the following purposes:

To aid in the alleviation of human distress in the City and County of Honolulu; to serve in preventing social disorganization resulting from the inability of individuals and families satisfactorily to adjust themselves to their social or economic circumstances or to the broader aspects of community life; to care for children requiring the community's interest, such care to be provided either in their own homes or in foster families or institutions; to protect children from cruelty and abuse; to assist in reducing juvenile delinquency; to stimulate greater interest in good standards for the training and guidance of children; to work either directly or by co-operation with other persons or agencies, as far as the resources of the corporation permit, that persons requiring the community's interest may obtain the form of services of most value to them; to aid in initiating and advancing social legislation; to undertake or aid the establishment, development and maintenance of surveys, demonstration projects, programs and courses of study designed to further an understanding of social problems; and to further in all other practicable ways the welfare of the people of Hawaii to the end that they may become useful members of society.[35]

We see a broadening of philosophy by comparing these purposes with those the Associated Charities adopted in 1900 and slightly modified in 1915. There is now little stress on the financial aspects of relief; more emphasis is given to standards in child welfare, and the Child and Family Service is to co-operate further with other organizations in the common aim of social betterment. Judge Dole's spirit must have been happy indeed with the reference, slight as it was, to government's participation through legislation in social welfare.

By 1942 the Child and Family Service had a staff of twenty-six professional caseworkers, an office manager, and a clerical staff of eleven. Its activities are limited to Oahu.

With a governmental organization responsible for dispensing relief to the indigent, the workers of the Child and Family Service have increasingly emphasized services of a psychological and preventive nature. This is exemplified in marriage and family counseling.

Occasionally a young couple, contemplating marriage, will seek counsel because they want to talk things over with someone outside their own families. But most of the marriage counseling is after—rather than before marriage. It concerns conflicts between husband and wife, between children and parents, brothers and sisters, relatives and in-laws. Casework and counseling in this regard is toward prevention of breakdowns in family life.

WORLD WAR II

In July 1940, the month in which the Honolulu Plan was submitted, a group of representative men of the community met with the mayor to discuss the possibility of the United States' being drawn into the war then raging in Europe, and its implications for Hawaii. As a matter of fact, plans for defending the Islands had begun in 1939 with the arrival of construction workers from the mainland; their number increased in the ensuing months until at one time an estimated 82,000 defense workers were in the territory.[36] Thousands more passed through, en route to and from other areas in the Pacific. Likewise, the armed services mushroomed the population still higher. Periodic blackout practice was going on and plans were under way for feeding the civilian population in case of emergency. Selective Service and the registration of men between twenty-one and thirty-six years of age began in October 1940; [37] those of Japanese ancestry were excluded. Suspicion and hatred of the Japanese race grew apace as defense preparations were speeded up. These fears concerning the Japanse in Hawaii proved to be groundless.

A special session of the legislature met in September 1941 and enacted the Mobilization-Day Law, giving the governor wide emergency powers in case of war. Early Sunday morning, December 7, 1941, Pearl Harbor was bombed by Japanese military planes and the United States was drawn into World War II.[38] In addition to Pearl Harbor and several other military posts, a number of civilian areas suffered attack or caught fire, which entailed the evacuation of persons from the areas in imminent danger to schools and buildings in safer localities.

For ten days after the "blitz," the majority of the staff of the Child and Family Service worked at the City Hall, helping with the evacuees. By setting up a file of missing persons, they brought together members of families separated during the hours immediately following the assault. They also helped with plans for possible evacuation on a much larger scale.

With the bombardment of Pearl Harbor, defense construction boomed, and thousands more war workers poured into the territory, bringing not only needed skills and labor, but creating a plenitude of social problems. One of the most acute was the housing shortage; this in turn, made for family and neighborhood conflicts. *Malihini* (stranger) war workers were at loose ends, homesick, and disgruntled. Curfew and complete blackout by military order restricted freedom after dark. Employment and wages were at an all-time high and their effect on the resident population was not altogether wholesome. Instances were common of little children being left at home with insufficient care—or none—while their mothers went out to work. The demand for foster homes increased, but none were available, for few women wanted to be foster mothers at agency rates of $30 a month per child when they could earn many times that amount in some war-connected activity. Domestic discord was a common symptom of a profound social upheaval. Oriental parents with high standards of behavior saw their daughters cheapening themselves in promiscuous dates with strange *haole* (white foreigner) men. Interracial marriages became so numerous that the Army and the Navy ruled that, for those below a certain rank, official permission must first be obtained. Many of these marriages went on the rocks as soon as the husbands were transferred elsewhere. It was by no means uncommon for men in higher ranks, some with families on the mainland, to become involved with women in the islands, *haole* and otherwise. Babies were born without benefit of marriage. All this was reflected in the types of problem referred to the Child and Family Service. But V-J Day did come at last and, with it, attempts to gather up the strands in a Hawaii that would never be the same again.

PROFESSIONAL COLLABORATION

The Child and Family Service recognizes the need in the community for greater collaboration between the legal, medical, and social work professions. In this regard they are concerned about the looseness of adoption procedures.

There are two axioms governing adoptions which if disregarded may lead to serious consequences. (1) Histories should be obtained, without disclosing identities each to the other, of the natural and adopting parents, so as to satisfy the natural parents, especially the mother, that her child will have a wholesome development and to let the adopting parents know whether or not the child has a normal heritage. (2) Though the adopting parents may be granted temporary legal custody of the child, adequate time for the assurance of these facts should elapse before a decree is issued.

The following is an example of what is known to happen without due regard to these axioms. A strange woman came to the Social Service Department of The Queen's Hospital asking if she could return a child she had legally adopted. She said "it had been given to her by a doctor and looked good," and the adoption took place within a few days. The baby proved to be an idiot. There was little the social worker could do under the circumstances other than to explain to the caller why she and her husband, having assumed legal responsibility, could not "give the baby back," and to tell her of Waimano Home [39] and how to make application for the child's admission there.

The Child and Family Service reports a growing collaboration in adoption cases between their agency and the medical profession. Since 1950 they have charged for these services; they feel this has strengthened collaboration—as one worker remarked, "We appreciate more that for which we pay."

CONCLUSION

In a final word for this chapter the reader is reminded of what was expressed in the Introduction: that it would be impossible for me to write definitively of the agencies included in Part I of this volume. Speaking for the Child and Family Service, it well deserves a history of its own. Perhaps the abbreviated account given here will inspire another to assume this important task.

[1] Information not specifically documented was obtained by reviewing the records at the office of the Child and Family Service.

[2] *Pacific Commercial Advertiser,* March 28, 1899; Public Archives of Hawaii.

[3] Mary E. Richmond, *The Long View, Papers and Addresses* (New York: Russell Sage Foundation, 1930), pp. 574–79.

[4] Frank Derker Watson, *The Charity Organization Movement in the United States* (New York: The Macmillan Company, 1922), p. 179.

[5] Margaret Bergen, *Twenty-five Years of Service of the Social Service Bureau;* address given at the Territorial Conference of Social Work, Honolulu, March 19, 1925.

[6] Son of the Reverend Daniel and Mrs. Dole, who were sent to the Sandwich Islands in 1841 by the American Board of Commissioners for Foreign Missions. *Portraits and Biographical Sketches of American Protestant Missionaries to the Hawaiian Islands* (Honolulu: Hawaiian Missionary Children's Society, 1937), p. 75.

[7] Ralph S. Kuykendall and A. Grove Day, *Hawaii: A History* (New York: Prentice-Hall, Inc., 1949), p. 297.

[8] Culled from documents and reports of the Associated Charities; filed in the office of the Child and Family Service.

[9] See Appendix I for population statistics.

[10] A technical device operated from a central office by which a social agency registers new cases or is informed whether or not an applicant for service is known to other social agencies. It not only avoids duplication but makes for co-ordination among organizations.

[11] Now the Booth Memorial Home for unmarried mothers.

[12] Annual report of Judge Dole, president of the Associated Charities; filed at the Child and Family Service.

[13] *Report of the Board of Health,* June 30, 1903.

[14] Founded in Palama district in 1896 under the auspices of Central Union Church. Known first as Palama chapel, it changed its name (1906) to Palama Settlement, in keeping with an expanded program of group work, recreation, and medical care. It has long since become an autonomous organization.

[15] *The Queen's Hospital Charter of Incorporation;* Public Archives of Hawaii.

[16] Regarding domiciliary care for people of other races, see chapter X.

[17] Kuykendall and Day, *op. cit.,* pp. 143–44.

[18] *Thrums Annual,* 1883, p. 62; 1910, p. 105; 1929, p. 127.

[19] Aldyth V. Morris, *History of King's Daughters' Home;* also conversations with Mrs. J. H. Bowman, president, and Mrs. Morris, secretary.

[20] Governor of the Territory, 1903–7.

[21] Charles Stewart Loch (1849–1923) was knighted in 1915 in recognition of his humanitarian leadership. Mary E. Richmond (1861–1923) pioneered in America for training in social work. Her best-known publication is *Social Diagnosis,* published in 1917. See also her *The Long View,* already cited.

[22] Kuykendall, *Hawaiian Kingdom,* p. 329.

[23] Tin Yuke Char, "Immigrant Chinese Society in Hawaii"; paper read Oct. 9, 1952, to the Hawaiian Historical Society.

[24] *T.H. Session Laws* (1919), Act 129, p. 72.

[25] *Ibid.* (1921), Act 37, p. 52.

[26] Wm. R. P. Emerson, "Malnutrition and the Schools," *The Friend,* Sept. 1922, p. 206.

[27] Information received from B. E. Astbury, general secretary, Family Welfare Association, London, England.

[28] Information obtained in correspondence from the Family Association of America, April 12, 1951.

[29] *T.H. Session Laws* (1943), Act 77, p. 33.

[30] Known since 1948 as St. Anthony's Home.

[31] *T.H. Session Laws* (1933), Act 208, p. 253; amended 1933. During a special legislative session, also in 1933, the act was amended to combine under one administration the Child Welfare and Old Age Pensions boards. *Ibid.,* Special Session, Act 39, p. 51.

[32] *Ibid.* (1937), ch. 259A, Public Welfare, p. 272.

[33] *The Honolulu Plan—A Program of Community Welfare Organization,* developed by Community Chests and Councils, Inc., July 1940.

[34] In 1944 it became known as Catholic Charities; see chapter VII.

[35] "Five Years of Community Service," *Child and Family Service Report 1941–1946.*

[36] Gwenfread Allen, *Hawaii's War Years 1941–1945* (Honolulu: University of Hawaii Press, 1950), p. 233.

[37] *Ibid.,* pp. 264–65.

[38] *Ibid.,* pp. 1, 2.

[39] A territorial institution established in 1921, for the feeble-minded.

VI

Central Committee on Child Welfare
(Period included: 1914–1937)

About 1910, a group of women, residents of the then sparsely populated Manoa Valley, organized the Manoa League, "to make this district a safe place in which to raise our children." They held their meetings in the homes of members and had the use of Kawaiahao's chapel in upper Manoa Valley for sewing classes and Sunday evening singing, "for the benefit of the less privileged."

By 1914 these cause-inspired women decided to establish an organization on a much wider basis. Calling themselves the Central Committee on Child Welfare,[1] they drew into membership representatives of every woman's organziation in Honolulu, lay and professional, directly or indirectly "interested in any form of child welfare." This was spelled out in a *Statement of General Policy:*

We women of Honolulu banded together in a Central Committee of Child Welfare believe that whenever the rights of the child are involved, it is essential to the purposes of this organization to take cognizance of those social questions which affect the integrity of the family and to do our part in the up-building of a vigilant public opinion.

We believe the young of both sexes are the peculiar prey of evil men and women who would profit to the destruction of society, and that society owes to all youth the protection of sound social customs, embodied in and enforced by law, and sustained by public opinion. We deprecate alike the injustice which insolent and aggressive [2] shields the boy at the expense of the girl, and the vindictive desire to get even which too often lurks under the cloak of the avowed champion of the girl. An unprejudiced hearing and justice are rights of every girl and boy alike.

With this strong motivation, the Central Committee initiated or furthered numerous programs in behalf of children, which have continued over the years in one form or another. Conspicuous contributions were made in three areas—nutrition for undernourished children, institutional care of the mentally defective, and the Juvenile Court.

NUTRITION FOR UNDERNOURISHED CHILDREN

The preceding chapter noted a general concern in the community about the prevalence of poor nutrition among school children. The Central Committee raised the money for supplementary food used in a joint experiment conducted in 1921 by the Associated Charities of Hawaii and certain public schools. The furnishing of hundreds of half-pint bottles of milk was a prime factor in establishing the milk habit among school children.

Relevant to this interest in nutrition was a project initiated by another member agency of the Central Committee on Child Welfare, the International Institute of the Young Women's Christian Association.

The majority of parents of school children in that period were first-generation Orientals in Hawaii. As they did not speak English, and did not have time to attend cooking classes at the YWCA, the classes went to them in "The Little House on Wheels" (toward the cost of which the Central Committee raised $500). This mobile cottage consisted of a livingroom and a kitchen simply but tastefully decorated, even to window curtains. Mrs. Nellie Russell—a warm, outgoing, motherly person, who somehow got children to like carrots and spinach —was in charge of the Little House on Wheels. She insisted on simplicity of equipment. Pots and pans and dishes had to be of the grade within the economic range of the people in the neighborhood, and cooking of course had to be done on a kerosene stove. At night, when traffic was lightest, the Little House was hauled from one poor and congested district to another.

The time came when the feeding of undernourished children seemed the responsibility of other agencies, particularly the Department of Health, which had a natural entree to homes through its public health nurses. The Board of Health therefore assumed this obligation, assisted at first by a contribution of $150 a month from the CCCW. In time the Department of Public Instruction assumed the responsibility of school lunches on a much wider and more professional scale.

INSTITUTIONAL CARE FOR MENTAL DEFECTIVES

The second major project of the Central Committee was undertaken when America was becoming interested in the tests developed by Alfred Binet for ascertaining the mental age of individuals. The first known person in Honolulu to have taken more than a passing interest in the Binet test was Dr. A. L. Andrews, Dean of the College of Arts and Sciences, University of Hawaii. His wife, Harriet C. Andrews, was a leading spirit and for years the president of the Central Committee on Child Welfare.

Collaborating with Dr. Andrews in research in feeble-mindedness was Miss Sadie Sterrit, Superintendent of the Girls' Industrial School. Miss Sterrit was concerned about girls who she felt were feeble-minded being committed by the Juvenile Court to the Industrial School. As they could not be held beyond the chronological age of majority, 18 years,[3] they were released into an unprotected environment when they reached this age. This same picture was true in the Boys' Industrial School.

Through the application of the Binet test to girls at the Girls' Industrial School, Dr. Andrews confirmed Miss Sterrit's opinion and encouraged the Central Committee to take steps for the establishment of institutional care for feeble-minded persons.

In 1918 the Legislature met in special session "to consider appropriate measures indicated by the effect of the war[4] on Hawaii.[5] Through pressure brought by the CCCW, Governor Lucius E. Pinkham was mandated at this special session to appoint a Commission to Investigate Feeble-Mindedness in the Territory of Hawaii.[6] Dr. Andrews, a member of the Commission, advised that in the interim between the special and regular session in 1919, data should be gathered showing the need of institutional care for the feeble-minded.

Toward this end letters were written to interested people throughout the territory—teachers and others—asking for lists of persons who were obviously feeble-minded. The commission's direct method convinced the Legislative Committee. As Dr. Andrews read out the names from the collected lists, some legislator would remark, "I know that boy (or girl). Sure, he (or she) is *lolo* (stupid)."

Added impetus was provided when several CCCW members took a number of low grade feeble-minded persons to a meeting of the special legislative committee. One of these persons, twenty-three years of age, sat on the floor and played with his toes, reciting the nursery jingle, "this little pig went to market, this little pig stayed home, etc." That was enough to bring success to the sustained efforts of these crusaders.

Home for the Feeble-Minded

The Legislature of 1919 appropriated $60,000 for the next biennium [7] and 500 acres of territorial land at Pearl City were acquired for the establishment of the Home for the Feeble-Minded. Later its name was changed to Waimano Home.[8]

The home was opened in March 1921. The original capacity was 64. At the end of the first fiscal year there were 45 feeble-minded residents. By 1952 the capacity was increased to 534; at that time there were 697 feeble-minded persons in the home, and a waiting list of 500, including 100 urgent cases.[9] Since 1941 Waimano Home has been under the jurisdiction of the Department of Institutions. Prior to that date it was under the control of an unpaid board of five commissioners appointed by the governor of Hawaii.

Advocacy of Sterilization

The Central Committee on Child Welfare did not stop with the establishment of an institution for the feeble-minded. There was a conviction, rather general during those years, that feeble-mindedness was inheritable and that to allow the propagation of human beings unable to manage their lives would increase not only social and economic problems but also the tensions in families which had feeble-minded members.

Several physicians, as well as various organizations represented by the CCCW, were strongly in favor of sterilizing the feeble-minded in general and those in Waimano Home in particular. They went so far as to get a legislative bill drafted for this purpose.

The minutes of the Central Committee record the dissenting voice of one member—a Roman Catholic—and the remark of a prominent politician who said the introduction of such a bill would be political suicide. The story ends when the ladies retired gracefully behind their decision to refer the matter to the Honolulu County Medical Society—there it died a natural death.

THE JUVENILE COURT

The third major concern of the Central Committee on Child Welfare was the Juvenile Court. Although that title was generally used, there were no juvenile courts in the territory at that time. Children's cases were assigned to the judges of circuit courts on the respective islands. Sessions concerning children were always held in chambers [10]—the Judge's office.

Rumors were current in Honolulu of substandard probationary practices—juveniles being whipped or "railroaded into the Industrial Schools," low standards in the Detention Home, inadequate physical examinations, poor food, indiscriminate mixing of ages and of delinquents and dependents, and so forth. The Central Committee decided to correct this state of affairs. I had just returned from a two-year graduate course at the New York School of Social Work and was ready to assist on a professional level.

Obtaining the co-operation of the judge of the Juvenile Court, the CCCW began a project in 1919 which ended with the legislative session in 1921. In this period I had the status of "special probation officer." Expenses were met by the CCCW. My duty was to gather facts upon which to base recommendations toward the enactment of appropriate Territorial laws in 1921.

ANALYTIC STUDY OF 100 JUVENILES

A room at the Associated Charities, then on Miller Street, was prepared at nominal cost and as complete a study as possible—social, physical, and mental—was made of 100 unselected boys and girls brought into the Juvenile Court. Helping in this undertaking were four physicians: Drs. Edwin R. and Margaret C. Lewis,[11] who gave the children thorough physical examinations; Dr. Eric A. Fennel,[12] who donated his services for the serological analyses; and Dr. Ernest Hoag, psychiatrist of the Los Angeles Juvenile Court, at the time a visitor in Honolulu, who likewise volunteered to give mental examinations.

Social Examinations

The social histories of the 100 juveniles revealed the shocking environments in which some were living. Cases were brought before the judge and summarily disposed of. De-

cisions were based upon the most superficial histories from
one or the other of the two probation officers—a man for the
boys and a woman for the girls—neither of whom had the
requisite training or experience for such a responsible position.
Some children were sent to the Detention Home or even committed to the Industrial Schools on nothing other than a complaint of "disobedience" by a parent or one in authority.

One morning a kindly speaking woman in a clean, crisp
holoku [13] sought adoption of a new-born baby whose mother,
she said, had died the day before in childbirth. The judge
told one of the probation officers to get the necessary adoption
papers ready for him to sign. Seeing my expression, the judge
remarked, "You don't seem to approve. Why?" I replied,
"What of the veracity of this woman's story? How do we
know whether or not the baby's mother is dead; and, if so,
what of possible relatives who might have something to say?
Despite Mrs. —'s good appearance and kindly manner, what
do we know of her suitability as a foster mother?" The judge
was irked. He snapped, "Very well, I'll assign the case to you,
but I want your report in 24 hours." He got it.

Confirmation of the baby's birth and the mother's death was
obtained. The mother was a very attractive, illiterate Spaniard
who had come to Hawaii with her husband, and both had
entered as laboring immigrants. She had divorced him to
marry an American soldier, since transferred to the Philippines.
I visited the home of the applicant for the baby—a single,
dirty, shabby room in a congested part of the city. In the
course of the interview the applicant revealed a probable
syphilitic history as she told of repeated pregnancies which
resulted in either abortions or stillbirths. Her husband, she
said, drank heavily. A trunk in the room belonged to the baby's
deceased mother. Looking in it for clues, I found well-expressed
letters from the soldier husband, begging his wife to get someone to write for her as he was anxious about her approaching
confinement. There were also letters from his sister, a teacher
in Texas.

Next morning I made my report to the judge. "Now, what
do you propose be done?" he asked. I suggested that the Court
place the baby, upon discharge from the hospital, in the Salvation Army Girls' Home, [14] and that letters be written to both
father and paternal aunt asking their wishes in the matter.

This was done. The aunt, whose credentials proved good, wanted her niece, and the baby's father wanted it that way. In a matter of weeks the infant was on her way to Texas, shepherded en route by a suitable person. What this child's life would have been had the adoption paper been signed without investigation is left to the reader's imagination.

Physical Examinations

The physical defects among the 100 juveniles included abnormal tonsils, decayed teeth, pediculosis, and ruptured hymens. Aside from these impairments noted in his report, Dr. Edwin Lewis had something to say on the credit side of the account about the general appearance of the boys.

It was a constant source of pleasure to observe the marvelous muscular development of the boys. Many, while slight in stature displayed the hard firm muscles, common to all, which the out-of-door life and exercise gives. The Hawaiian boys were the pictures of physical perfection with their broad deep chests and the slender waist so much admired in the athlete. The Japanese were more generally developed, lacking the beauty of the Hawaiian, but built for strength and endurance. Chinese, Korean, Filipino and Portuguese were hard and firm, though wanting in the spectacular. Boys from the mainland suffer in comparison.[15]

The most significant findings of the physical examinations of those 100 juveniles are contained in Dr. Fennel's report. By the Wassermann test he found that "23 of the children had syphilis, 8 more probably had it, 8 more were very doubtful, and 61 did not have syphilis."

Mental Examinations

In the report of mental examinations, and with the most liberal interpretation (because of language difficulties and racial differences), Dr. Hoag rated the children he examined as follows:

Above Normal	1 case
Normal	6 cases
Dull-Normal	5 cases
Dull	20 cases
Border-Line	11 cases
Feeble-Minded	55 cases

He found that 79.33 per cent were retarded in school, most of them by several years. He stated further:

All studies of Juvenile Court cases coincide in respect to the fact that the majority are much retarded in school and subnormal in intelligence. It seems remarkable that this relation between school retardation, mental incapacity, and delinquency has not in the past attracted more attention from school and court authorities, and the general public.[16]

Colin J. Herrick, Ph.D., Director of the Psychological and Psychopathic Clinic, who read the manuscript, stated:

Dr. Hoag's ratings of these 100 children are probably not far different from ratings by other authorities in Juvenile Courts in various parts of the country during that period. Investigations since that time, including follow-up studies on some of the earlier reported cases, make it abundantly clear that feeble-mindedness is not more frequent in the delinquent than in the nondelinquent population, i.e. from 0.5 per cent to 1.5 per cent.[17]

In the analytical study of the 100 juveniles, there were instances of a lack of co-ordination among several courts, in every one of which might be a member of the same family—one or both parents arraigned in the Police Court, later seeking a divorce in the Circuit Court, and a child or children brought to the Juvenile Court as delinquents or dependents.

With this piecemeal handling of families, good probationary standards were impossible. A court of domestic relations was indicated as a means of co-ordination, but for any such court to function adequately there must be at least a minimum number of probation officers who are qualified caseworkers.

RECOMMENDATIONS

As noted in the preceding chapter, a natural sequence to casework is the discovery of needs and the extension or organization of social services to fill these needs. As the two years for which I was employed drew to a close, I made, in consultation with the executive board of the Central Committee on Child Welfare, the following recommendations:

1. That a court of domestic relations be established for the adjudication of all cases of a domestic or family nature, including delinquent and dependent children.

2. That probation officers be graduates of schools of social work and that five be appointed—a chief and four assistant officers.

3. That an advisory board be appointed, composed of persons of special fitness and of which the judge would be a member ex-officio.[18]

4. That a venereal disease clinic be established.

5. That a mental hygiene clinic be established.

Appropriate bills for the enactment of these recommendations into laws were introduced into the 1921 legislature. The main results are described below.

Court of Domestic Relations

A Court of Domestic Relations was established in 1921 in Honolulu by adding a fourth judge to the First Circuit. All cases of a domestic or family nature, including dependent and delinquent children, were thereafter to be heard in the Court of Domestic Relations.[19] Five probation officers, as recommended, were appointed and were paid salaries comparable to those of professionally educated social workers. The legislature refused, however, to make training a mandatory qualification.

The recommendation of an advisory board to the judge of the Court of Domestic Relations fell on deaf ears. Though the Central Committee had ample factual evidence for the advisability of establishing such a board, particularly in matters concerning probation standards, they could make no impression on the lawyer chairman of the legislative committee to which the bill was referred. To him and his legal colleagues such an innovation would be interference with the authority of a judge.

The first judge of the newly established Court of Domestic Relations incurred so much criticism for his lack of qualification in this field that he resigned before the end of his second term. It was said that his chief probation officer had come from a job in a lumberyard. When a member of the Central Committee remonstrated with him upon such an appointment, he replied in effect, "Politics gave me this job and I have to play politics."

In 1945 the Court of Domestic Relations was disestablished—owing, it was said, to the congestion of the calendar because marital and juvenile cases were adjudicated by the same judge.[20] A Juvenile Court was therefore established in 1945 by the addition of a sixth judge to the First Circuit to give full time to juvenile cases, while domestic relations rotated among the other circuit judges. Seven adult probation officers serve the First Circuit, none of them professionally qualified for the type of casework family problems require. There was no longer a Central Committee on Child Welfare to block this regression.

In 1939, when the Territorial Civil Service was established, government employees then on the payroll were given permanent civil service status, regardless of qualifications. As of June 1, 1952, inclusive of the chief, subexecutive and supervisory officers, the probation staff of the Juvenile Court numbered twenty-seven, none of them graduates of accredited schools of social work. Despite this fact there has been improvement since 1921 in probationary standards, but lack of professional qualifications is reflected, to mention but one example, in restricted opportunities for field training in social work.

Hawaii needs social workers. The School of Social Work, University of Hawaii, needs diversified field work resources and these must be found in agencies that can offer adequate professional supervision. The Courts of the First Circuit do not yet meet this requirement.

Venereal Disease Clinic

As to the fourth recommendation of the CCCW mentioned above, the 1921 Legislature established by law a venereal disease clinic. Because venereal disease was then not commonly mentioned in public, it was thought inadvisable to identify this clinic; it was therefore merged with the dispensary of Palama Settlement, which at that time had the only outpatient general dispensary in Honolulu. In 1942 the Territorial Department of Health established a bureau of venereal disease, since when all this work has been concentrated there.

Mental Hygiene Clinic

Concerning the establishment of a mental hygiene clinic, the last recommendation, the legislature in 1921 established the Psychological and Psychopathic Clinic to "investigate the nature, causes, treatment, and consequences of mental disease and defect within the Territory of Hawaii." [21] As a deterrent to political pressure the control of this clinic was vested in the Board of Regents of the University of Hawaii. Accepting the advice of the CCCW, the legislature appropriated funds to bring to Honolulu a consultant to organize the Psychological and Psychopathic Clinic. This is where trouble began.

PSYCHOLOGICAL AND PSYCHOPATHIC CLINIC

In the early 1920s there was still comparatively little understanding of feeble-mindedness and mental illness. The consultant recommended by the Central Committee on Child Welfare was Dr. Harold Williams, of Whittier, California, a psychologist. A very different situation would have evolved had the consultant been a psychiatrist. Dr. Williams advised an initial staff of three for the proposed clinic—a chief and an assistant psychologist and a social caseworker. He recommended Stanley D. Porteus [22] as chief psychologist and director and me as the social worker.

Dr. Porteus arrived in Honolulu in 1922 and was joined later by Miss Marjorie E. Babcock (Mrs. Wm. F. Robertson) as assistant psychologist. Social casework was not considered necessary to the clinic's program and I was not a psychologist, so I resigned in less than two years.

Although the intent of the promoters was a treatment as well as a research clinic, it was never so set up. Psychotherapy presupposes psychiatrists and social caseworkers as well as psychologists; but, with the exceptions of six months in the early 1940s when a psychiatrist, the wife of an army officer, was temporarily employed, and of a short time when a research psychiatrist was employed in 1953, the clinic's staff never has included a psychiatrist or a social caseworker since I resigned in 1923.

It was inevitable that dissatisfaction should arise in the community regarding the limitations of the Psychological and Psychopathic Clinic. This was accentuated as mental illnesses increased with the increase in population. A movement was therefore initiated by the Medical Social Service Association of Hawaii, which brought about the establishment of the Bureau of Mental Hygiene in 1939 (see Chapter XIX).

But here, too, were limitations for, with an older governmental organization staffed with psychologists, the legislature made no allowance for those in the younger Bureau of Mental Hygiene. Thus we had a Psychological and Psychopathic Clinic with no psychiatrist and for years a Bureau of Mental

Hygiene with no psychologist. Since January 1952 the staff
of the Bureau of Mental Hygiene has included a psychologist.

Though never stated as such, the very human factor of pre-
rogatives asserts itself in the "mental hygiene" of the participants in this problem. With the Psychological and Psychopathic Clinic strongly entrenched before the establishment in
1939 of the Bureau of Mental Hygiene, it was not to be expected that the director would take a position subordinate to
that of a psychiatrist, nor would a psychiatrist consent to be
secondary to a psychologist—and there cannot be two masters.
Irrespective of cost and treatment limitations, the Psychological
and Psychopathic Clinic and the Bureau of Mental Hygiene
continued to function as separate territorial entities until 1955.
It became a habit, not confirmed by statute, to eliminate
"Psychopathic" from the title of the Psychological and Psychopathic Clinic.

In 1948 Dr. Porteus, who had given outstanding service to
the community as a psychologist, retired and was succeeded
by Dr. Colin J. Herrick as Director of the Psychological Clinic.

The clinic by 1951 had eight psychologists, six on Oahu
and one each on Hawaii and Maui. Periodic visits were made
from Oahu to Kauai. The clinic's program included services
to courts and correctional institutions and public and private
agencies. Before a minimum sentence was imposed, for example, the accused underwent a psychological examination
by a member of the Psychological Clinic. A psychologist was
also in weekly attendance at the Juvenile Court for the purpose of counseling. About 40 per cent of the clinic's referrals
in 1952 came from schools—requests for psychometric testing
for retardation and consultation with teachers about children
manifesting psychological problems. A number of referrals
came from private agencies concerning adoptions, and occasionally an individual sought counseling of his own accord,
or a child was brought to the clinic by a parent. Some referrals
were from physicians in private practice.

In addition to these clinic services the agency conducted
research in its particular field and gave courses in psychology
to graduate and undergraduate students of the University of
Hawaii. University students also sought personal consultation
at the Psychological Clinic.

REORGANIZATION OF PSYCHOLOGICAL SERVICES

Under the auspices of the Oahu Health Council, Inc., a survey of public health was made in 1950 by Dr. Ira V. Hiscock.[23] Giving credit to the Psychological Clinic for the essential services rendered by it, Dr. Hiscock questioned its continuance as a separate unit and advocated a reorganization of psychological services.

Because of pressure building up in the community, as well as Dr. Hiscock's recommendation, the Oahu Health Council and the Mental Health Association combined efforts through special committees to bring about "integration, co-ordination, and unification of governmental services in mental health." This was finally accomplished in 1955 when the legislature of that year abolished the Psychological and Psychopathic Clinic by transferring its services to the Bureau of Mental Hygiene. At the same time it was ruled that the director and one other psychologist should remain on the staff of the University of Hawaii and should be assigned to appropriate positions on the faculty.[24]

CENTRAL COMMITTEE ON COMMUNITY WELFARE

As the years passed, the scope of the Central Committee on Child Welfare had broadened to include the welfare of adults as well as of children. It was, for example, helping to organize classes in Braille to teach the blind. It was helping financially to get occupational therapy established at The Queen's Hospital, and was co-ordinating its efforts for better laws with those of the League of Women Voters. A change of name had been discussed and was so voted at a special meeting in June 1925. With a revision of by-laws to embrace a wider scope, the Central Committee on Child Welfare became the Central Committee on Community Welfare.

But times were changing. In 1914, when a group of zealous women united in the cause of underprivileged children, social service was still in swaddling clothes. With the passage of years social casework began to meet professional criteria in techniques and skills; concurrently the acceptance of community organization was expressed in councils of social agencies.[25] A waning of the crusading spirit of earlier years was evident.

Dissolution

The Central Committee on Community Welfare felt it had served its purpose and should disband. This was effected at a special meeting on February 19, 1937. Reflecting on the general apathy in the territory today regarding the enactment of sound social laws and the repeal or modification of unsound ones, one could wish for a return of those crusading spirits who fearlessly and tenaciously held on whenever a cause needed the kind of social action to which the Central Committee on Child Welfare was dedicated.

[1] The organization was not incorporated.

[2] A word or phrase is missing in the statement consulted at the Archives.

[3] In 1949 majority was raised to 20 years. *T.H. Session Laws* (1949), Act 96, p. 20.

[4] The United States entered the first world war on April 5, 1917.

[5] "Purpose of Special Session 1918," *Senate Journal*, p. 3.

[6] *T.H. Session Laws* (Special Session 1918), Act 18, p. 23.

[7] *Ibid.* (1919), Act 102, p. 137.

[8] Hawaiian for "head of distributing waters." It is thought the name originally referred to ditches, at one time the common method of irrigating plantations. (Information given by Mr. Thomas B. Vance, director, Department of Institutions.)

[9] Information given by Mr. Vance.

[10] *T.H. Session Laws* (1909), Act 22, p. 23.

[11] No longer in the territory.

[12] Late member of the Straub Clinic, Honolulu.

[13] The Mother Hubbard gown fashioned by the early missionaries to replace the scant clothing of Hawaiian women.

[14] A function of the Salvation Army Girls' and Boys' Home was the foster care, temporarily or permanently, of children placed there by the Juvenile Court.

[15] Margaret M. L. Catton, *Report to the Central Committee on Child Welfare 1921*, p. 85; Public Archives of Hawaii.

[16] *Ibid.*, p. 89.

[17] Communication from Dr. Herrick.

[18] Since political pressure was anticipated, the advisory board was recommended (1) to help the judge in the appointment of qualified probation officers, and (2) to advise the officers.

[19] *T.H. Session Laws* (1921), Act 183, p. 238.

[20] *Ibid.* (1945), Act 142, p. 260–63.

[21] *Ibid.* (1921), Act 140, p. 184.

[22] Then Director of Research, Psychological Laboratory, Training School at Vineland, New Jersey.

[23] Ira V. Hiscock, *Public Health in Hawaii* (New Haven: Yale University Press, 1950), p. 11.

[24] *T.H. Session Laws* (1955), Act 182, p. 151.

[25] The Honolulu Council of Social Agencies was organized in 1927.

VII

Catholic Social Service [1]

(Period included: 1917–1951)

In 1917, when America entered the first world war, the National War Service Division of the Knights of Columbus, needing a canteen and recreational center for servicemen and their families, financed the erection of the building at 1183 Fort Street now known as the Catholic Center. The war over, the Columbus Welfare Association donated this building to the Catholic Church for the Association's use as headquarters for its clubs and classes and, by 1921, for such family service as one worker "without complete professional training" was able to render.

By 1942, during World War II, the Columbus Welfare Building was among those needed by the United Service Organization, so the lone social worker and secretary moved to other offices next to the Roman Catholic Cathedral.

CATHOLIC CHARITIES

Pressure by their church and by community agencies for more adequate social service to Catholic families and children had been slowly mounting. In recognition of this need, Bishop Sweeney in 1942 appointed Father Hubert Winthagen as Diocesan Director of Catholic Charities. This led in turn to an agreement by the Maryknoll sisters to furnish a social service staff to the Catholic Charities. They sent Sister Victoria Francis and three additional sisters to Honolulu in 1944. In the same year the Columbus Welfare Association was re-organized into the Catholic Charities, the first name under which these Maryknoll sisters functioned.

CATHOLIC SOCIAL SERVICE (1948)

In 1948 this division of the organization took the name Catholic Social Service. The word "division" is used because,

77

contrary to the general impression among non-Catholics, the name Catholic Social Service did not supplant that of Catholic Charities. The latter designates the whole organization of which social service is one part. Other divisions within the Charities are health (St. Francis Hospital and its various departments), child caring institutions (St. Anthony's Home on Oahu and the Maui Children's Home at Paia), and the Catholic Youth Organization.

According to Article I of its charter, the purposes of the Catholic Charities include the following:

e) To co-ordinate and correlate charitable agencies, to direct the work of the Roman Catholic Diocese of Honolulu in the major functional fields of health, social action, social group work and social casework, including child placing and child care in institutions and family foster homes;

f) To function as the official representative of the Roman Catholic Diocese of Honolulu, in its dealings with kindred agencies in the Territory of Hawaii and in its participation in community movement for the promotion of the general welfare;

i) To organize and direct any subsidiary agencies, units or auxiliaries needed to carry out any of the above works.

Support

A considerable portion of the support of Catholic Social Service is through the Honolulu Community Chest. Its budget includes an allowance for supplemental payments, if necessary, to certain relief cases and for the care of the children in St. Anthony's and family foster homes.

Persons needing basic support are referred to the Department of Public Welfare. When, in the furtherance of treatment, supplementary financial assistance is indicated, the agency may draw upon other Catholic organizations and clubs. As a means of stimulating interest in their work, as well as for financial resources, the Catholic Social Service conducts an annual membership drive.

Administration

The Catholic Social Service functions as such only on Oahu, from its office, formerly at 258 South Vineyard Street and now at 1660 Kalakaua Avenue. It is governed by an advisory board of men and women, with not less than ten, nor more than thirty members. The Bishop of the Roman Catholic Church, the most Reverend James J. Sweeney, as titular head of all its diocesan activities, is the honorary president of Social Service; the active president must be a layman.

As Diocesan Director of Catholic Charities Father Winthagen was given responsibility for the over-all planning of its social service. This is in accordance with the general pattern of Catholic Charities throughout the United States. Serving under the Diocesan Director is the executive secretary responsible for its casework program. Sister Victoria Francis was the first executive secretary of Catholic Social Service.

In the development of a social agency there is usually an outstanding personality. That person in the Catholic Social Service was Sister Victoria Francis. She is remembered not only as an able executive but also as a member of the Hawaii chapter of the American Association of Social Workers. She took an active part in discussions of general professional interest. It caused real regret to many Honoluluans when in 1950 Sister Victoria Francis was transferred back to the mainland.

In 1951 the professional staff of Catholic Social Service, including the executive secretary, consisted of nine sisters (four of whom had degrees in social work), one lay worker, and three students from the School of Social Work, University of Hawaii. In addition there were eight volunteers.

Functions

The casework functions of the Catholic Social Service are those of a general family agency. There is also an active foster-care program. St. Anthony's Home, situated in Kalihi Valley, was known before 1948 as the Kalihi Orphanage. It accepts boys from age five to twelve and girls from five to seventeen. Any social agency is free to apply, but all applications must be channeled through Catholic Social Service. The majority of the young ones in St. Anthony's are of the Roman Catholic faith, but there are also children of Protestant parents or guardians; they are free to attend their own churches.

Catholic Social Service designates one caseworker as a liaison between St. Anthony's and community agencies who use this home as a resource. The agencies are responsible both for support and casework of the children they place in St. Anthony's Home. Those who reach maximum age and are still in need of foster care are still the responsibility of the placing agency.

In addition to St. Anthony's Home, Catholic Social Service has an affiliation, though a less direct one, with the parochial schools. The schools send to Social Service students who manifest social or emotional problems. If a mental examination is indicated the caseworker prepares the social history, makes the referral to the Bureau of Mental Hygiene or the Psychological Clinic [2] and follows through with suggested plans for treatment.

Catholic children in public schools are also referred to Catholic Social Service, usually through the Division of Pupil Guidance of the Department of Public Instruction.

UNIQUE FEATURES OF A RELIGION-BASED ORGANIZATION

The operations of the Catholic Social Service are indicative of a high grade of work. Meeting accepted standards for child welfare, the agency is licensed in this regard by the Department of Public Welfare. A further criterion of the caliber of this organization is the fact that Catholic Social Service is used for field work placement of students attending the School of Social Work, University of Hawaii.

Were the word "Catholic" eliminated, this chapter, so far, might be the history of any approved social agency, but there are basic differences which make for the uniqueness of this one, and for that matter, of any organization under the control of a religious body.

In schools of social work that bear the stamp of approval of the American Association of Schools of Social Work—and there are Catholic ones among them—comparable knowledge and skills are taught all students, Catholic and Protestant alike. There is nothing unique about that.

The distinction is one of basic philosophy between a religious-controlled (not necessarily Roman Catholic) and a lay institution. For example, an applicant for a position in a church organization is expected to have an affiliation with the church and the conviction of a spiritual ultimate, something beyond the material world, whereas this certitude is not of cardinal importance to a nonsectarian organization. Some of the workers have it—reflected as a plus in their practice—while others with knowledge and skill as caseworkers are agnostics—their practice sometimes reflects a minus. (See "Religion as a Resource in Social Work," Part II, Chapter XX.)

One may mention incentive as another distinction. At one time social work was chosen as a career principally for the opportunities it offered for service. Over the years another motivation has come into prominence, that of ego satisfactions such as professional advancement with accompanying higher salaries which are to be had more easily in secular than in church-governed institutions.

But though many individuals in secular organizations may be motivated by worldly gratifications, there are others to whom, across the ages, the Voice still rings clear: "Inasmuch as ye have done it unto one of the least of these, my brethren, ye have done it unto me."

[1] This chapter is based on *Short History of Catholic Social Service* (copy at headquarters of agency) and conferences with sisters of the organization.
[2] Disestablished 1955.

VIII

Liliuokalani Trust

(Period included: 1935–1951)

Close to where The Queen's Hospital stands, a Hawaiian Chiefess was born on September 2, 1838. The newborn baby was wrapped in fine tapa cloth and taken to the home of Paki, whose wife was a direct descendant of Kamehameha the Great. Paki and Konia had an only daughter, Bernice Pauahi (Mrs. Charles R. Bishop), who, through her inheritance of Kamehameha lands, formed the Bishop Estate, and became the largest landowner in the Territory.

Liliuokalani was educated at the Chiefs (later known as the Royal) School. With financial support and building provided by the chiefs, the school was conducted for children of chief's or royal blood by Mr. and Mrs. Amos Cooke, sent to Honolulu by the American Board of Commissioners for Foreign Missions.

In 1862 Liliuokalani married John Owen Dominis, son of a well-to-do sea captain who had settled in Honolulu. In January 1891, following the death of her brother, King Kalakaua, Liliuokalani was crowned queen in Iolani Palace. John Dominis died seven months later. The queen inherited the political unrest of her brother's reign and was herself to reign for less than two years. She was deposed in January 1893, and the Hawaiian monarchy came to an end.

The dethroned queen returned to the Dominis family home, Washington Place, where she was kept under guard until the monarchists had lost hope of restoring her to the throne. Here she wrote *Hawaii's Story by Hawaii's Queen*. Washington Place was later acquired by the territory and still serves as the official gubernatorial residence. Close to its Beretania Street boundary, in a paved spot embowered with Hawaiian verdure, a stone stands to commemorate the queen. On a bronze tablet are engraved the words of the most famous of many songs she composed—*Aloha Oe*.

82

The Queen's Trust

In 1909 Liliuokalani executed a trust deed which provided that at her death all her property not included in specific bequests should be used for the benefit of orphan children in the Hawaiian Islands, "preference being given to Hawaiian children of pure or part aboriginal blood," this to be done as soon as practicable through the establishment of one or more fireproof institutions, each to bear the name "Liliuokalani." The deed was modified in 1911 to include destitute as well as orphan children in the Hawaiian Islands, the preference to be given to children of pure or part-Hawaiian blood.[1]

Queen Liliuokalani died in 1917. She had no children, nor did she possess great wealth. Since there were at the time insufficient funds to carry out her wishes in the interest of children, her trustees decided to let income accumulate against the day when there would be enough to provide, not only land, buildings, and equipment for an institution, but also for its maintenance and for staff.

That the trustees gave a good account of their stewardship is evidenced by the fact that the value of the estate, which was $125,000 when the original deed was executed in 1909, had risen by 1933 to $835,330. By this time the trustees were becoming convinced that institutional care of children *per se* was obsolete; foster homes and boarding schools were taking its place.

It was felt, therefore, that this trust deed should be interpreted in accordance with modern ideas of child welfare. This would also mean a saving in the overhead costs of maintaining an institution such as the one first envisioned.

In September 1934 the requisite legal steps were taken, and a decree was duly entered giving the trustees of the Liliuokalani Trust full power to use the whole or any part of the current net annual income for the benefit of "orphan and other destitute children." Although the court saw no need to dispense permanently with the idea of an institution, the decree authorized the trustees to provide for care in foster homes, boarding schools, or other suitable institutions which the circumstances might dictate as the wisest choice.[2]

In January 1935 the Liliuokalani Trust commenced a child welfare program with an office in the Inter-Island Steamship

Company Building on Fort and Merchant Streets. Miss Nora Lange, an Island-born woman whose professional training had been in child welfare, was its first executive director.

Later in 1935 another important event took place—the establishment of the Children's Service Association (chapter IX), of which the Liliuokalani Trust was a constituent. When the Children's Service Association was dissolved in 1941, the Child Welfare Services of the Liliuokalani Trust functioned for several years as a distinct unit within the Child and Family Service.

The trust members became increasingly dissatisfied with this arrangement. One reason given was that the caseload was decreasing instead of increasing; another was the feeling that, with the merger, family problems took precedence over those of children. These reasons would hardly hold today.

In the 1930s there was mass unemployment, and caseloads in social agencies were correspondingly high, whereas during the war years (1941–45) unemployment was practically nil and caseloads fell correspondingly. As for the second reason, although in that period of social welfare segmentation into specialized fields was common, the approach became increasingly a more generic one. Even though the emphasis might shift from one to the other as circumstances indicated, child welfare and family welfare are not divisible.

The Liliuokalani Trust disassociated itself in 1946 from the Child and Family Service. It withdrew its records from the unit system installed at the time of consolidation but, by paying rent, maintained headquarters in the same building with the Child and Family Service until 1948 when, needing more space, it moved to 1160 Bishop Street. (In 1952 it moved again, to property owned by the Liliuokalani Trust at 1218 Young Street.) Another incentive for these moves was to enhance its identity as an autonomous agency, the better to preserve the intent of a memorial to Queen Liliuokalani as expressed in the original trust deed.

Administration

The governing board of the Liliuokalani Trust consists of three trustees, one of whom is a social worker of part-Hawaiian blood, Clorinda Lucas; one a former delegate to Congress, also part-Hawaiian, Captain Victor S. K. Houston, U.S. Navy, retired; and the third the Cooke Trust Company.

Though the terms of the trust deed give preference to children of "pure or aboriginal blood," they do not debar those of other ancestry; however, in order to do a better job with a lesser number, intake is limited to "preference." Service is also limited to children under the age of majority, which in Hawaii is twenty years.

Staff

Miss Lange, who for some ten years had not been with the Liliuokalani Trust, returned to it in 1946 on a part-time basis, as executive director of its child welfare services. Otherwise the professional staff consisted in 1951 of a supervisor who had a degree in social work, three caseworkers with one year of graduate training at the School of Social Work, University of Hawaii, and one worker without graduate training.

Functions

The Liliuokalani Trust limits its activities to Oahu. Children from the neighbor islands are accepted, provided arrangements can be made for them in boarding schools. If a study indicates factors in the family as the source of maladjustment, the case is referred to the Child and Family Service.

The trust has agreed to help the Kamehameha Schools in obtaining social histories of applicants for scholarships awarded by those schools. They also accept "care and custody" for dependent minors referred by the Juvenile Court, provided, however, the dependents qualify as "orphan or other destitute children." Such children are placed in boarding institutions or foster homes, with the Liliuokalani Trust taking responsibility for any indicated casework.

Hanai Children

There are certain complications peculiar to *hanai* (foster) children. According to an old Hawaiian custom, parents often give their children to grandparents, or others, to be reared. Hawaiians are particularly fond of children and the matter of racial background is unimportant. In answer to a question I once asked a Hawaiian about her *hanai* daughter of Japanese parentage, she replied, "It makes no difference; I love her just like my own child."

Liliuokalani was herself a *hanai* child. Though the custom

of *hanai* made no difference so far as affection between foster parents and children was concerned, complications arose when the white man took over in the Islands and promulgated laws in accordance with the mores of his culture. Among these were adoption laws which discriminated against *hanai* children in the matter of inheritance. Unless legally provided for by will, a *hanai* child may not inherit property from his *hanai* parents. This can create serious dissension, especially if there are natural children who have not been so close to their parents as have their *hanai* siblings.

Aside from the matter of inheritance, a *hanai* child may be overindulged by its grandparents and, should the latter die, it is not always wise to return the child to its natural parents, especially if there are other natural children and adjustments have to be made between them and one who is actually a stranger in their household. The question of paternity, legal or *hanai*, thus has a bearing on decisions made by the Liliuokalani Trust regarding children.

PROPOSED PLAN FOR OPERATION

In September 1950, a Proposed Plan of Operation was submitted by Miss Lange to the trustees of the Liliuokalani Trust to the effect that "any child living in his own home with one or both parents would not be eligible for assistance from the Trust. Assistance would be offered only to the child without a satisfactory home of his own."

The idea of this proposal was, it seems, to keep in mind the original purpose of the trust, namely, an institution for "orphans and other destitute children," and it was thought that, if children were living in their own homes with one or both parents, they could be neither orphaned nor destitute. In current practice, however, the agency is giving some support to minors in the homes of destitute parents.

ACCREDITATION

The Department of Public Welfare has legal responsibility for licensing children's institutions and agencies. Owing to certain technicalities that had to do with the policies of the governing board, the Liliuokalani Trust operated under a temporary license until the regular license was granted in 1952.

The accreditation of institutions and agencies through licensing has made for uniformity as to standards and cost of care. Budgets set up by the Department of Public Welfare do not include such items as spending money, school fees, or an adequate allowance for clothing. The Liliuokalani Trust can afford to be liberal in these respects.

1 Equity No. 1748, pp. 1, 2, Circuit Court of the First Judicial Circuit; recorded in Registry Office of Honolulu, Liber 319, pp. 447–59.
2 Extract in Child Welfare Department, Liliuokalani Trust.

LITERATURE REVIEWED

Liliuokalani. *Hawaii's Story by Hawaii's Queen—Liliuokalani* (Boston: Lothrop, Lee & Shepard Co., 1898.)
Kuykendall and Day. *Hawaii, A History.*
Kuykendall. *The Hawaiian Kingdom 1778–1854.*

IX

Children's Service Association [1]

(Extant: 1935–1941)

In 1935 there were in Honolulu three separate agencies which included child welfare programs—Hawaiian Humane Society, Social Service Bureau, and the newly established Liliuokalani Trust Child Welfare Department.

The United Welfare Fund and the Honolulu Council of Social Agencies were concerned about the overlapping functions and cost of three organizations with certain similar activities. They therefore engaged Mr. C. C. Carstens, Executive Director of the Child Welfare League of America, to come to Honolulu in January 1935, to make a study of "agencies and institutions dealing with dependent and delinquent children of Honolulu." [2]

FOUNDING OF CHILDREN'S SERVICE ASSOCIATION (1935)

Mr. Carstens' principal recommendation was the founding of a special agency to be known as the Children's Service Association, its nucleus to be the Children's Bureau of the Social Service Bureau, the Children's portion of the Hawaiian Humane Society, and the child welfare services of the Liliuokalani Trust. Other recommendations included: follow-up with families of children accepted for care; shortened residence of children in institutions; more individualization to discover capabilities as well as limitations and needs; placement of wards of the Juvenile Court by the Children's Service Association instead of by the court; raising the standards in the Detention Home; replacement of truant officers by visiting teachers; a more adequate parole system; and the furtherance of psychological services. By September 1935 the Children's Service Association was established.

88

Support

This new agency was supported chiefly by the United Welfare Fund. The Liliuokalani Trust took responsibility for the salaries of a staff and the cost of services to implement its particular program within the Association. Sometimes parents made reimbursements for boarding their children, sometimes the Juvenile Court assumed this cost.

Administration

Representatives of the agencies incorporated into the Children's Service Association formed its board of directors. Dr. A. L. Dean was appointed president. Miss Alida Winkelmann, (who came from a similar position in the Children's Bureau of Delaware), was executive secretary. The initial staff were the workers of the three constituent bodies.

The agency's first headquarters were on Punchbowl Street between Beretania and Hotel Streets. In March 1937 the office was moved to South Beretania Street, opposite Central Union Church. This building had been a private residence which, after the death of its owner, was bought by Mr. Frank C. Atherton and later deeded to the United Welfare Fund. It became the headquarters of the Boy Scouts of America.

FUNCTIONS

The Children's Service Association was incorporated for the following purposes:

1. To care for children requiring the community's interest, such care to be provided either in their own homes or in foster families or institutions.

2. To protect children from cruelty and abuse.

3. To assist in reducing juvenile delinquency.

4. To stimulate greater interest in good standards for the training and guidance of children by community education and by suitable legislation or by any other means found necessary.

5. To work in all suitable ways either directly or by co-operation with other agencies, and as far as the resources of the corporation permit, that any child requiring the community's interest may obtain the form of service which will be of most value to him.

6. In all practicable ways to further the welfare and the improvement of children in the Territory of Hawaii to the end that they may become useful members of society.[3]

In accordance with the first purpose, an appraisal was made of foster homes and institutions, and of those in charge. As a result of this study the association reiterated the opinion of every preceding social agency interested in children; the need for a shelter home for the temporary placement of dependent minors where case studies could be made pending more permanent placement.

The Children's Service Association initiated the practice of casework service for children who were placed in foster homes and institutions. The experiment proved so successful that it became the association's major program and much pressure was exerted for its continuance when, due to lack of funds and personnel, the association had to limit its service.

Social Legislation

The association was concerned about the abuse and neglect of children. This brought them into close relationship with the Juvenile Court and also emphasized the need for the adoption or modification of laws in behalf of minors. One modification in which it was particularly interested was the extension—from six months to two years after date of birth—of the period within which an unwed mother could bring legal action against the father for the support of their child. The law was so amended in 1947.[4] Undoubtedly the amendment would have been made earlier had the Children's Service Association not been disincorporated in the meantime.

Another concern was the problem of illegitimate children of normal intelligence born as a result of feeble-minded women mating with men of mentality superior to theirs. As these mothers lacked the mental capacity to raise their offspring, the Children's Service Association felt that Waimano Home should be enlarged and feeble-minded women committed there during the child-bearing age.

In line with this philosophy of prevention the association was acutely aware of the relationship of inadequate relief to need and disease. This was particularly evident in the number of dependent children whose parents were tuberculous.

In furthering child welfare the association set high school as the educational standard for children able to benefit thereby, reasoning that not only would their own lives be enriched but they in turn would be better prepared for parenthood.

The Children's Service Association came into being just one month after the enactment of the Federal Social Security Law, August 1935, and less than two years before territorial law established the Board of Public Welfare and County Welfare Commissions, making possible participation in the federal program.

This was the decade of the great depression, a time of mass unemployment and of rising relief rolls, and a time when there were too few qualified workers to carry the load. The United Welfare Fund was having its troubles campaigning for support of voluntary agencies. Public Welfare relieved pressure on the Children's Service Association by accepting transfers that came within the former's category of Aid to Dependent Children, but even so, the association continued to run on a deficit and had to apply to the Territorial Relief and Welfare Commission for supplementary funds.

Getting under way was no simple matter for the Board of Public Welfare, either. It was necessary to close intake, which of course shut off referrals from the Children's Service Association. In addition to financial stringency, the association suffered severely from professional turnover. At a time when help was most needed, the association lost to the Board of Public Welfare four workers, including two in key positions; thus the thwarting effect of monthly deficits was aggravated by the depressing number of unserviced applications.

The Social Service Bureau was likewise unsettled regarding its survival as a voluntary agency; it, too, was feeling the effects of the depression and was also losing workers to the newly formed governmental organization.

Question of Consolidation

These circumstances suggested a merger of the Social Service Bureau and the Children's Service Association in the interest of both stability and economy. In January 1939 the problem was brought before the directorate of the Children's Service Association. The directors of both agencies asked representative workers to express their opinions on a merger.

The family agency's workers thought in terms of the family; they said that, as a matter of fact, they had, since the begin-

ning of the Children's Service Association, been receiving referrals of cases in which the emphasis was as much, or more,
on the family than on the child. Conversely, they were referring children to the other organization. The workers whose
specialty was child welfare were averse to a merger; one went
so far as to say that the Humane Society had become a constituent of CSA only on the understanding that its identity as a
children's agency would be maintained. This feeling was
shared by the workers of the Liliuokalani Trust.

In developing skills in casework various philosophies come
into practice, some to remain, others to be modified, and some
to be discarded; it is thus that the profession of social work
evolves.

There were different techniques practiced at that time in
the Children's Service Association and the Family Consultation
Service; [5] one a positive, the other a passive relationship between worker and client.

In contradistinction to the aggressiveness of the charity
visitor of an earlier period and a still thoughtless dominating
attitude of a later period, a school of thought had arisen, holding that, in order to ensure better adjustability, the client
should take responsibility in making application and in interviews.

At the time that a merger of these two organizations was
being discussed, the passive attitude assumed by workers in
the family agency was very much to the fore. It was not always a success. One patient of mine, though no longer in
need of medical social service, did require family consultation.
I retain a vivid picture of an irate man coming back to tell
me that "the family worker was dumb; she didn't say anything,
she just looked at me."

The Children's Service Association submitted that children
needing a positive approach would be the losers through the
passive attitude practiced by the Family Consultation Service.
The latter, however, voiced the assurance that this would not
necessarily be its technique in establishing a casework relationship with children. Careful thinking went into the idea
of consolidating the two agencies, and they were finally merged
by February 1, 1941, as a result of the Honolulu Plan. The
Children's Service Association thus came to an end after only

six years, but in that brief span it had set an excellent standard for child welfare in Hawaii.

[1] The files of the CSA were made available to me. These files have since been deposited at the School of Social Work, University of Hawaii.

[2] *A Brief Study of Children's Organizations, City and County of Honolulu,* January and February, 1935, Child Welfare League of America, Inc., p. 1.

[3] *Charter, Children's Service Association,* Territory of Hawaii, 1935, pp. 1–2.

[4] *T.H. Session Laws* (1947), Act 57, p. 393.

[5] The name adopted later in 1939 by the Social Service Bureau.

X

Medical, Rehabilitation, and Domiciliary Services

(Period included: 1860–1953)

Essential to the practice of social casework are facilities for meeting the hazards of illness, crippling conditions, and old age. This chapter will describe what has been done in Hawaii in this regard.

MEDICAL

Limited medical services are supplied to the indigent and medically indigent [1] by the federal, territorial, and city and county governments. Categorically, the indigent are without means for such necessities as food, shelter, and clothing; recipients of public welfare, for example, are indigent persons; the medically indigent are economically independent so far as ordinary living expenses are concerned, but cannot meet the extraordinary costs of illness.

Prior to 1947, no general hospital in Honolulu had outpatient services. Ambulatory patients in need of free treatment had to get it at Palama Settlement, where a dispensary financed by the city and county had been in operation since 1915. Before that the government operated a part-time clinic held in a building adjacent to the Board of Health. In 1947 Palama closed its dispensary with the opening of outpatient departments at The Queen's and St. Francis hospitals. In rural Oahu and on the neighbor islands private physicians are subsidized by the Territory, through the Department of Health, to see needy patients in their offices, call upon them at home, and hospitalize them in county general, plantation, and private nonprofit hospitals. On Oahu, subsidy and administration are shared jointly by the Territory and the county.

As the population of Honolulu increased, so did the number

94

of indigent persons. Costs of medical care were likewise mounting. The various counties could require a certain period of residence before paying for medical care, and in the city and county of Honolulu this was the rule.

The Department of Public Welfare, operating on a Territorial level, had to accept responsibility of medical care for indigent persons in any county irrespective of how long they had lived in it; but what of the medically indigent as defined above?

Immediately before and during the war years, when there was no unemployment and the Department of Public Welfare was still receiving one-half of one per cent Territorial tax on compensation and dividends, it accumulated a surplus of some three million dollars. (See p. 123.) With pressure brought to bear by the counties, the 1943 legislature authorized the DPW to spend this surplus for the medical care of both the indigent and medically indigent.[2] Public Welfare paid the bills, but the counties continued to administer the programs. Payment was quite liberal, including, in addition to medical and dental care, special appliances and burials.

When the war had ended, unemployment rose and so did the relief rolls of DPW. By 1949 the organization was no longer receiving a special share of the tax on compensation and dividends. Its surplus began to diminish and a deficit loomed; it had to curtail expenditure, and one way to do this was to relinquish financial responsibility for a large share of the program covering medical care and burials. By June 1949 the DPW had ceased to be responsible for the medical costs of any non-Welfare recipients, and by June 30, 1951, recipients, too, were eliminated.[3]

The counties reassumed the load of the indigent. Again there were restrictive policies, particularly in the County of Honolulu. To the extent possible a negligible number of the medically indigent were helped by endowments to The Queen's Hospital and by contributions through voluntary organizations, but the program was confusion confounded; this was reflected particularly in services to the medically indigent.

In 1949 the legislature appointed a hold-over committee with certain investigatory duties including the problem of medical care to the indigent and medically indigent. Accepting the recommendations of this hold-over committee, the

1951 legislature created, within the Territorial Department of Health, the Division of Hospitals and Medical Care for the Indigent and Medically Indigent.[4] Under this law, costs of medical care are paid, subject to a means test, and without free choice of physician. This law, and its provisions and limitations, are gone into more thoroughly in Part II, chapter XIX.

Hospitals: General

There are general hospitals on all the islands. A few are owned by private nonprofit associations, others by plantation corporations, a number by county governments, and some small ones by private individuals. Included here are closed and open hospitals on Oahu, exclusive of Tripler U. S. Army Hospital and those owned by plantations.[5]

In Hawaii closed hospitals include the government-owned and tax-supported ones in which patients, irrespective of economic status, come under the care of full-time salaried physicians. Leahi Hospital is an example of a closed institution. Included in this category are the corporation-owned plantation hospitals in which employees are treated by doctors hired by the respective corporations. Open nonprofit hospitals are administered by voluntary directorates and supported by endowments, fees of private patients, and governmental subsidies common to all hospitals in the territory.

Private patients in open hospitals are attended by personal physicians, whom they pay for services as rendered. In closed hospitals social service may have automatic contacts with new admissions, whereas in open ones contacts are by referral. In the former, the social worker is a member of the professional team attending a patient; in an open hospital this is not the usual custom.

The Queen's Hospital: Open (1860): In 1790 the ship *Eleanor* came to anchor in Kealakekua Bay, Hawaii. Its boatswain, John Young, an Englishman, went ashore on a visit and was forcibly detained by Kamehameha I. After waiting several days, the *Eleanor* sailed away without her boatswain. John Young so proved himself that Kamehameha gave him the rank of chief and made him a principal adviser. He married Kaoanaeha, a niece of Kamehameha. She was the maternal grandmother of Queen Emma, after whom The Queen's Hospital is named.

Emma was raised by Dr. and Mrs. T. Charles Byde Rooke.

Mrs. Rooke was Emma's maternal aunt. Dr. Rooke, an English-man, came to the Islands in 1827 as surgeon on a south sea whaler. The Rookes had no children of their own and in ac-cordance with Hawaiian custom of *hanai* Emma was brought up in the Rooke household. (Queen Emma is generally con-sidered to have been adopted by Dr. and Mrs. Rooke. There is reason for doubting that this was an adoption in the accepted meaning of the term. The first adoption law in Hawaii was enacted in 1846, ten years after Emma's birth—January 2, 1836.)

Health in the Islands was an abiding concern with Dr. Rooke, particularly as it affected transient seamen, or was affected by them. He described how the sick had to be boarded with such individuals as could be found to undertake the care of them, "sometimes in hovels of natives and sometimes in those of foreigners. One was a thatched building so pervious to the weather that in particular cases they had to hang an old garment, or mat, against the side of the house to ward off the damp wind during the inclement season. This abode was in the same enclosure with a grog shop, subject to the noisy and often dangerous intrusion of drunken sailors." When, in 1850, cholera threatened the islands, Dr. Rooke and several other physicians were appointed by Kamehameha III to act as a board of health.

Diseases introduced by transient seamen and other foreigners took a heavy toll of the Hawaiians, but there was no hospital to which they could be admitted and the need was great. Dr. Rooke, by his marriage to an *alii* (of chief's heritage) could easily identify with the Hawaiians, and they sought his advice in health as well as in illness. In those days, offices of physicians were located in their residences. This was true of Rooke House.[6] A childhood companion of Emma Rooke was Alex-ander Liholiho, who ascended the throne in 1854 as Kame-hameha IV. It is understandable how these young people were influenced by the environment of Rooke House, by the sick and troubled folk coming to consult the doctor, and by the discussions they heard between him and others about the affairs of the kingdom, not the least of which was the health of its subjects.

Kamehameha IV and Emma Rooke were married in 1856. In 1855 a law was enacted for the establishment of a hospital in Honolulu for "sick and destitute Hawaiians." This law was

contingent upon an incorporated association raising $5,000,
whereupon the government might convey to the association
lands of equal value in which case it would have a voice in the
management of the corporation. The royal couple each contributed $500 and the king personally solicited funds from the
residents of Honolulu.

In 1859 a charter was issued to The Queen's Hospital "for
the purpose of creating a fund for the erection and establishment of a hospital at Honolulu for the relief of indigent sick
and disabled people of the Hawaiian Kingdom, as well as such
foreigners and others as may desire to avail themselves of the
same." [7]

Against a colorful Hawaiian pageantry and using the ritual
of the Masonic Order of which he was Past Master, Kamehameha IV laid the cornerstone of The Queen's Hospital on
July 17, 1860. [8] The original building of The Queen's Hospital
consisted of two stories, built of native coral rock. It had a
bed capacity of 100. In keeping with the times, the first building gave place to larger and more modern ones. By 1952 the
capacity of Queen's was 365 adult beds and 49 bassinets. On
July 10, 1953, ground was broken for an additional four-story
wing. Its main features are surgeries and their contributory
facilities.

From the time of its founding until 1909, The Queen's Hospital received a legislative subsidy in behalf of the indigent, [9]
these then became a City and County responsibility [10] and,
in 1951, again a Territorial one. That Queen Emma's interest
in the hospital she helped to found was an abiding one is
evidenced by her will. She bequeathed her estate to The
Queen's Hospital, subject to certain annuities and an annual
provision of $600 to St. Andrew's Priory. All the annuitants
have since died. In 1950 the hospital became the owner of
an estate at the appraised value set by the court of $2,750,000. [11]
It has other endowments, it is supported also by fees from
private patients, by a Territorial per diem subsidy of 75 cents
per ward bed, whether or not occupied, [12] and by the Territorial
Division of Hospitals and Medical Care for the Indigent and
Medically Indigent. [13] Needy Hawaiians no longer receive
preferential consideration by The Queen's Hospital.

In the beginning The Queen's Hospital was governed by a
directorate composed of ten voluntary subscribers and ten gov-

ernmental representatives appointed by the legislature.[14] After 1909, when the legislative subsidy was withdrawn, the governing board became entirely a voluntary one. Not until 1952 did it include a woman. In the following year, 1953, two women were elected to a board of 15 directors. The Queen's Hospital has long been accredited by the American College of Surgeons.[15] Many practicing physicians in the Territory receive all or part of their hospital training at Queen's. It has had a School of Nursing since 1916.

Medical Social Service was introduced in 1923 to The Queen's Hospital by an extramural organization, the Hospital Flower Society, from which grew the Medical Social Service Association of Hawaii. Part II of this volume is exclusively the history of medical social service in Honolulu.

Kuakini Hospital and Home: Open (1900): This institution, previously known as the Japanese Hospital, had its inception with the bubonic plague scare and the incidental fire in 1900. Among those made homeless at this time were 3,500 Japanese. As a result of this catastrophe and a growing awareness of the needs of their sick and aged, the Japanese Benevolent Society founded the Japanese Charity Hospital in Kapalama. In 1902 the hospital expanded to larger facilities on Liliha Street, and again in 1917 to a new hospital, named the Japanese Hospital, built on Kuakini Street, its present location. In 1942, following the outbreak of the second world war, the hospital was renamed Kuakini Hospital and the Japanese Benevolent Society, which operates the hospital, was renamed Kuakini Hospital and Home.[16] In 1952 the capacity of the hospital was 115 beds and 30 bassinets. It has no outpatient department as such, but by arrangement with the city and county, Kuakini will give follow-up care to discharged county patients.

Kuakini Hospital and Home is supported by fees of private patients and the governmental subsidies common to other hospitals. It has become an accredited, open general hospital, both in regard to services and racial backgrounds of patients. The institution was a member of the Medical Social Service Association of Hawaii. Since 1949, when the latter withdrew from its member hospitals, Kuakini has had an interrupted history as far as social service is concerned.

Kauikeolani Children's Hospital: Open (1909): In December 1850, a small boy sailed from Honolulu on the bark Croton—his father was taking him to Boston for the correction of club feet. That child of nearly seven years was Albert Spencer Wilcox, a son of Abner and Lucy Hart Wilcox, missionaries to the Sandwich Islands under the American Board of Commissioners for Foreign Missions.[17]

As a man, Albert Wilcox was closely identified with the development of the Islands' sugar industry. He served in the legislature of the Hawaiian Kingdom and, though his home was on Kauai, he gave liberally to religious and educational institutions on Oahu. Boyhood friends of comparable missionary backgrounds were Sanford B. Dole and William O. Smith, both eminent in the political and humanitarian activities of their day.

During much of the time that Mr. Dole was president of the Associated Charities, his wife was active in the Hawaiian Humane Society, whose program included children as well as animals. A further influence in the founding of the Children's Hospital was that of Mrs. Elizabeth Napoleon Low, sister of Mrs. Albert Wilcox. In girlhood, Mrs. Low was a member of the Dole household for many years and an active participant in the Hawaiian Humane Society. She, too, saw the need for a children's hospital.

In a letter to Mr. Dole, dated June 12, 1907, Mr. Wilcox said that, provided an endowment of $50,000 was first assured, he would himself contribute $50,000 to establish a children's hospital, open "to children of all nationalities and races, but preference always given to children of Hawaiian parentage." Mr. Wilcox added that he would give an additional $5,000 for initial expenses.[18] The required endowment having been raised among private subscribers, Mr. Wilcox gave $55,000 to buy several acres of land and to erect a two-story building on Kuakini Street, its present site. Its name, Kauikeolani, was the given name of Mrs. Wilcox. It was incorporated in 1908 "for the relief, care, and treatment of children suffering from disease, injuries and deformities." [19]

In the early decades of this century it was unusual for women to be hospitalized for childbirth; general practitioners and private nurses took care of them in their homes. Women in poorer circumstances were delivered in their homes by midwives, or perchance a friend or the husband. This is not to forget the mores of Oriental women, stringent in those days, which forbade delivery by male physicians.

As obstetrics became increasingly specialized, hospital deliveries became increasingly common. The Kauikeolani Children's Hospital was small and friendly and homelike, and physicians practicing there were among Honolulu's leading doctors. It was a simple matter for them to have facilities added for the admission of private obstetrical patients. However, with scientific progress in obstetrics, the modification of cultural patterns, and the addition of maternity wards to general hospitals, the maternity service at the Children's Hospital was discontinued in 1929.

An outpatient department was opened by the hospital in 1949. It includes a well-baby clinic and a rheumatic fever clinic, the latter subsidized from the Children's Bureau through the Territorial Department of Health.

In 1950 the comparatively small and homelike building of 41 years was replaced by a completely new and modern institution with a bed capacity of 99. It is an accredited open hospital. Admission is limited to children whose ages range from the newborn through sixteen years.

The hospital is supported by fees for private patients, interest from endowments, and the governmental subsidies common to other hospitals. Hawaiian children are no longer given special consideration. The Kauikeolani Children's Hospital is governed by a board of twelve members, only three of whom are women (1953). Social Service was introduced into the Children's Hospital by the Medical Social Service Association in 1928. Since 1949, when the association withdrew from its member hospitals, Children's has not had a professionally qualified social worker. (In January 1958, Miss Helene Morgan became the social worker.)

St. Francis Hospital: Open (1927): This hospital, situated on Liliha Street, is owned by the Roman Catholic Community of the Third Franciscan Order of Syracuse, New York. It was opened in 1927 with a bed capacity of 50. By 1952 this was increased to 255 beds. It is an accredited open hospital governed by a board of Franciscan sisters in Hawaii; the sisters have a lay advisory board. Support is by fees of private patients, some endowments, and the Territorial subsidies common to other hospitals.

In 1928 a plan was consummated with the Hospital Social Service Association of Hawaii for a social worker to divide her time between the St. Francis and Kauikeolani Children's Hospitals. In 1934 St. Francis Hospital terminated this arrangement because at that time—a time when the great depression was keenly felt in Hawaii—the association was collaborating with a number of doctors and social agencies in furthering a maternity health clinic at The Queen's Hospital, where, in accordance with some case histories, birth control was being advocated.

Since the opening of an outpatient department in 1947, St. Francis Hospital has employed a social worker, but her function is limited to means reviews of patients applying for treatment. Since 1934 the professional staff of the Hospital has not included a medical social worker for inpatients.

Wahiawa General Hospital (1945): Following the outbreak of the second world war, a school building in Wahiawa was commandered by the Office of Civilian Defense to serve as an emergency hospital. In 1945 it was incorporated as the Wahiawa General Hospital, an open nonprofit institution, which has since become accredited by the Joint Commission on Accreditation of Hospitals. Its professional staff does not include a medical social worker. The Wahiawa General Hospital is administered by a board of nineteen directors, two of whom are women. At the time of writing plans were in progress for the old rambling one-story school building to be replaced by a modern three-story 80 bed hospital.

Gynecological and Obstetrical

Kapiolani Maternity and Gynecological Hospital: Open (1890): In 1890 King Kalakaua and his queen, Kapiolani, opened the Kapiolani Home of the Hoolu and Hoola Lahui Society [20] "for the purpose of benevolence and charity and for the special object of providing a maternity home where Hawaiian women can receive proper care and treatment during the period of childbirth, and for such other benevolent and charitable purposes as may be consistent with the maintenance of such Maternity Home." In 1918 the name was changed to Kapiolani Maternity Home, the purposes remaining the same. [21]

In 1929 the home moved from the original site on Beretania Street to a newly erected building on Punahou and Bingham streets, its present location. [22] On May 6, 1931, by further amendment of the charter the name was again changed, and it has since been known as Kapiolani Maternity and Gynecological Hospital. It is an open accredited hospital limited to gynecology and obstetrics, open to women of all races. It is supported by fees of private patients and by the usual governmental subsidies. The directorate consists of five men, one of whom is president, and five women.

The staff of the Kapiolani Maternity and Gynecological Hospital has never included a medical social worker, notwithstanding that adoptions from a hospital of this nature are a common occurrence. Arrangements for these adoptions are usually made by the attending physician, generally without consultation with an accredited casework agency. A contributing influence in this regard is the common practice that in adoption cases all medical and hospital costs are paid by the prospective parents on condition that they obtain the baby.

Tuberculosis

Leahi Hospital: Closed (1900): Each island county operates a hospital, or section of one, for treatment of tuberculosis (Appendix III). The largest institution for this disease, and the only one in which there is social service, is Leahi Hospital on Oahu.

The history of this hospital dates back to Queen Victoria's Diamond Jubilee in 1897. A group of Island residents decided to commemorate the occasion with the establishment of a hospital "for the care and treatment of persons suffering from incurable diseases except leprosy and for the relief of those excluded from other hospitals." [23]

It took a frightening experience, however, to make the hospital become a reality. In December 1899, bubonic plague, or the black plague as it was first called, broke out in Honolulu, chiefly in the thickly populated Chinatown. By order of the Board of Health, as patients died, buildings were burned—the other dwellers having been transferred to the "pest house," quarters temporarily opened in "the old kerosene warehouse" in Kakaako. In January 1900 a fire got beyond control, completely destroying a large congested area. Those made homeless included chronic invalids. They were housed in warehouses in Kakaako later acquired by the Victoria Hospital Association and named the Victoria Hospital. [24]

In 1901, when the political character of the Islands was becoming predominantly American,[25] the name was changed to the doom-connoting "Honolulu Home for Incurables." In 1902 the "Incurable Hospital," as it was called for short, moved to Kaimuki. In 1906 the name was changed to Leahi Home [26] and again in 1942 when in order to "qualify for war time priorities available to hospitals" it become known as Leahi Hospital.[27] It covers sixteen and one-half acres at the foot of Diamond Head, the district known in old Hawaii as Leahi.

From its humble beginnings in Kakaako with less than twenty beds, by 1951 Leahi Hospital had a bed capacity of 770.[28] As the curability of tuberculosis was realized, other diseases have been eliminated so that for many years only tuberculous patients have been admitted there. Leahi is an accredited closed hospital, staffed by full-time salaried specialists. It has an outpatient department for the purpose of observing ex-patients over a period of time.

Leahi Hospital is supported almost entirely by Territorial funds [29] and, irrespective of economic status, residents of Hawaii are not required to pay for their care; but nonresidents are—a policy adopted to inhibit tuberculous persons coming from elsewhere to receive treatment in Hawaii. Though a closed governmental hospital, Leahi is still administered by a voluntary directorate, a carry-over from its founding days. As of 1953, its governing board numbered fourteen trustees, one of whom is a woman.

Social service was initiated in Leahi Home in 1926 by the Hospital Flower Society, since known as the Medical Social Service Association of Hawaii. The value of the service being recognized by the governing board, Leahi decided in 1928 to assume full responsibility for social service.[30] The social service staff, Miss Helene E. Morgan, director, numbers five professionally qualified caseworkers, who serve with doctors as members of professional teams. (In January 1958 Miss Morgan became the social worker at the Kauikeolani Children's Hospital.)

Mental

Territorial Hospital: Closed (1930): The Territorial Hospital in Kaneohe is an accredited closed governmental institution for treatment of the mentally ill. It replaced, in 1930, the Oahu

Insane Asylum established in Honolulu in 1866, an institution which was no exception to the ignorance of that era in the treatment of mental illness. At the time of transfer to Kaneohe, 549 patients were taken over the Pali to the new institution. In May 1953 the census was 1,160.[31]

The Territorial Hospital is the only institution in Hawaii for the care of mentally ill persons. Temporary detention of mental patients on the other islands is the responsibility of the respective counties, as is also the safe conduct of patients to Oahu for admission to the Territorial Hospital.

In addition to the original eight buildings and those that have since been added, there is the Goddard Building, named in memory of Oscar F. Goddard, first director of the Department of Institutions, established by legislative enactment in 1939. This building, opened in 1950, is a modern diagnostic and treatment center.

The Territorial Hospital is under the jurisdiction of the Department of Institutions, which appoints the medical director; he in turn selects the other members of the resident staff, all of whom must have minimum professional qualifications.

In compliance with stated regulations, patients are admitted to the hospital either on a voluntary basis or by court commitment.[32] In accordance with a means review, they pay in full, in part, or nothing at all for their care; the chief support of the hospital comes from territorial funds.

The Territorial Hospital has no outpatient department. Such service is given by the Bureau of Mental Hygiene and the outpatient departments of The Queen's and St. Francis hospitals. As to follow up of patients on convalescent status (a more pleasing appellation than the older "parolee"), some consult private physicians, some report to the medical officer of the day at the Territorial Hospital, while most attend either one of two clinics in Honolulu. These clinics are staffed by psychiatrists and social workers from the hospital and are held monthly in Honolulu, in space alternately and voluntarily made available by the Department of Public Health and Palama Settlement.

As of 1953 there are four qualified social workers, one a man, to fill seven listed positions. Workers are civil service appointees, the minimum requirement is a master's degree, preferably in psychiatric casework. Irrespective of economic status, a caseworker makes contact with every newly admitted patient. Social histories are incorporated with the medical records. The social workers are members of professional teams inclusive of psychiatrists, psychologists, occupational therapist, and others in regular clinical conferences.[33] This idea of teamwork is carried into the community; families or relatives are prepared for the reception of patients on convalescent status, and representatives of social agencies participate with psychiatrists and social workers in preconvalescent planning for patients who are their clients.

In 1950 the School of Social Work, University of Hawaii, began placing students at the Territorial Hospital for field work training.

Hansen's Disease [34]

Kalaupapa Settlement and *Hale Mohalu Hospital:* There are two closed hospitals in the territory for the treatment of Hansen's disease, the earlier one at Kalaupapa, on the Island of Molokai, and the second at Pearl City in Honolulu.

Leprosy, or Hansen's disease,[35] appeared first in Hawaii during the reign of Kamehameha III (1825–54). It was said to have been introduced from China, hence its Hawaiian name, *mái-pake* (Chinese disease). It was taking such a heavy toll of the Hawaiians that, in 1865, during the reign of Kamehameha V (1863–72), a law was enacted giving the Board of Health authority to enforce segregation of lepers.

With the enactment of the segregation law, and pending transfer to a cliff- and ocean-bound peninsula on the north coast of Molokai, patients were isolated in a receiving station and hospital at Kalihi in Honolulu. In 1910 this institution was combined with the newly established Leprosy Investigation Station, staffed by the U.S. Public Health Service, which provided medical supervision and laboratory services for patients in the adjacent Kalihi Receiving Station.

During World War II, the United States Navy acquired some eleven acres at Pearl City on which they erected barracks to house waves. It was occupied by these women for one year, then by civilian workers from Pearl Harbor. In 1946 the use of this property was granted to the Territory on a revocable permit by the Navy. For two years the barracks was operated by Leahi Hospital as an annex for convalescents. In 1949, under the name of *Hale Mohalu* (house of relaxation), it took over the functions of the Kalihi Receiving Station which closed in that year. In 1956 the property was declared surplus by the federal government and deeded to the Territory by the U.S. Department of Health, Education, and Welfare, with a 5 per cent annual credit on its assessed valuation for continued use as a hospital.

Patients having the infectious form of Hansen's disease (bacteriologically positive) are admitted to Hale Mohalu Hospital for treatment. All patients under compulsory isolation have the option of remaining at Hale Mohalu Hospital or transferring to Kalaupapa Settlement. Those patients found to have the noninfectious (bacteriologically negative) form of the disease upon initial diagnosis, are not hospitalized but are treated throughout their illness as outpatients. When hospitalized patients become bacteriologically negative they are granted temporary release and may return home. If at the end of five years a patient is still clinically and bacteriologically negative, he may be medically discharged, but the present trend is to continue medical supervision indefinitely. Among the "wonder drugs" credited to the war years are the sulfones, considered the chief means of checking Hansen's disease, with reasonable assurance of eventual recovery.

Prior to the scientific discoveries by modern medicine, leprosy was a threat to the people of these islands. In the beginning, patients were sent to several centers on the Molokai peninsula, but chiefly to Kalawao on the eastern side. Because the western side offered a more sheltered and drier environment, there was a gradual shift to Kalaupapa. The last patient quarters at Kalawao were vacated in 1932. Since then all Hansen's disease persons who go to Molokai live at Kalaupapa.

In the early decades of segregation, patients were allowed to have their spouses, relatives, or close friends live permanently with them as *kokuas* (helpers). This custom, with the advancement in knowledge and treatment of the disease, has been abolished.

No social history of the leper settlement on Molokai, however abbreviated, can omit mention of a Roman Catholic priest —Father Damien. Joseph de Veuster was born in Belgium, January 3, 1840, and was ordained to the priesthood in Honolulu in May of 1864. As Father Damien he went to Molokai in

1873 and labored for more than 800 isolated persons, at a time when and in an environment where proper provisions were lacking in shelter, food, and clothing. He contracted the disease and died on April 15, 1889. He was buried in the little cemetery next to the church he had started at Kalawao. At the request of the Belgian government, Father Damien's body was returned to Belgium in 1936 and interred there with national honors.[36]

The Territorial Department of Health receives an annual federal grant of $1,000,000 for the treatment of Hansen's disease. Kalaupapa has two, and Hale Mohalu one, full-time physician. These institutions depend upon community hospitals, where special arrangements are made, for particular services to Hansen's disease patients, e.g., childbirth, surgical operations, and mental illness. As far as possible patients are encouraged to lead normal lives. It is not uncommon for marriages to take place among them; babies born of these unions are removed directly after birth and placed in foster homes. Consideration is given the wishes of the natural parents in placement of their babies with relatives or friends. Where this is impossible referral is made to the Department of Public Welfare for foster home placement. Until they reach majority (20 years) these children receive annual check-ups by representatives of the Department of Health. District physicians in rural parts and neighbor islands take responsibility for outpatient services. Mrs. Ruth L. Rath, the social worker, Division of Hansen's Disease, has responsibility for social services to both inpatients and outpatients at Kalaupapa and Hale Mohalu.

At Hale Mohalu, where children are hospitalized, schooling is given from the elementary through high school grades and vocational rehabilitation services by instructors furnished by the Department of Public Instruction. There are also programs in occupational therapy, recreation, and hobbies. Patients are encouraged to accept suitable employment, for which they are paid, at both Kalaupapa and Hale Mohalu.

From a beginning of stark privation and loneliness, conditions have so improved over the years that Kalaupapa has come to resemble a modern village, with cottages for patient couples, group houses for those who do not live independently, com-

Left: Rooke House; childhood home of Queen Emma. Born January 2, 1836, died April 24, 1885. (Robert Van Dyke Collection.)

Center: The Queen's Hospital about 1890.

Bottom: The Queen's Hospital in the early 1940's.

Kuakini, formerly the Japanese Hospital.

Kuakini Hospital, dedication of the new wing opened in 1939. The Japanese characters state that the Japanese Emperor Hirohito contributed to the cost of the new wing.

Right: Kuakini Home. Leaving the temple (Buddhist).
Lower right: A dormitory, Kuakini Home.
Below: Residents of Kuakini Home. (Three lower photos courtesy The Honolulu Advertiser.)

Kauikeolani Children's Hospital; taken in 1946.

New Kauikeolani Children's Hospital; taken in the early 1950's.

Above: Grass house.*

Above left: Hawaiian woman weaving a fish net.*

Left: Making poi. Poi, the Hawaiian staff of life, is made from cooked taro corums pounded and thinned with water.*

Right: Field laborers.*

Lower right: Field workers in early decades of the sugar industry.

Below: Women worked in the cane fields, too.
(* Bernice P. Bishop Museum photos.)

munity resources, shops, administrative offices, a Roman Catholic and two Protestant churches, and a hospital. Under provisions made by the administration, patients may be visited by relatives and friends both at Kalaupapa and Hale Mohalu.

The largest number of persons isolated on Molokai was about 1,180 in 1878 and the smallest number prior to 1953 was 252. At Hale Mohalu, between 1949 and 1953 the patient load varied between 57 and 97 persons. Contrary to the general opinion, some persons holding temporary release, and even medical discharge, prefer to remain for life at Kalaupapa among those with whom they have established empathy and in an environment which is the quintessence of the "welfare state," where all material needs are met at government expense.

Boards of Management

Allusion has been made to the predominantly male composition of boards of management of the hospitals included in this chapter. An important subject. What seems to be a general belief is that the most important element in hospital administration is business acumen, but though matters of consequence concerning finance must necessarily arise, a hospital or domiciliary home is not a commercial organization. Quite as significant are matters related to the housekeeping and homemaking, to the psychological adjustment and daily living of diverse personalities closely associated. It is important, therefore, that boards of management include both men and women and not predominantly one sex or the other; otherwise, good opinions may be lost or not expressed where one sex predominates. A board is strengthened, too, if its members include representation of both industry and the professions.

Dental Care

Dental care in Honolulu for the indigent and medically indigent began under voluntary auspices serving only children.

Strong-Carter Dental Clinic (1920): This clinic was founded in 1920 by Mrs. George R. Carter in memory of her parents, Henry A. and Helen P. Strong, of Rochester, New York. At first functioning from a cottage on Hotel Street, where the City Hall now stands, it moved in 1925 to Palama Settlement, where it still remains.[37] The Strong-Carter Clinic provides treatment and repair work for children in public and private schools, from kindergarten through the sixth grade. Parents are processed through a means test. Those who can afford to pay a small fee are charged; those who are indigent, e.g., clients of the Department of Public Welfare, are automatically eligible for free care.

Even though dental services are included in the Division of Hospitals and Medical Care for the indigent and medically indigent mentioned before, the facilities for juveniles above the elementary grades and for adults who need dental care are extremely meager on all the islands. The City and County of Honolulu has a mobile unit for rural areas and a unit at Maluhia Home. Treatment, however, is limited to the relief of pain, extractions, and simple fillings.

On the neighbor islands a person who urgently needs but cannot afford care may go to the dentist of his choice and receive limited service, the account being paid by territorial funds via the Department of Health through the Division of Hospitals and Medical Care for the indigent and medically indigent.

REHABILITATION

Shriners' Hospital for Crippled Children: Closed (1923): In 1923 the local Board of Governors of the National Board of Trustees of Shriners' Hospitals rented an annex of 10 beds, inclusive of surgical facilities, at the Kauikeolani Children's Hospital. In 1930 this order of Freemasonry acquired its present site on Punahou Street. The hospital, with a capacity of 30 beds, is an accredited, closed, nonprofit institution supported entirely by Shriners and limited to needy crippled children under 14 years of age. In 1925, at the request of the hospital, the Department of Public Instruction began to supply them with a teacher. Since then, two teachers are in attendance with classes from kindergarten through the 10th grade. A comparable provision has not been made for the equally important function of social casework. The professional staff of Shriners' Hospital does not include a social worker.

Vocational Rehabilitation Service (1936): Congress enacted a vocational rehabilitation bill in 1920, but covering only a limited period. With the passage of the Social Security Act of 1935, vocational rehabilitation became a permanent service.

In 1936 the Vocational Rehabilitation Service was established as a unit of the Territorial Department of Public Instruction. In 1949 it became the Division of Vocational Rehabilitation, still within the DPI.[38] For war-disabled civilians, the program is supported 100 per cent by federal funds; for all other persons the cost is met 50 per cent by territorial funds and 50 per cent by federal grants-in-aid.

Eligible for this service are men and women injured in industry or by accident, or handicapped by illness or congenital defects. In 1943 the federal act was so amended as to include both the mentally and the physically handicapped. Included in the program are medical and psychiatric diagnosis and treatment, and hospital and convalescent care. If necessary, maintenance and transportation are provided during the period of training. Tools and artificial limbs are also supplied. If the handicapped person is financially able, he pays for physical or mental restoration; otherwise it is provided for him.

Other than the Hauola Business College located at McKinley High School, the Division of Vocational Rehabilitation has no training center; rather, it purchases training through job apprenticeship or instruction at established institutions such as the University of Hawaii. It furnishes tutors, if indicated, and will send handicapped individuals to the mainland for rehabilitation instruction. At the completion of the instruction period, assistance is given in getting suitable employment, and the counselor's interest continues as long as is necessary to obtain a satisfactory adjustment. The staff of the division includes a medical social consultant. Training and counseling is free to all rehabilitees irrespective of economic resources.

Rehabilitation Center of Hawaii (1953): This center, an accredited, open institution, was the consummation of several years' work by a special committee of the Oahu Health Council, to achieve a much needed co-ordinated rehabilitation service "to help all types of handicapped persons make physical, emotional, and social adjustments." [39]

A number of organizations contributed funds to bring as consultant to Honolulu Dr. Howard A. Rusk, professor and chairman of the Department of Physical Medicine and Rehabilitation of the New York University-Bellevue College of Medicine.[40] Dr. Rusk approved the plans submitted by the Kauikeolani Children's Hospital for the establishment in 1953 of a rehabilitation center in their grounds,[41] to be administered by their board of directors.

The center has facilities for 20 inpatients and 50 outpatients, with no restriction as to age and sex. The inpatient service is limited to a twenty-four hour routine in which the patient learns to care for his physical needs. It does not provide hospitalization to those who become ill in the ordinary sense of the term. The organization has consulting medical specialists in physical and occupational therapy and in placement and vocational counseling. In accordance with a recommendation by Dr. Rusk, a qualified social worker is a member of the professional staff. Private physicians or interested agencies may refer a patient to the center for an evaluation of his ability to benefit by the program. Responsibility for the medical care of private patients remains with their own physicians. Those not so designated are on staff service, i.e., interns and residents supervised by an honorary staff of practicing physicians.

The Rehabilitation Center of Hawaii is supported by fees of patients; the cost for those unable to pay is assumed by relevant voluntary or official organizations. Any deficit is underwritten by the Kauikeolani Children's Hospital.

The Honolulu Chapter of the National Foundation for Infantile Paralysis (1939): The first Island chapter of this national organization was established in Honolulu in 1939. Since then, chapters have been established in other counties under the names of the respective islands.

The program is a broad one covering treatment of both adults and children stricken with poliomyelitis. Eligibility for assistance is flexible. If the government is short of funds, the foundation will accept financial obligation for the care of patients who would otherwise qualify under a governmental plan. The foundation will also accept financial responsibility for the medical care of patients who are above those classified as "medically indigent." Patients may be hospitalized in any open hospital with free choice of doctor.

In addition to medical treatment, the foundation issues grants for surveys and research and educational scholarships in medical and allied fields. It is supported entirely by the annual "March of Dimes."

The Hawaii Chapter, National Society for Crippled Children and Adults (1947): This society will accept patients for medical care in any open hospital with free choice of physician. However, the medical care part of its program has become negligible with the development of schools for crippled children. These schools offer a program which includes physical, speech, occupational, recreational, and functional therapies.

RELEVANT ORGANIZATIONS

Bureau of Maternal and Child Health and Crippled Children (1925): In 1925 the Territorial Legislature allotted funds to the Department of Health to make possible participation in the Federal Maternity and Infant Hygiene program of the Sheppard-Towner Act of that year. By 1926 the Bureau of Maternal and Infant Hygiene was organized in the Territorial Department of Health.[42]

Under the Social Security Act, the name of this program was changed in 1936 to Maternal and Child Health. Its activities cover a wide latitude, including prenatal and postnatal conferences with mothers and demonstration clinics in child health for infants and preschool children. The bureau does not pay for medical treatment or hospitalization. Those unable to meet such expenses are referred to their respective counties for free service.

In 1939 the Territorial Legislature, by matching funds of the Federal Children's Bureau, made possible the creation of the Bureau of Crippled Children. A condition of the Children's Bureau for participation was the inclusion on the staff of a professionally educated medical social worker. The first one was Elizabeth Leong Lee, who was at that time on the staff of the Hospital Social Service Association of Hawaii. The services for crippled children include diagnosis and treatment of crippling conditions. The orthopedic part of the program for children under 14 years is shared with Shriners' Hospital for Crippled Children; the Bureau of Crippled Children provides care from birth to 21 years.

Diagnostic service to crippled children is rendered irrespective of a family's circumstances. The cost of treatment is borne by the family, but if they are unable to assume it, the bureau will meet the cost so far as allotted funds permit, after which it becomes the responsibility of other organizations, governmental or voluntary.

The Department of Health now administers both programs—

under the combined name of Maternal and Child Health and Crippled Children. In its program are integrated medical, psychiatric, nursing, and social casework services.

Bureau of Sight Conservation and Work with the Blind (1932): The first autonomous territorial casework organization supported solely by taxation is the Bureau of Sight Conservation and Work with the Blind.

Largely through pressure by community groups, the Departments of Health and Public Instruction requested the National Society for the Prevention of Blindness to send a representative to Hawaii. Mrs. Winifred Hathaway, associate director of the National Society, came to Honolulu in 1932.[43]

The Governor's Committee on Conservation of Sight was a recommendation of Mrs. Hathaway's carried out by Governor Judd in the appointment of such a committee in 1933. As a result of the efforts of this committee, the legislature of that year included in the General Appropriation Act (Education) a specific appropriation for the conservation of sight. Since territorial funds may be allotted to governmental institutions only, this appropriation was channeled through the University of Hawaii to the (voluntary) Hospital Social Service Association of Hawaii[44] for the employment of a medical social worker as a member of this committee. Mrs. Dora Zane, at that time on the staff of the association, was given a seven months' leave of absence to go to the mainland for postgraduate work in eye service.

Upon her return, a three-point program—medical, social casework, and shop—was organized under the supervision of Dr. F. J. Pinkerton, the Hospital Social Service Association, and the Lions Club respectively.

In 1935 the Governor's Committee on the Conservation of Sight was dissolved. The legislature of that year appropriated funds for a program in behalf of the blind, the funds to be expended by the governor of Hawaii.

Mrs. Grace C. Hamman, having also taken special training on the mainland, became director of this program, with Mrs. Zane as assistant director. Under Governor Joseph B. Poindexter, a committee was appointed, known as the "Bureau of Sight Conservation and Work with the Blind."[45] Assistance was available to persons of any economic status and consisted mainly of visual testing, training for vocational and recreational pursuits, and casework services. A workshop begun some years before was further developed. Since there were no funds for relief and only a negligible amount for medical treatment, clients in need of these services were referred to other community agencies. The organization had a staunch ally in the Lions Club, whose interest in the blind and the prevention of blindness has continued throughout the years.

Between 1937 and 1945 the "Bureau" functioned within the Department of Public Welfare, presumably in its program Aid to the Blind. It continued, however, to receive specific Territorial appropriations. In 1945 an "independent Bureau of Sight Conservation and Work with the Blind" [46] was established. In accordance with this law the director, who is "appointed and removable by the governor, . . . shall be a member of the civil service system. . . . [He] shall administer work with and for the blind including registry of [the] blind, vocational guidance, training and placement in employment, and other services including conduct of activities for sight conservation and prevention of blindness, but not including public assistance or medical care."

Mrs. Hamman has continued to hold the position of director of the Bureau of Sight Conservation and Work with the Blind.[47] Though not required by law to do so, she organized a voluntary advisory board composed of subcommittees (including one of medical specialists), which advise on three general areas in which the bureau functions—social service, vocational rehabilitation, and employment opportunities.

Social Service works toward achievement of social and emotional adjustment of the individual—and those nearest to him—to the handicap of blindness. The bureau has no funds for maintenance assistance or medical care. Clients in need of these services are referred to the Department of Public Welfare under its Aid for the Blind program and to appropriate voluntary or governmental organizations for medical care. A qualified social worker from the bureau attends the Eye and Glaucoma Clinics in the outpatient department of The Queen's Hospital.

In connection with registering the blind, the bureau has established a vision-testing service available to all public schools and to the private ones which request it.

A Rehabilitation Center for the Blind and Visually Disabled

was founded in 1951 at Farrington High School in Honolulu. The center is in session for eight weeks during the summer vacation when teachers and facilities are available. The program emphasizes prevocational and personal adjustment training.

Blind and visually disabled persons come from all counties of the Territory and live at the school for the entire session. Classes are conducted in group therapy, travel training (to help the blind to find their way about), personality development, Braille, sewing, homemaking, workshop, mechanics, typing, and Dale Carnegie's course in public speaking.

Employment opportunities are fostered by a committee known as Business Enterprise. It includes the Territorial Shop for the Adult Blind, vending stands in public buildings, and home industries.

The Bureau of Sight Conservation and Work with the Blind is now functioning in all Island counties. Where there is no hospital outpatient service, the bureau fosters rural clinics served by local doctors, chiefly for diagnostic purposes.

DOMICILIARY SERVICES

In Hawaii there is much confused use of the word "convalescent." It means returning to health after an illness,[48] but locally, "convalescent home" is the common term for an institution which cares for persons with long-continued illnesses or for whom care for life is necessary.

Convalescents may not require nursing service, whereas the chronically ill usually do. Strictly speaking then, a convalescent home is for those who are recovering from illness, while a nursing home is equipped to take invalids whose conditions are of long duration or for whom recovery is not expected.

In Honolulu some so-called convalescent homes are in fact nursing homes for the chronically ill or for domiciliary care of the aged. In Appendix III are mentioned some homes wrongly named "convalescent," and which the Department of Health, therefore, classifies as "chronic."

Maluhia Home (known since 1956 as Maluhia Hospital)

In the early decades of this century—when the population in Honolulu was smaller and younger and the cost of hospitalization was only a few dollars a day—the convalescent, the chronically ill (exclusive of tuberculosis and mental illness), and the aged who were without families were boarded in The Queen's Hospital. By 1931 the city and county were using two private boarding homes[49] for such persons under their care. In that year, Dr. Robert B. Faus, then city and county physician, drew the attention of the Board of Supervisors to the increasing number of indigent incurables and convalescents, and the increasing cost of maintaining them in privately owned hospitals or homes.[50] As a result, late in 1931, the municipality acquired property in Honolulu, including several buildings formerly occupied by the Oahu Insane Asylum (which in the meantime had moved to Kaneohe and was renamed the Territorial Hospital).

The vacated buildings were opened by the city and county as the Indigent Invalid Home, to give nursing and domiciliary care to the convalescing, the chronically ill, and the aged without other resources. The home's name was later changed to Maluhia (peace, serenity), and offered services to convalescing patients, the chronically ill, and only those aged persons who are in need of medical care.

In 1949 Maluhia Home opened a new building with modern facilities for a limited amount of medical treatment. In 1952 its bed capacity was 265. It was caring for 310. Originally admissions to the home were limited to the indigent, but the need for similar facilities for those of limited means has become so great that Maluhia began to admit patients who could pay a per diem rate of $4.50. There is no difference in accommodation or treatment for those who can and those who cannot pay for their care. All patients are under the medical supervision of the city and county physician.

The aged do not all require continuous nursing care, but they do need a sense of protection—physical, mental, and economic—with their advancing years. This is possible only where adequate provision is made in their own, or in residential, homes.

As seen above, Maluhia Home will not admit the aged unless they require medical treatment. What provision is made for those who do not so qualify? This recalls Hawaii at the time when races were not so intermingled as they have since become, and when residential homes were established according to racial ancestry. Elsewhere in this volume are described

homes for the aged—Hawaiians, Caucasians, and Chinese—
and are available to acceptable persons from any island. Following are illustrations of two homes, for aged Japanese and
Korean men, respectively.

Kuakini Home (1932): In 1932 the Japanese Benevolent Society, administrators of the Japanese Hospital, established the
adjacent Japanese Home of Hawaii to give domiciliary care "to
aged Japanese men who had neither savings nor relatives and
were not bedfast." Following the outbreak of the second
world war, the Japanese Benevolent Society became the
Kuakini Hospital and Home. By 1953 the capacity of the home
was 35.

In conformity with a tradition of older generations, the responsibility for elderly parents devolved upon their children;
this was especially true of eldest sons in Japanese families, and
was the reason for making indigency both in regard to money
and relatives a controlling policy for admissions to the Japanese
Home of Hawaii. But times are changing and we change with
them. No longer is it a disgrace for children to express disinclination for the acceptance into their own homes of the
care of aged and helpless parents, nor are parents willing in
this day to be dependent upon their children.

Since World War II, Kuakini Hospital and Home are accepting for domiciliary care elderly Japanese men who are
not indigent and who have relatives. Those in the home who
have neither means nor relatives are supported by the Department of Public Welfare and the Honolulu Community Chest.

Korean Old Men's Home (1938): This home, situated on
School Street, grew out of the "Mutual Aid Society" organized
by Koreans in 1927. A purpose of the society was to help with
burial expenses. By 1938 control was voluntarily given to the
Korean Christian Church which administers the home. The
majority of the 40 old men are supported by the DPW, the re-
mainder have pensions or are supported by relatives.

Maunalani Hospital and Convalescent Home: The emphasis
on men in homes according to race is due to the immigration
of single men in the early years of agricultural and commercial
development of the Hawaiian Islands. It is now an accepted
fact that residential homes for the aged have a more normal
atmosphere if inhabited by both men and women. At one time
even married couples might be separated. With this in mind

there was opened in 1950 a nonprofit, corporation-owned home, the Convalescent-Nursing Home (now known as Maunalani Hospital and Convalescent Home), offering care on a fee basis to convalescents, the chronically ill, and the aged of both sexes, and of any race.

Kauai has no domiciliary homes, as such, for their elderly folk. Some are cared for in the G. N. Wilcox Memorial Hospital in Lihue. The DPW may board others in private homes on Kauai or transfer them to any of the homes on Oahu mentioned above.

Maui County, which also includes the islands of Molokai and Lanai, has two domiciliary homes: the Fred Baldwin Memorial Home, a private institution at Paia, Maui, limited to Caucasian men; and Hale Makua, or Old Folks' Home, at Wailuku, Maui, owned by the county and admitting persons of both sexes and of any racial background.

The County of Hawaii gives domiciliary care to needy old men and women of any racial ancestry at the Olaa Old Folks Home, administered as a section of the county-owned Hilo Memorial Hospital.

The Department of Public Welfare also makes use of a number of privately owned, so-called convalescent homes in Honolulu for those of its clients who require nursing or domiciliary care (Appendix III).

THE POTTER'S FIELD

So much for medical care, rehabilitation, and domiciliary services for those in need. There is still another service before a human's chapter is closed. As a medical social worker, I used to wonder why some patients were so concerned about their burials. I remember one man who was partially supported by his church, but the time came when he needed domiciliary care. The county accepted his application for this, but intimated he first spend toward his support about $100 he had saved for his burial. He had a strong emotional block against using up this money. We finally compromised when his pastor assured him that if he would spend his savings as advised, his church would give him "a decent burial." When he died he was buried in a private cemetery in a plot acquired by his church.

Recently I attended the funeral of a man I had known for

many years. He was a client of the Department of Public Welfare and, when taken ill, was hospitalized at government expense. Since he was a Roman Catholic, the body was not cremated but was buried in a county cemetery, one of unspeakable shabbiness and neglect, overgrown with weeds and brushwood. Neither churches nor social agencies are obliged to dispose of the remains of those supported through public welfare but surely decency and order may be expected, even in a graveyard.

[1] Terms in common use. Social workers prefer the more respectful ones: needy and medical needy.

[2] *T.H. Session Laws* (1943), Act 36, p. 237; *Revised Laws* (1945), Sec. 4828, p. 551.

[3] Newton R. Holcomb, *Statement for the Hold Over Committee of the Territorial Legislature,* Nov. 28, 1949.

[4] *T.H. Session Laws* (1951), Act 129, pp. 162–65.

[5] Appendix III.

[6] Located at the corner of Nuuanu and Beretania streets; no longer existent.

[7] "The Queen's Hospital" (*The Commercial Advertiser,* 1859); Archives of Hawaii.

[8] Dr. Rooke did not live to witness this momentous occasion; he died in Kailua, Hawaii, on November 28, 1858. Kamehameha followed him on November 30, 1863; Queen Emma 22 years later, in 1885.

[9] *Charter and By-Laws of The Queen's Hospital,* Archives of Hawaii.

[10] *Minutes of Board of Supervisors,* July 9, 1909, vol. II, pp. 675–76.

[11] Information obtained in the administration office, The Queen's Hospital.

[12] These subsidies are paid to all open nonprofit hospitals.

[13] *T.H. Session Laws* (1951), Act 129, creating the Division of Hospitals and Medical Care for the Indigent and Medically Indigent.

[14] *Charter and By-Laws of The Queen's Hospital.*

[15] A constituent of the Joint Commission on the Accreditation of Hospitals, established in 1951.

[16] Kuakini Hospital and Home, Annual Report, Fiscal Year 1956–57.

[17] Elsie Hart Wilcox, *A Record of the Descendants of Abner Wilcox and Lucy Hart Wilcox* (Honolulu Star-Bulletin, 1950); private circulation.

[18] *Children's Hospital for Honolulu,* a communication signed by Sanford B. Dole and E. A. Mott-Smith, November 2, 1907; pamphlet 362 D. 68, Hawaiian Mission Children's Society Library.

[19] *Ibid.*

[20] Founded in 1874 by King Kalakaua; the title means "to propagate and perpetuate the Hawaiian race."

[21] *The Honolulu Advertiser,* June 13, 1890.

[22] *Ibid.,* March 26, 1929.

[23] Gwenfread Allen, *The Story of Leahi; Fifty Years of Service, 1901–1951* (Honolulu Star-Bulletin), p. 6.

[24] *Ibid.*

[25] Hawaii was annexed to the United States August 12, 1898, but the Territorial Government was not established until June 14, 1900. Ralph S. Kuy-

kendall and A. Grove Day, *Hawaii: A History, From Polynesian Kingdom to American Commonwealth* (New York: Prentice-Hall, Inc., 1949), p. 297.

26 Allen, *Story of Leahi*, p. 9.

27 *Ibid.*, pp. 18, 19.

28 Information given by Dr. Hastings H. Walker, administrator.

29 Allen, *op. cit.*, pp. 34–37.

30 Letter, dated Jan. 23, 1928, from P. E. Spalding, secretary of Leahi Home, to Mrs. F. J. Lowrey, president, HSSA File, Hospital Social Service Association 1927–37, Honolulu County Medical Library.

31 Printed guide furnished visitors to "Open House" at the Territorial Hospital on May 23, 1953, p. 4.

32 *Report of the Territorial Hospital of Hawaii*, Central Inspection Board, American Psychiatric Association (Honolulu, Aug. 1951); copy at Territorial Hospital.

33 *Ibid.*, p. 16.

34 Acknowledgement is made to Dr. Ira D. Hirschy, director of the Division of Hansen's Disease, Department of Health, for his courtesy in giving me information and reprints of publications on Hansen's disease and for reviewing what I have written; also to Mrs. Ruth L. Rath, social worker for the division, for information regarding social service functions. Ethel M. Damon's *Siloama: The Church of the Healing Spring*, published by the Hawaiian Board of Missions in 1948, was also a valuable resource for history.

35 Since 1949 leprosy has been officially called "Hansen's disease" in Hawaii, after the Norwegian physician Gerhard A. Hansen, who discovered the *Bacillus leprae* in 1868. Ralph S. Kuykendall, *The Hawaiian Kingdom 1854–1878* (Honolulu: University of Hawaii Press, 1953), p. 73.

36 Sister Martha Mary McGraw, A.S., *Stevenson in Hawaii* (Honolulu: University of Hawaii Press, 1950), p. 60. See also Ethel M. Damon, *Siloama The Church of the Healing Spring;* Hawaiian Board of Missions, Honolulu 1948.

37 *Strong-Carter Dental Clinic, Thirty-first Annual Report*, Aug. 31, 1951; copy in Honolulu County Medical Library.

38 *T.H. Session Laws* (1949), Act 219, p. 102.

39 *Oahu Health Council Bulletin VII* (March 1953), p. 1.

40 *Ibid.*

41 At first in temporary quarters. On June 1, 1957, the center opened a new and permanent building in the grounds of the Children's Hospital.

42 Ruth Ackland, *A Century of Public Health in Hawaii*, Department of Health, Territory of Hawaii, Aug. 1949, p. 13. Honolulu County Medical Library.

43 *Prevention of Blindness in Hawaii*, Publication 151, National Society of the Prevention of Blindness; Honolulu County Medical Library.

44 Known since 1944 as the Medical Social Service Association of Hawaii.

45 As it was generally understood that the Bureau of Sight Conservation and Work with the Blind was a title established by territorial statute in 1935, an exhaustive but vain search was made to find this law. The assistance of the attorney general, Mr. Edward N. Sylva, was finally sought and, through his courtesy, a chronological list of laws was received relating to the blind since 1917. It disclosed that the Bureau of Sight Conservation and Work with the Blind was not established by law as an independent department of the territory until 1945. Because of its potential interest to others, the list is here given in full.

Chronological list of laws:

(1) *T.H. Session Laws* (1917), Act 133; provided for the establishment and maintenance of a school for the training and instruction of the blind and other defective children.

(2) *Ibid.* (1927), Act 77; amended the above act, but provided for the instruction to all persons. It also specifically provided for the training and instruction of the blind, deaf, and dumb and other defective or mentally defective persons to be under the direct supervision of the Department of Public Instruction.

(3) *T.H. Regular Session* (1931), Act 275, and *Special Session* (1932), Act 9; appropriated funds under the General School Budget for the Territorial School for the Deaf and Blind and to the Shop for the Adult Blind.

(4) *T.H. Session Laws* (1933), Act 188; under the General Appropriation Act (Education), a specific appropriation was made for the conservation of sight.

(5) *Ibid.* (1935), Act 142; a general appropriation was made for the conservation of eyesight and for the blind with a proviso that said sum was to be expended by the governor of Hawaii, and that no portion of said sum was to be expended by the Department of Public Instruction or the Board of Health.

(6) *Ibid.* (1937), Act 242; created a Territorial Board of Public Welfare and Public Welfare Commissions, and specifically provided for the public assistance to the aged, to the blind and dependent children, for the conservation of sight, and work with the blind for the Territory of Hawaii. (*T.H. Session Laws* (1937), Act 205; appropriated the funds to the Board of Public Welfare. Said funds were to be expended by said board with the approval of the governor of Hawaii.)

(7) *Ibid.* (1939), Act 238; amended above Act 242 and created in the Territorial Government a Department of Social Security and provided for a Bureau of Sight Conservation and Work with the Blind. (*T.H. Session Laws* (1939), Act 244; appropriated the funds for said bureau.)

(8) *Ibid.* (1941), Act 296; amended Act 238 and created a Department of Public Welfare. (*T.H. Sessions Laws* (1941), Act 273 and (1943), Act 191; appropriated funds for the Bureau of Sight Conservation and Work with the Blind.)

(9) *Ibid.* (1945), Act 113, p. 134; amended the above act and provided for an Independent Bureau of Sight Conservation and Work with the Blind.

[46] See (9) under note 45.

[47] Mrs. Hamman retired in 1955 and has since been succeeded by Mrs. Vivien Castro.

[48] W. A. Newman Dorland, *American Illustrated Medical Dictionary*, 22nd ed. (Philadelphia: W. B. Saunders Company, 1951).

[49] The Robinson Home on Kinau Street and the Minaoka Home on Young Street. Both have been razed.

[50] Robert B. Faus, *Excerpts of Communications to the Board of Supervisors* (1931); loaned by T. M. Mossman, M.D., city and county physician.

XI

Social Security
(Period included: 1933–1953) [1]

The concept of government's responsibility for the welfare of its people has been evolving, in one shape or another, for centuries. In the United States it was accentuated by the greatest economic depression in the history of the country. Beginning on the mainland in the late 1920s, it reached these islands in the early 1930s. To cope with the problem, the federal government established various relief programs; Hawaii participated in all of them.

On the territorial level, the legislature of 1933 levied a tax of one-half of one per cent on earned and unearned income, the proceeds to be used to pay wages on work projects for the unemployed.[2] To administer these funds, the same legislature created the Unemployment Relief Commission, a body composed of seven members from Oahu and one each from Kauai, Maui, and Hawaii, with Walter F. Dillingham as chairman.

The commission soon found the law governing their operation restrictive. In addition to able-bodied persons, there were many unable to work who needed relief. The statute was therefore amended in 1935 to enable the commission to provide direct relief throughout the Territory, subject to the governor's approval. To indicate this wider range of function, the name was changed to "Territorial Relief and Welfare Commission."

SOCIAL SECURITY SYSTEM (1935)

In the meantime it was becoming increasingly evident in Hawaii, as well as on the mainland, that voluntary agencies were unable to cope with mass unemployment and the socio-economic hazards inherent in sickness and disability, death of the breadwinner, needs of dependent children, and old age. A conviction was taking shape that these hazards should be an abiding concern of government. This realization led to the Social Security Act signed by President Franklin D. Roosevelt on August 14, 1935.[3]

Any state[4] desiring to participate under this act in federal grants-in-aid first had to submit a plan of operation. Though the states were allowed considerable latitude in formulating their individual policies, in order to be eligible for federal grants-in-aid, they first had to meet certain requirements. The program of public assistance had to be administered through a single governmental agency with state-wide responsibility for its supervision or administration. Any person wishing to apply for assistance had to be given the opportunity to do so, with assistance to be given in cash. If the recipient was a minor or was *non compos mentis,* payment was to be made through a natural or appointed guardian. Opportunities had to be allowed for appeals against what might seem an unfair decision. Social histories and records were confidential, and were not to be divulged to politicians or others interested in discrediting the program at the expense of the recipients of aid.

TERRITORIAL BOARD OF PUBLIC WELFARE AND COUNTY PUBLIC WELFARE COMMISSIONS (1937)

Hawaii's first step was to prepare herself to participate in the federal social security program. In July 1936 acting Governor Charles M. Hite appointed a governor's advisory committee on public welfare, representative of all the islands.[5]

The group was asked to study the existing territorial laws, the relationships among private, public, and semipublic agencies, and the Federal Social Security System from the point of view of territorial participation, and to make recommendations for amending present laws or enacting new ones to meet the territory's relief needs. Based on evidence obtained and the recommendations of the Governor's Advisory Committee on Public Welfare, the legislature of 1937 established a Territorial Board of Public Welfare and County Public Welfare Commission.[6] It also enacted the Unemployment Compensation Law.[7]

The Governor's Advisory Committee recommended the continuance of the one-half of one per cent tax on earned and unearned income as a means of obtaining funds to qualify for federal grants-in-aid in the implementation of this new territorial law.[8]

Administration

The Social Security Administration, now a constituent of the U.S. Department of Health, Education, and Welfare, has ultimate responsibility for the administration of most social security programs. Supervision of these programs at the state level is provided through regional offices of the federal department. Hawaii has a resident deputy representing the regional director in San Francisco.

On the territorial level the public assistance and child welfare programs are administered by the Department of Public Welfare, subject to federal and territorial laws and policies, including those adopted by the Public Welfare Board.[9] The territorial legislature sets the number of members of this board and the governor appoints them. He also appoints the executive director of the department. Each county has a county administrator who in turn is responsible to the executive director.

The first chairman of the Territorial Board of Public Welfare and County Public Welfare Commissions was Dr. A. L. Dean, former president of the University of Hawaii. Dr. Dean, who took an active part on preliminary committees, gave much careful thought to the organization of this new governmental agency.

The first director of the Department of Public Welfare was Miss Pearl Salsberry, a social worker previously employed by the Works Projects Administration in St. Louis. In December 1936, Miss Salsberry was asked to come to Hawaii to administer the Boards of Child Welfare and Old Age Pensions with the understanding that, if the proposed social security legislation was enacted in 1937, she would be appointed director of the Territorial Board of Public Welfare.[10] Miss Salsberry worked closely with Dr. Dean formulating a comprehensive plan or manual of operation which, as already noted, was obligatory for participation in the grants-in-aid from the federal government.

Notwithstanding the constructive thought that is given to the formulation of welfare legislation, there is always the danger that for selfish political purposes standards will be lowered by a succeeding amendment to the original statute. This was true of the Territorial Board of Public Welfare. The law enacted in 1937 was amended in 1939 to reduce the number of board members from seven to five, and tenure from four years to one year. The board from then on met only at the call of the executive director, who was given practically complete control of administration.[11] This state of affairs prompted the resignations of Dr. Dean and Miss Salsberry from their respective positions as chairman and executive director of what became known in 1939 as the Department of Social Security.

The executive director of the Department of Public Welfare is appointed by the governor and has cabinet status. For this very important position, professional education and experience in social welfare is not considered to be a prerequisite. In the sixteen years from 1937 to 1953, five executive directors followed Miss Salsberry in turn, all of them political appointees.

Headquarters

The headquarters of the Department of Public Welfare has progressed from basements of public buildings in Honolulu to shacks hurriedly erected during World War II and, since July 1950, into handsome permanent offices in the new Queen Liliuokalani Building.

Professional Staff

With the establishment of the Board of Public Welfare in 1937, Hawaii was faced with the problem of inadequate staff for the anticipated caseload. Here, as on the mainland, private agencies released workers to form the nucleus of public welfare organizations. In June of that year the majority of the staff went for this purpose from the Social Service Bureau to the newly created Board of Public Welfare. At the same time the bureau transferred its assistance cases to the governmental agency, retaining a limited number in which financial aid was not a dominant factor.

Otherwise, public welfare had to do its best with apprentice-trained workers. But the picture is changing. In 1950 the Department of Public Welfare had a staff of 158, all holding baccalaureate degrees. Some had taken postgraduate courses in social work and thirty-two held master's degrees in the profession. All personnel below the executive director are qualified by civil service examinations for their respective positions.[12]

STANDARDS OF LIVING

In the beginnings of organized charity in the last century, the general belief was that the cause of poverty existed in the individual seeking relief—if a man would work he needn't beg—and the principle of charity workers was to give as little as possible, and never in cash.

Social philosophy has come a long way since that era. Two world wars and a great economic depression, together with the emergence of social work as a profession, have established the conviction that socio-economic conditions occur over which the man in need may have no control. There is also a greater appreciation for the dignity and worth of the human being, and today cash, not food orders, is the medium of help. But after all, workers must have criteria by which to gauge the amount of help an applicant needs.

In 1937, the same year in which the Board of Public Welfare was established, the Honolulu Council of Social Agencies appointed a committee of specialists to study minimum standards of living. They included in a family budget costs of food, housing, clothing, household operations, transportation, education, recreation, and health needs.[13]

In 1941 a territorial law was enacted stating, in effect, that assistance granted by the Department of Public Welfare must not exceed a minimum amount compatible with "decency and health." [14] A client may be given less, but he must not be given more. But translating decency and health into dollars' worth of aid is difficult, and subject to varied interpretation.

In 1947 another committee of specialists was appointed by the Honolulu Council of Social Agencies to make a further analysis of the minimum content of living. This committee recommended that in particular circumstances, to be decided upon an individual basis, a budget that would include (in addition to the basic items) special care, insurance (health, life, property), telephone, laundry and cleaning, medical and dental care, taxes, educational and school supplies, and housekeeper or nursing services.

Prior to the days of scientific nutrition, social agencies varied their estimates according to racial backgrounds, it being thought that an Oriental or a Hawaiian, for example, required neither the same kind nor such costly food as an Occidental, nor should his standard of living be as high. No such distinction is made today. The Committee on the Minimum Content of Living based their decisions on factual analyses of nutrition and welfare for human beings as such, and not on racial bases. It was not their concern whether or not an agency or a family could meet the minimum standards set. The Department of Public Welfare could not do so; therefore it eliminated some items and reduced others. Even so, by 1949–50, Public Welfare fell to 70 per cent of their own minimum standard of what it takes to be "decent" and "healthful." [15]

HAWAII HOUSING AUTHORITY (1935) [16]

Not only children but families, as families, need the security of belonging somewhere, a home that is more than mere shelter in a crowded slum. An essential element of social security therefore is housing. With the increase in Honolulu's population (Appendix I) came congestion in certain areas, which took on the worst features of slums. The condition led to the enactment of a law in 1935 establishing the Hawaii Housing Authority.[17] This was in anticipation of the United States Housing Act of 1937. In 1947 the federal program became known as the Public Housing Administration, and it has since been changed to the Housing and Home Finance Agency.

The Hawaii Housing Authority is an autonomous governmental agency, supervised by five commissioners appointed by the governor with the consent of the Senate. The Authority has the right of eminent domain. It receives no territorial funds nor federal grants-in-aid. Construction of multiple dwellings is financed by loans procured through the National Public Housing Administration and refunded through rentals.

The purpose of the Hawaii Housing Authority is to provide decent housing to low-income families at rentals they can afford. No discrimination is made on the basis of race, color, or creed. Tenant selection is governed by policies established by federal law, and is subject to maximum net income restrictions. Special rates are made for clients of the Department of Public Welfare.

In 1953 the Hawaii Housing Authority was operating over

5,000 dwelling units, most of them on Oahu, but some also on Hawaii and on Maui. Many of these were erected during World War II by the federal and territorial governments and operated as emergency housing by the Hawaii Housing Authority. Emergency housing for returning veterans was also provided, and in 1946 temporary dwelling units were furnished to Hilo families made homeless by a disastrous tidal wave.

Temporary buildings are now being replaced by permanent ones, as and where needed. The Hawaii Housing Authority was housed for some eight years in temporary buildings erected during World War II on Iolani Palace grounds.[18]

SOCIAL INSURANCE

Unemployment insurance and old age and survivor's insurance, though not administered by the Department of Public Welfare, are within the Social Security System and are of significance to Public Welfare in estimating budgets of relief for applicants who carry one or both insurances.[19]

Unemployment Insurance

Not infrequently when a person loses his job he will get another in a matter of days or weeks; in the meantime he may need support. Provided an employee has lost his job involuntarily and that he will accept work for which he is reasonably fitted (the local agency includes an employment service) he is entitled to receive cash for a limited number of weeks, based upon his previous earnings.[20]

The program is administered jointly by state and federal governments. In Hawaii the employer alone is taxed. The Unemployment Insurance and Employment Services are managed by the Bureau of Employment Security of the Territorial Department of Labor and Industrial Relations.[21]

Old Age and Survivor's Insurance

Social workers know that nothing causes greater anxiety than facing an old age of want. The framers of the Social Security System were aware of this when they included old age and survivor's insurance in its provisions. This insurance is contributed to by a tax paid by both employer and employee on an equal basis.[22] All employees, irrespective of the amount of salary or wages, are taxed on the first $4,200 earned during each year, their employers contributing an equal amount. Coverage under this law is more extensive than in unemployment insurance. In successive years it has been extended to practically all types of occupation. It includes the self-employed as well as regularly employed agricultural and domestic workers. There are still some exceptions, principally among the professions, but the trend is consistently toward universal coverage. Insurance benefits are related to length of employment and the average monthly wage or salary.

The insured is not eligible for benefits until he has reached his sixty-fifth birthday, women 62 years, and has stopped working, or if working is not receiving more than $75 a month in covered employment.[23] The plan includes policies granting death benefits to the widowed (applicable also to widowers dependent upon working wives) and children under eighteen years of age. It covers dependent parents who are over sixty-five. Payments to the insured are made directly by the federal government.[24]

Two public assistance programs are administered by the Department of Public Welfare: Federal Public Assistance, which is supported by federal and state matching funds, and General Assistance and Child Welfare Services, supported entirely by state appropriations.

FEDERAL PUBLIC ASSISTANCE

Old Age Assistance

This category does not include persons under the Old Age and Survivor's Insurance mentioned above, except those whose insurance and other resources are not enough to meet their minimum needs and who must, therefore, have supplementary income. In this regard there is a territorial law which makes it mandatory for adult children to support to the extent of their financial ability needy aged parents,[25] sociologically a questionable law.

An applicant for old age assistance must have reached his sixty-fifth birthday. He may be living with relatives or in a boarding home, but there are some limitations as to the type of institution in which a person can live and still be eligible for old age assistance. An example is a voluntary hospital treating conditions for which resources are provided by the government in tax-supported institutions.

An analysis of each of the two systems, public assistance and old age and survivor's insurance, as a means toward security, brings out strong psychological reasons in favor of insurance. Based upon employment, insurance gives a predictable income, preserves self-respect, and does not require a means test.

In old age assistance there is no such predictability, and the means test or financial investigation required under that program is repellent to most people. An important fact is that in the years ahead there will be decreasing applications for old age assistance and aid to dependent children because of the increasing numbers covered by old age and survivor's insurance.

Aid to Dependent Children

Children in Hawaii reach legal majority at twenty, but so far as the Social Security Act is concerned the Department of Public Welfare must limit minority to persons under sixteen, or, if regularly attending school, eighteen years of age. By this act, aid to dependent children is granted to needy minors "who have been deprived of parental support or care by reason of the death, the continued absence from the home, or the physical or mental incapacity of a parent." The Social Security Law prohibits aid to dependent children who are placed in an institution or with anyone who does not come within a comprehensive list of natural or legal relatives. The objective of this is to preserve family unity.

Aid to the Blind

This is provided to persons diagnosed as blind by competent physicians or optometrists if their income is insufficient to provide a subsistence compatible with "decency and health." Beginning July 1, 1952, the first $50 a month of earned income was not taken into account when determining the need of a blind person or his dependents.

The organization now known as the Bureau of Sight Conservation and Work with the Blind was transferred to the Department of Public Welfare in 1937. This loss of autonomy was a source of such dissatisfaction to personnel of the bureau that they were able by legislative enactment in 1945 to reestablish it as a separate organization.[26]

Aid to the Permanently and Totally Disabled

This program was added in 1950 to the Social Security System. Grants-in-aid are available to states for needy persons who are eighteen years of age and older and who are permanently and totally disabled. This statute has the same restrictions as Old Age Assistance regarding care in non-tax-supported institutions.

GENERAL ASSISTANCE AND CHILD CARE WELFARE SERVICES

General Assistance

In addition to state appropriations to match federal grants-in-aid for public assistance programs, states also appropriate funds direct to the Boards of Public Welfare for general assistance and child welfare services. The territorial legislature made its first such appropriation in 1937.[27] The purpose of this additional sum is to supplement the restrictive federal programs; for example, a person lacking one year of age eligibility (sixty-five) for old age assistance, a partially incapacitated single person, a temporarily unemployed man with a family, or a young person out of a job,[28] could all be assisted, although ineligible for federal programs.

Child Welfare Services

The funds appropriated for child welfare services are for the "protection and care of children who are homeless, neglected, abandoned, or in danger of becoming delinquent." [29] The program includes casework and financial assistance for minors under twenty years of age in their own homes, in foster homes with persons in no way related to them, and in child-caring institutions.

Child Welfare Services also include casework where no financial help is involved; it offers services to unmarried mothers, is active in the field of adoptions, irrespective of indigency; and is the official agency for clearance of applications and evaluations of adoptive homes for babies sent to Hawaii from foreign countries.[30] Thus this program has greater latitude than Aid to Dependent Children under the Social Security Act, which is limited to financially needy children under sixteen years of age and to placement with relatives or family connections.

RELATED CHILDREN'S PROGRAMS

In addition to the programs cited, the Federal Children's Bureau [31] makes an outright grant to the Territorial Department of Public Welfare. This is used for the administration of Child Welfare Services, the salaries of workers in rural areas, and the furtherance of professional education.

The Department of Public Welfare is responsible for the annual inspection requisite for the licensing of agencies, homes, and institutions concerned with the foster care of children.[32] The Department of Health has the same authority but, except where health is concerned, it plays a passive role in this regard. This licensing law is an example of overlapping of function and responsibility.

There are no governmental institutions in the Territory for the foster care of children other than those for delinquent boys and girls committed by juvenile courts to either the Koolau Boys' Home or the Kawailoa Girls' Home, both on Oahu. Delinquent minors from the other islands are also committed to these homes. Such enforced separation from the home island and family ties can do psychological damage.

The court gives care and custody of dependent wards to the Department of Public Welfare which may use any one of the following private institutions for their care. On Oahu, the Salvation Army Boys' and Girls' Homes, St. Anthony's Home for both boys and girls, the Susannah Wesley Home for girls, all in Honolulu; on Hawaii, the Salvation Army Girls' Home in Hilo, and Kohala Girls' Seminary in Kohala; on Maui, the Maui Children's Home in Paia for both boys and girls. On Hawaii, dependent boys are generally placed in foster homes; occasionally they are brought to Honolulu; on Kauai, if suitable foster homes are not available, both boys and girls are brought to Honolulu.

Since 1947, the Department of Public Welfare has been using three private homes in Honolulu for temporary emergency care, one each for adolescent boys and girls, and one for younger children. Any nongovernmental agency or individual may apply to the Department of Public Welfare for emergency or temporary care of a dependent child in one or another of these foster homes.

For years, social workers in Honolulu have discussed the

need of a study home, i.e., a place in which a child would receive through qualified staff individualized study for placement in accordance with his emotional and physical requirements. No such home has been created, although a law was enacted in 1943,[33] mandating the Department of Public Welfare to establish a home for the temporary care of dependent children. In the midst of World War II, with a housing shortage and construction costs very high, it was an inauspicious period for the enactment of any such law.

At that time, too, John H. Wilson, director of Public Welfare, was convinced of the need of what was described as a "flop house," for an increasing number of unattached, homeless men. For this purpose he secured the two-story Kapiolani Girls' Home in Kalihi. Since 1912 it had been administered by the Sisters of St. Francis as a boarding home for children born at Kalaupapa—"nonleprous children of leprous parents." In 1938 this home was closed and its charges transferred to the more normal environment of foster homes.

Lacking anything better, Mr. Wilson decided to use the upper story of this building for minors, keeping the lower one for men. This decision brought about his head a veritable storm of abuse for "mixing children with old derelicts." In the circumstances of that time, and when social workers offered nothing better than opinions, this seemed unfair; however, Mr. Wilson, a man of determination and not unaccustomed to abuse, went ahead with his plans, and children were sheltered —but not "studied"—at the Kapiolani Home from January 1, 1944, until November 30, 1947, when arrangements were made for the above-mentioned foster homes.

As for the "flop house," the Kapiolani Home continues, under the aegis of the American Legion, to shelter transient or homeless men, while the need for a study home for certain children continues to be a perennial subject for discussion among social agencies.

In May of 1952 the Family and Children's Division of the Honolulu Council of Social Agencies organized a Residential Treatment Home Committee representative of public and private social agencies. Its aim is toward a controlled environment where disturbed children may spend a period under specialized treatment; but, as one social worker remarked, "when you get the youngsters studied, what are you going to do with them?" Thus the problem includes, not only the cost and staffing of so very specialized a project, but also the resources to carry on, if necessary, where the home leaves off.

Adoption Procedures

The history of adoption laws in Hawaii stems from an era when adoptions were legalized with no more than one appearance of a petitioner in court and no verification of the suitability of adoptive parents to rear a child. Pressure over the years by voluntary organizations, including the Honolulu Council of Social Agencies, has brought about amendments in successive legislatures.

The legal profession, on the other hand, is not generally amenable to changes which threaten a judge's authority. Adoptive proceedings are held in the Juvenile Court (formerly in the Court of Domestic Relations). The presiding judge (1953), Gerald R. Corbett, takes an active interest in social welfare and is likely to accept the findings of the DPW or other recognized social agencies regarding the suitability of an adoptive home under observation.

In accordance with a law enacted in 1945 [34] a judge might request a social history from the DPW, but this was not mandatory, nor did it require a recommendation for disposition. In 1953 this law was amended [35] to make mandatory the referral of petitioners to the DPW for investigations. Public Welfare was authorized to refer cases to other accredited agencies for investigation, but all petitions for adoption had to be channeled through the DPW. Recommendations were required in all reports. There is still a loophole, however. The judge is permitted to dispense with social histories and waiting periods if he finds it "in the best interests of the child." [36]

WORLD WAR II (1941–1945)

With the outbreak of hostilities in December of 1941, the Department of Public Welfare, no less than other social welfare organizations, found it necessary to assume war-connected responsibilities. Unemployment had dropped to a minimum, which in turn had decreased the caseload in relief, but an entirely new function in social service was induced by what seems to have been war hysteria.

The largest racial element in Hawaii's population is Japanese (Appendix I) and there was fear of sabotage in Hawaii, fanned by the fact that California had forcibly evacuated from the coastal areas all its Japanese, including the second and third generations and those of mixed blood. There was thought of taking the same action in Hawaii, but the immensity of such an undertaking, and the fact that there was no proof of sabotage and that most of the local Japanese were loyal American citizens, put a stop to wholesale evacuation. Nevertheless, some three hundred Japanese were interned and a number of them were sent to internment camps on the mainland. Families were broken. In some instances the close relatives of internees asked to be sent to Japan, rather than to hostile or unfriendly environments on the mainland. At the end of the war, homes that were broken had to be re-established. The DPW was active in this program of rehabilitation.

Aside from the social problems of broken Japanese homes, there were innumerable problems concerning the living and working conditions of war workers, many of whom sought transportation back to the mainland. This became a problem serious enough for the establishment of the War Workers' Service Bureau, composed of twelve organizations, governmental and voluntary. In a few months its functions became the sole responsibility of the DPW. If a war worker was injured or became ill in line of duty, the contracting firm had to pay his transportation back to the mainland, but if, as was so often the case, a man had become disgruntled or homesick, he would importune doctors and social agencies to "get him back." The federal government had alloted funds to meet the cost of transportation approved by the DPW.

In 1943 the territorial legislature passed a joint resolution establishing the War Records Depository at the University of Hawaii.[37] Organizations throughout the Territory were asked to send to the War Records Committee of the University reports of their activities during the war years. In 1947 the legislature authorized the publication by the University of Hawaii Press of a history based upon these reports. Gwenfread Allen's *Hawaii's War Years—1941–1945* [38] is the result. In this compendium are accounts of the programs of Hawaii's welfare organizations, governmental and voluntary, as they related to World War II.

AN ADMINISTRATIVE SURVEY (1949)

A disturbing attitude about social welfare developed in Hawaii, as well as on the mainland, after the war. This was one of the incentives for an administrative survey in 1949 of the Department of Public Welfare. This was a year in which a new board of directors was confronted with rising unemployment, increased applications for relief, and decreased means to meet them. A lively exchange of correspondence started in the daily press. Public Welfare was accused of "supporting charity wards in prosperity"; its workers were criticized for such "unrealistic thinking" as to include telephone, radio, and lodge dues in a recipient's budget. Plenty of free advice was given on the conduct of a public welfare agency. Some thought all funds to recipients, including the payment of rent, should be subject to the control of the caseworker. Some recommended food orders instead of cash; others, that relief should not exceed what a recipient could normally earn in wages, even if these were below the department's standard of "decency and health." There were those who felt that case records should be open for inspection. It was reminiscent of the long ago when "charity" was authoritative, niggardly, punitive, and lacking in a sense of human dignity.

This seemed like a ground swell from the mainland. In order to receive grants-in-aid from the federal government for certain programs under the Social Security Law of 1935, states had to respect the confidential nature of social histories and case records. By the Jenner Amendment in 1951, Congress made it possible for states to give out information concerning assistance disbursements without jeopardizing their rights to participation in federal funds.

In the *Social Work Journal* for April 1952, under the title "Confidentiality of Assistance Records," there is a succinct statement by Elizabeth Wickenden of what brought about this return to seventeenth-century Poor Law psychology and its implications for those concerned. When uninformed politicians need a scapegoat to further their ends, the public assistance program provides an easy victim. Unfortunately, they are too often aided by the press and national magazines competing for sensational news.

The Jenner Amendment was brought about through attacks

by politicians in various states on the secrecy provision in public assistance. They wanted names and amounts of payments to be made public in order "to smoke out chiselers, reduce caseloads through shame of exposure, force persons to support their aged relatives and assure good administration." True, the amendment prohibits making lists of names or other information available for commercial or political purposes, but social workers know full well that this is but the thin edge of the wedge for further weakening the basic principle of confidentiality.

Already the legislatures of several states have made assistance information accessible to the public. This threat hovers over Hawaii. The National Association of Social Workers is much concerned.

The Department of Public Welfare Board that came into office in 1949 during this rising tide of criticism realized the limitations of inexperience and, wishing to know how efficiently the department was being run, requested the Senate Hold-over Committee to analyze its administration. This was undertaken by a competent team under the direction of the Legislative Reference Bureau, University of Hawaii.[39]

The analysts found the Department of Public Welfare's basic problem to be, not administration—which they thought good on the whole—but the need for Hawaii's people to determine the kind of public welfare laws and program they wanted. It was felt that, until a consensus on eligibility and basic standards for public assistance could be arrived at, the Department of Public Welfare would continue susceptible to criticism, particularly in times of financial crisis. Unless a consensus is reached under qualified leadership its value is open to question.

Rated according to expenditures, the Department of Public Welfare ranks third among territorial institutions. The two with higher expenditures are the Department of Public Instruction and the Department of Public Works. The report cited the ambiguity of the board's governing power and made recommendations to strengthen its authority.

It had been stated that the primary function of the Department of Public Welfare is to determine eligibility for relief, and obviously there are recipients who need casework as well as financial assistance. Because of load pressure the survey team recommended that more use be made of private agencies for casework services.[40] Another recommendation was to expedite the processing of applications; they found that for almost a third of these it took more than one month to establish eligibility or to issue income maintenance.

This habit of slowness in processing applications for relief seems to be general, and it can be the cause of acute suffering, mental as well as physical. It is not limited to governmental agencies. By the Social Security Act Amendments of 1950, states are now required to be reasonably prompt in furnishing assistance.[41]

Accretion of Family Agencies

The accretion of welfare organizations and programs over the years has caused some confusion and overlapping of function. There are three voluntary casework agencies—Child and Family Service, Catholic Social Service, and the Liliuokalani Trust—and one governmental organization, the Department of Public Welfare.

What has taken place in Hawaii has also happened in America, and before that in Great Britain and continental Europe. Governmental organizations were formed when voluntary agencies could no longer cope with needs incidental to world wars and the development of technological and scientific knowledge. Nevertheless, governmental organizations have not eliminated the voluntary ones, especially those of long standing or with unique programs.

Granted, therefore, that all four of Honolulu's agencies have comparable standards as to education and experience of staff, and accepting the fact of a religious affiliation of one and the inheritance of a trust by another, wherein do the policies and functions differ between private and governmental organizations?

The frames of reference are dissimilar. In one, policies are made or approved by a board of voluntary directors; in the other, rules and regulations are promulgated by government or a board acting for it. In the one, support is obtained (with the exception of the Liliuokalani Trust) by voluntary contributions, chiefly through the Honolulu Community Chest, which does not always achieve its goal. In the other, support is by taxation and is therefore assured.

Historically, voluntary agencies have been more flexible in

experimenting with new ideas and establishing concepts which might be frowned upon by governmental authorities as the frills of impractical idealists. The Child and Family Service, for example, can adopt policies and modify them as circumstances indicate, while the Department of Public Welfare to do so may first have to obtain the approval of the legislature, the majority of whose members are inadequately informed on social welfare. Further, private agencies can choose administrators who combine executive ability with training and experience in social work, whereas, in Hawaii at least, the administrator of the Department of Public Welfare is a political appointee who, lacking such qualifications, may fail to gain the respect of those of his subordinates who are qualified social workers.

The primary function of the Child and Family Service, the Catholic Social Service, and the Liliuokalani Trust is casework to families and children. The two first named also provide services to those who are neither children nor have families but who, nevertheless, need consultation regarding personal or social problems. The Department of Public Welfare has a comparable function, so the question remains, "When does one refer to governmental and when to private organizations?" There are no categorical answers, only some general guides; and these are not consistent.

The activities of the Child and Family Service, the Catholic Social Service, and the Liliuokalani Trust are concentrated on the Island of Oahu and the first two are available to persons of any financial status. The programs of the Department of Public Welfare are territory-wide and with two exceptions are restricted to the indigent. One exception is the Child Welfare Services of the Department of Public Welfare, which are available to children on all islands, irrespective of economic status. The second exception is caused by the fact that only on Oahu are there voluntary casework agencies; the DPW will, therefore, accept referrals on the neighbor islands of adults who are not indigent.

SUMMARY

The title of this chapter, "Social Security," is used in its broadest sense to include basic services established in the Territory, within a given period, that are essential to the welfare of human beings.

Above: Loading cane by hand, prior to 1925.

Left: Loading cane by machinery.

Right: Interior of laborer's dwelling.

Below and lower right: Laborers' camps in the early days of the sugar industry.

Above, and upper right: Modern homes of plantation laborers.

Right: Fred Baldwin Memorial Home; Paia, Maui.

Lower right: A Japanese lady, taken prior to World War II.

Below: An *Issei* (born in Japan) carrying her *nisei* (born in Hawaii) child.

The great economic depression of the 1930s, leading in 1935 to the Federal Social Security System, strengthened the concept that the welfare of a people is the responsibility of their government. To provide the organization required by the Social Security Act to receive matching funds, the territorial government established, in 1937, the Board of Public Welfare and County Public Welfare Commissions, known since 1941 as the Department of Public Welfare.

In 1935 the Hawaii Housing Authority was established by legislative enactment to provide decent housing to low-income families at rentals they could afford.

The Federal Social Security Law includes two social insurance programs applicable to all employees in certain covered employment. One is the Unemployment Insurance, a short-term plan for the involuntarily unemployed, and the other is Old Age and Survivor's Insurance, applicable for life to retired employees upon reaching the age of sixty-five, women at 62 years. Both these insurances are pertinent to the programs of the Department of Public Welfare, but are managed by other governmental agencies.

The programs of the Department of Public Welfare are known as Federal Public Assistance and General Assistance. In addition, the DPW administers the Child Welfare Services. The Federal Public Assistance and Child Welfare Services are supported jointly by federal and state funds. General public assistance is supported entirely by state funds and is used to supplement the more restrictive programs under Federal Public Assistance.

An administrative survey of the Department of Public Welfare was made in late 1949 under the direction of the Legislative Reference Bureau. This study attested that the administration of the department is on the whole sound.

---

1 The reader is reminded that research regarding this subject terminated several years before the book was published. Modifications of earlier, as well as later programs are, therefore, not included in this chapter.

2 *T.H. Session Laws* (1933), Act 209, p. 259; amended 1935 *Session Laws,* Act 135, p. 323.

3 For data regarding the Social Security Act the writer has reviewed *Social Welfare Administration in the United States of America,* prepared by the Social Security Administration at the request of the United Nations, Washington, D.C., June 1950, copy in office of Deputy Regional Director, Social Security Administration, Honolulu; Eveline M. Burns, *The American Social Security System* (Cambridge, Mass.; The Riverside Press, Houghton Mifflin Company, 1949); Eveline M. Burns, *The Social Security Act Amendments of*

1950 (Cambridge, Mass.: The Riverside Press, Houghton Mifflin Company), copy in Honolulu County Medical Library; data on social security in Hawaii from a perusal of official papers of the various agencies.

4 For convenience the Territory of Hawaii is here included as a state. comes . . .")

5 Governor's Advisory Committee on Public Welfare appointed July 1936; Walter F. Dillingham, chairman; Minutes of Meeting filed with the Department of Public Welfare.

6 Known 1937–39 as the Board of Public Welfare; 1939–41 as the Department of Social Security; since 1941 as the Department of Public Welfare. *T.H. Session Laws* (1937), chapter 259A, p. 272.

7 *Ibid.*, p. 293.

8 This tax was originally imposed as a two-year emergency measure, but with modifications it has been continued. In 1943 it was increased to two per cent, a continuing allotment of one-half of one per cent going to the Department of Public Welfare and the balance going to the General Fund of the Territory. In 1949 the total amount of this tax was allotted to the General Fund. Since then the Department of Public Welfare has received regular appropriations from the General Fund of the Territory. Information obtained at the office of the territorial auditor.

9 A board of directors and not to be confused with the original name of the organization; i.e., Board of Public Welfare. See note 6, above.

10 Information through correspondence with Miss Salsberry.

11 By legislative amendments in later years these faults have been corrected.

12 *The Department of Public Welfare, An Administrative Survey*, Legislative Reference Bureau, University of Hawaii Report No. 3, 1951; copy Honolulu County Medical Library.

13 Honolulu Council of Social Agencies, *Minimum Standards of Living and its Cost*, 1937.

14 *T.H. Session Laws* (1941), Act 296, part of Sec. 1, p. 339.

15 Information supplied by the Territorial Auditor's Office shows in contrast that, beginning in 1942, territorial employees were allowed a cost-of-living bonus in varying amounts. By 1945 this was incorporated in an increment to base pay. In 1951 the bonus was eliminated through an increase of $25 in the monthly pay of all territorial employees.

16 Information and reports regarding this section were given by Mr. Lee Maice, executive director, Hawaii Housing Authority.

17 *T.H. Session Laws* (1935), Act 190, p. 243.

18 In 1954 it moved to Iolani Barracks, and since December 1955 it has been settled in its own building on School Street in the Kapalama district.

19 Limited, generally, to employees of commercial and industrial occupations. Hawaii's coverage includes employees of eleemosynary institutions.

20 Burns, *American Social Security System and Amendments of 1950*, p. 125.

21 Headquarters are in the Keeliokalani Building, 825 Mililani Street, Honolulu.

22 Burns, *ibid.*, pp. 65, 448 ff.

23 In successive years there have been increases in rate, wage base and benefits.

24 Old Age and Survivor's Insurance is processed through the local office of the Social Security Administration in the Young Hotel Building, Honolulu.

25 *T.H. Session Laws* (1933), Act 66, p. 62.

26 See chapter X.

27 *T.H. Session Laws* (1937), ch. 259A, Public Welfare, p. 272.

28 In 1951 a territorial law was enacted making it obligatory for physically

fit recipients of general assistance to be employed on government work projects as a condition for aid from the Department of Public Welfare.

29 *T.H. Session Laws* (1937), Act 242, p. 273.

30 An activity which developed subsequent to World War II and the Korean War.

31 In July 1946 the Children's Bureau was transferred from the Department of Labor to the Federal Security Agency, now called the Department of Health, Education, and Welfare.

32 *T.H. Session Laws* (1945), Sec. 4830, p. 551; amended 1949 *Session Laws*, Act 353, p. 280.

33 *Ibid.* (1943), Act 213, p. 236.

34 *Ibid.* (1945), Act 40, p. 301; amended 1947 *Session Laws*, Act 47, p. 392.

35 *Ibid.* (1953), Act 115.

36 The source for the interpretation of certain aspects of this law is an analysis of it in July 1953, by Judge Corbett.

37 *T.H. Session Laws* (1943), Joint Resolution No. 6, p. 329.

38 See also *Notes and References to Hawaii's War Years*, by Gwenfread Allen, revised and edited by Aldyth Morris (Honolulu: University of Hawaii Press, 1952).

39 *The Department of Public Welfare Administrative Survey*, Legislative Reference Bureau, University of Hawaii Report No. 31951, p. 2; copy in Honolulu County Medical Library.

40 Private agencies have the problem of pressure, too. The size of their staff is determined largely by Honolulu Community Chest allotments.

41 Burns, *Social Security Act Amendments of 1950*, p. 469.

XII

The Neighbor Islands
(Period up to 1954)

This chapter is a brief history of social service on three other major islands in the Hawaiian group, the islands of Kauai, Maui, and Hawaii.

Although the island of Oahu is only third in land area, its superior Honolulu and Pearl harbors have brought it the greatest concentration and diversity of population. While the other islands remained essentially agricultural and rural, on Oahu the economy became increasingly industrial, and the population more and more concentrated and urban. Hence, Honolulu, the capital of the Territory, had casework organizations long before the need for them became apparent on the neighbor islands. With the establishment of the territory-wide Board of Public Welfare and County Public Welfare Commissions in 1937, casework was organized on neighbor islands.

Any history of social service in the Hawaiian Islands must take into consideration the influence of the missionaries who were sent in companies from Boston to the Sandwich Islands (as they were then called) by the American Board of Commissioners for Foreign Missions. The first company arrived in 1820; the last in 1848.[1] Along with the propagation of the Christian Gospel came its corollary—charitable works.

AGRICULTURAL DEVELOPMENT

After Captain Cook's discovery of the Islands in 1778, traders and merchants, as well as missionaries, were landing on these shores. Among them were some with a vision of the wealth to be gained from the cultivation of sugar, and later of pineapples. With the vision came also the realization of the need for labor on a large scale. The Hawaiians were still too

144

closely identified with the economy of subsistence farming and fishing they had known before the coming of *haoles* (white people) to take part in heavy agriculture for the sake of profit. Also, serious epidemics introduced by traders had taken a heavy toll of the Hawaiians. The planters had to look farther afield.

In the second half of the nineteenth century and in the early years of the twentieth, thousands of Chinese coolies and laborers of other racial backgrounds—Portuguese, Japanese, Koreans, Filipinos, and others—were brought to the Hawaiian Islands to work on plantations.[2] They were settled according to race in communities or camps which, as might be expected, took on the atmosphere of the homelands from whence these immigrants came. Their camps were like villages of China or Japan, or any of the countries from which large numbers had come to labor on plantations.

Agricultural cultivation in Hawaii until after World War II was controlled largely by paternalistic corporations—some benevolent, some not so benevolent. It was the rule to provide laborers with free dwellings, free use of utilities, and medical care under a doctor employed by the corporation. The fear of losing both job and home in a strange country made for an imposed industrial stability.

By 1919 the concept of plantation welfare was taking shape in the minds of some of the members of the Hawaiian Sugar Planters' Association. In that year, through the recommendation of the Russell Sage Foundation, New York, the Planters' Association engaged Mr. Clinton S. Childs, a graduate of the New York School of Social Work, to undertake a welfare survey of their plantations. In varying degrees, on different plantations, Mr. Childs found much to be desired in the living and working conditions of plantation laborers.[3] One of the results of the survey was the employment of welfare workers; they were men who emphasized recreation, chiefly sports and games. For personal services the plantations depended largely upon nurses.

In Hawaii, as elsewhere, modern social work was preceded by an age of philanthropy based on the Christian gospel. As we have seen, the organized spread in the Hawaiian Islands of that gospel began with the missionaries sent here (1820–48) by the American Board of Commissioners for Foreign Missions. Among the descendants of these evangelists are some who have given outstanding service in government and social welfare on all the islands.

KAUAI

The most northerly of the islands is Kauai. Much of the social welfare on Kauai is traceable to the leadership given by two sisters, Elsie Hart Wilcox and Mabel Isabel Wilcox, direct descendants of missionaries alluded to above.

Mention must be made of a few of their many services. In 1932, Miss Elsie Wilcox was elected to the Territorial Senate, the first woman to hold this position; she was re-elected in 1936. During her incumbency Miss Wilcox was a member of the Judiciary, Health, and Education committees, and chairman of the Education Committee in the 1935–37 legislature.[4] She won the confidence of those on all the islands who were concerned with matters of social welfare. This included the important work that underlay the establishment by the 1937 territorial legislature of the Territorial Board of Public Welfare and County Public Welfare Commissions.

Miss Mabel Wilcox's major contribution to social welfare was in the field of health. From childhood it had been her desire to be a nurse. In 1911 she graduated from the Nursing School of Johns Hopkins Hospital. In 1917 she was active in getting a territorial law enacted for the registration of nurses trained in Hawaii.

By the second decade of this century the incidence of tuberculosis had increased to such an extent that an Anti-Tuberculosis Bureau was created within the Department of Health. The Bureau appointed a "TB nurse" for each island, with the responsibility of finding and reporting cases of tuberculosis and arranging for care of patients in their homes or in sanatoria.

The first nurse to receive an appointment for Kauai under this program was Miss Mabel Wilcox (1914). She was the first rural nurse on that island. Born and raised there, she quite easily identified herself with its people, especially the Hawaiians, who were shy of hospitals. They called her *Wilikoki Kauka Wahine* (woman doctor Wilcox) as she went among them getting them to accept treatment and to believe that a hospital did not necessarily mean death.[5] This experience laid the foundation in 1917 of the Samuel Mahelona Hospital, Kapaa, for the treatment of tuberculosis.[6]

Nurses as Social Workers

Nursing is a much older profession than social work. This is why nurses, in years gone by, combined social service with nursing and why they were employed as social workers when there were no qualified ones, as we understand the term today.

Miss Wilcox became increasingly convinced of the interdependence of nursing and social work. During these early years she took a leave of absence to attend talks given in Honolulu by Miss Margaret Bergen, manager of Associated Charities, and to work under her supervision. On at least two occasions she invited Miss Bergen to talk to the nurses of Kauai on the relationship between social conditions and illness.

Kauai is credited with the introduction of the plantation nurse as distinct from the public health nurse. In 1917 the Mokihana Club,[7] an organization founded twelve years earlier, chiefly for social and artistic activities, engaged Miss Fanny Kuhlig as a district nurse. In the beginning she worked in schools "cleaning children's heads and attending to sores and cuts." She found the school children's teeth in "such a shocking state" that the club arranged for dental care, parents paying what they could and the club contributing the balance. Miss Kuhlig also went into plantation camps where she so proved her worth that Lihue and Grove Farm and Kipu Plantation assumed the cost of her services. Other plantations followed suit in the employment of nurses whose functions included welfare services.

Governmental Organizations

Another casework function for which nurses on Kauai accepted responsibility was that of probation officer. Several nurses preceded Mrs. Claire Carra, currently in charge of the girls' division of the Juvenile Court. The probation staff in 1954 numbered four.

The programs of Child Welfare and Old Age Pensions mentioned before were implemented on Kauai by public health nurses, under the supervision of Miss Mabel Wilcox. Until the early 1920s public health nurses worked in specialized fields; there were school nurses, tuberculosis nurses, maternity and

infancy nurses, etc. By 1925 the nursing service was reorganized into one general program. The islands were redistricted,
making public health nurses responsible for any service in
any field that came to their attention.[8] Their training came
to include courses in social casework, thus increasing their
functional value to the Board of Child Welfare and Old Age
Pensions.

Miss Wilcox was a member of the Governor's Advisory Com-
mittee on Public Welfare, and likewise represented Kauai in
the formulation of policies which governed the establishment
of the Territorial Board of Public Welfare and County Public
Welfare Commissions. She was appointed chairman of the
Kauai Public Welfare Commission. The first Kauai County
Administrator for the Board of Public Welfare was Miss Alice
Bakeman, a qualified social worker.

MAUI

In 1831 the Reverend Dwight Baldwin and his bride, members of the fourth company of missionaries, arrived in the
Islands. The young theologian was also a doctor of medicine.[9]
The greater part of their lives was spent on Maui, where their
second son, Henry Perrine Baldwin, was born in Lahaina in
1842.[10] Grown to manhood, H. P. Baldwin gave outstanding
leadership in the development of the sugar industry in the
Islands. His name is also associated with the advancement of
social welfare, particularly on his native island of Maui.

In the year following the arrival in the Islands of Dr. and
Mrs. Dwight Baldwin came the Reverend and Mrs. William
Patterson Alexander. Several years later Mr. Alexander was
sent from Kauai to Lahaina, Maui, to take charge of Lahainaluna School for native boys. Emily, the daughter of Mr. and
Mrs. Alexander, became the wife of Henry Perrine Baldwin.
She, too, was deeply conscious of a philanthropic responsibility
which found expression in several organizations on Maui.[11] The
one with which social service was most closely identified for
many years was the Alexander House Settlement, named after
Mrs. Baldwin's parents.

Alexander House Settlement

The inspiration to found this organization came from the
vision of two devoted teachers, Miss Charlotte L. Turner and

Miss N. J. Malone, employees of the Hawaiian Board of Public Instruction. Part of what follows regarding the Alexander House Settlement is taken from a booklet written by Miss Turner, which describes her twenty-seven years on Maui.[12]

She went in 1893 to Waihee, populated largely by Hawaiians who dwelt usually in grass huts, each one containing one room, and each hut for a particular purpose—sleeping, eating, etc. Miss Turner's services were not confined to teaching. Riding horseback, she visited the rural homes, ministering to those in need, giving clothing, and teaching cleanliness. She brought people together at socials held in the teacher's cottage.

At the end of three years Miss Turner accepted an offer from the Hawaiian Board of Missions to live and work in a Chinese mission in Wailuku. Assisting her was a Chinese evangelist, Ting Ling, the father of Mrs. Goo, the first Chinese social worker in the Associated Charities, Honolulu. Miss Turner was a friendly visitor to Chinese families in Wailuku as she had been to the Hawaiians in Waihee. An example of the Chinese mores of that day is cited by Miss Turner. In approaching parents for contributions toward the support of mission work among their people, she would often get the reply, "I will give you so much for my boys, but nothing for my girls."

After a few years Miss Turner returned to the United States on a visit to her home. During this time she and Miss Malone, who had also gone home, decided to acquaint themselves with the settlement movement then taking shape in the United States. They visited several settlement houses, among them Hull House, founded in Chicago in 1889. Under Jane Addams it was to become the most famous of them all. They saw an analogy between the needs of European immigrants coming to America who suffered industrial exploitation and those of Asia and elsewhere coming to Hawaii.

These visits to settlement houses inspired Miss Turner and Miss Malone to get one established in Wailuku, where little children would have a kindergarten and where there would be classes in English and handcrafts for older ones, a reading room, and a small library.

Returning to Maui, these women set about raising funds. They received contributions from people of various racial backgrounds. The directors of the Wailuku Sugar Company gave the land and a building was erected and opened in September 1901 as the Alexander House Settlement. For many years the settlement was supported chiefly by the Baldwin family.

The first qualified social worker of the Alexander House Settlement was Mr. Clinton S. Childs, who became its director in 1920. The functions remained essentially of a community and group nature. The organization was responsible for similar programs on Molokai and Lanai.

The recreational programs developed for plantations were used as models throughout the territory. Under Mr. Childs' regime the Boy Scouts were reorganized and the Girl Scouts organized. In Lahaina a kindergarten that had been established in Baldwin Home (the old family residence of that name) came under the supervision of the settlement.

As for sports, there was no doubt that the Maui community was athletic-minded, even to the accompaniment of oaths and blows on athletic fields, among the spectators as among the players. It was the job of the Alexander House Settlement to bring about a changed attitude—that "it is better to play for fun than to win by any means."

The settlement took a leading part in the development of school health—nutrition, physical education, and summer health programs for underweight children. A co-operative program with the public health nurse led to the opening of children's wards at the Kula Sanatorium,[13] one for positive and another for nonpositive cases of tuberculosis. As a result of the TB Association's program, the time came when a children's ward at the sanatorium was no longer needed.

The staff of the Alexander House Settlement at one time totaled 35, with a peak of 1,500 volunteers. Though the functions were centered in group work, the organization did give casework service when the need was brought to their attention. Generally speaking, their policy was, "anything which could add to the happiness and welfare of the people of Maui."

But times were changing—the philanthropists of an earlier day had gone and a decentralization had come about with the development of local community associations. The establishment in 1937 of the Territorial Board of Public Welfare and County Public Welfare Commissions and the unionization of plantation workers in 1944–45 are among the reasons why the

Alexander House Settlement ceased to function as such in 1949. It has not been disincorporated; today its various buildings are being used as headquarters by different community groups.

Maui Aid Association

In 1909 the Maui Aid Association was incorporated for the purpose of "Americanization work" in the Wailuku Girls' Home, support of kindergartens, church aid, and theological training for local pastors. The association was affiliated with the Hawaiian Board of Missions and aided them in their church work on that island. The Baldwin family took a leading part in the organization and support of the Maui Aid Association.[14] This association is no longer extant.

Fred Baldwin Memorial Home

The Fred Baldwin Memorial Home was built in Paia in 1911 and endowed by Mr. Henry P. Baldwin in memory of his twenty-four year old son, who died in 1905. The policies of the home are still formulated by members of the Baldwin family. The primary object of the founder was to provide a home for elderly white men without money or relatives.

But the aging process is no respecter of wealth, and the time came when lonely elderly men of independent means were applying for admission to the Fred Baldwin Memorial Home. Provided they meet the requirements, among which is a year's residence in the Islands, aged Caucasian men from any island who can afford to pay a nominal sum have since become eligible for admission. This does not debar the indigent whose support includes clothing. When the indigent residents are in need of medical or hospital care, the Hawaiian Commercial and Sugar Company's hospital at Puunene assumes the expense if the patient is admitted to a ward; if to a private room, the home pays the difference between ward and private room rates.

The home has a capacity for fifteen Caucasian men, each having a separate bedroom. Four sitting rooms and a workshop are available for those who wish to make use of them.

One of the most appreciative letters to come to the Social Service Department of The Queen's Hospital was from a newly admitted resident to the Fred Baldwin Memorial Home. This elderly man had been a patient at Queen's. In planning for his discharge the social worker explained why it was unwise for him to continue to live alone and suggested the Baldwin Home. He agreed with everything but separation from his workshop and beloved tools—cabinet work was his avocation. When Mrs. H. A. Baldwin, daughter-in-law of the founder, wrote to say in effect "tell Mr.— to bring his tools, we'll give him all the room he wants," he consented to leave Honolulu. A few weeks later he wrote to tell us that he never thought he could be so content as he had become in the Fred Baldwin Memorial Home.

Mrs. Harry A. Baldwin (nee Ethel Smith) is the grand-daughter of Dr. James Smith, who came to the Islands as a member of the tenth company of missionaries. Dr. Smith was stationed on Kauai both as doctor of medicine and as a theologian.

Arrangements are under way for the closing in 1959 of the Fred Baldwin Memorial Home as a domiciliary home for aged Caucasian men. The trustees are taking legal steps to make possible its use as a dormitory for men students attending the adjacent Maunaolu Junior College, a private institution opened in 1950.

Hale Makua

Prior to World War II, the needy aged on Maui, irrespective of race and sex, were given domiciliary care by the county in a separate building on the grounds of the old Malulani Hospital in Wailuku. At the outbreak of hostilities every available hospital bed was required by military and civilian defense organizations for emergency needs. The old folk were therefore transferred to the basement of the Young Buddhist Association hall of Wailuku Hongwanji Mission. These quarters were quite inadequate but had to do for the time being. The Department of Public Welfare paid for their care, and the Salvation Army undertook their over-all supervision.

At the war's end the first project of the Maui United Young Buddhist Association was the erection of a suitable and adequately equipped home for the aged people of Maui County, "regardless of race, religious beliefs, or former walks of life— in more healthful and cheerful surroundings." They channeled an offer to build such a home through the Maui Community Council which, in the meantime, had made a survey of the needs of the aging on that island.

The offer was accepted and the young men went to work. The Wailuku Sugar Company furnished the land, which lay in a little village near Iao stream known as Happy Valley. It is said to have been so named because inhabitants too fond of the bottle became quite happy in consequence.

The Maui United YBA initiated in August, 1946, a drive for funds. Their goal was $10,000; they got $18,276.67. This enabled them to enlarge their anticipated capacity from 25 to 40 beds. The home was built by the volunteer labor of members of the United Young Buddhists Association and Buddhist Church members, and was dedicated on August 17, 1947.[15] The home was named *Hale Makua* (Home for the Aged). It has continued under the supervision of the Salvation Army, but with a governing board representative of both official and voluntary agencies.

By 1952 the county of Maui had erected a new hospital in Wailuku, the Central Memorial Hospital, in memory of its war veterans. The old Malulani Hospital, after basic repairs and alterations, was put in order for the old people in Happy Valley.

The Hale Makua of today (1953) has enlarged its capacity to about seventy residents, the chronically ill as well as the aged. The county owns the property, contributes toward maintenance, and assumes the cost of utilities. Otherwise, Hale Makua is supported by fees of residents who can afford to pay for their care, by the Department of Public Welfare for those who cannot, and by the Maui Community Chest.

Maui Children's Home [16]

The Maui Children's Home was opened in 1923 in Wailuku and has since been moved to Paia. Administered by the Maryknoll Sisters (Roman Catholic) it is a boarding home for dependent children from two to fourteen years of age. They attend the nearby Catholic school. The home is supported by voluntary contributions and the Maui Community Chest.

Governmental Organizations

Throughout its history Mrs. H. A. Baldwin was chairman for Maui County of the Board of Child Welfare and Old Age Pensions and Miss A. E. Dent, previously the public health nurse on that island, was its longest serving executive. In this position she led a staff of some fifteen volunteers.

In 1936 Mrs. Baldwin and Mr. Childs represented Maui County on the Governor's Advisory Committee on Public Welfare. Miss Dent was appointed the first administrator for the county of Maui of the Board of Public Welfare.

HAWAII

Hawaii is the largest and most southerly island in the group. Here, as on all the islands, the seeds of social welfare were planted by the missionaries sent to the Sandwich Islands by the American Board of Commissioners for Foreign Missions.

The missionaries came with a purpose of spreading the Christian gospel, but spreading the gospel among the Hawaiians depended to a large extent upon their learning how to read and write. Schools were opened on mission stations on the different islands. These came to be centers, not only for learning, but also for the furtherance of community welfare.

Hilo Boarding School [17]

One such school was the Hilo Boarding School, founded in 1836 by the Reverend and Mrs. David Belden Lyman, who were members of the fifth company (1832) of missionaries to arrive in the Sandwich Islands.

The object of the Hilo Boarding School was to train Hawaiian boys and to prepare scholars to enter the seminary at Lahainaluna on Maui. In addition to "reading, writing, and arithmetic," together with a strong emphasis on the Christian religion, a program was gradually developed in agriculture, dairying, printing, mechanics, blacksmithing, carpentry, and other vocations.[18]

The school progressed from small grass houses, with a total of twelve pupils, to governmental subsidy, substantial buildings, extended curriculum, and larger enrollments. It prepared Hawaiian boys to take leading roles in religious work, business, and politics.

But over the course of years public schools were being established with curricula which included vocational training. The need therefore, diminished for the Hilo Boarding School as originally planned. By 1929 it had become a home and "a Christian Social Service Center" for country boys attending Hilo Junior and High School, as well as for boys employed in Hilo. Since 1947 the buildings have been used, first as an extension of the University of Hawaii, and since 1950 as the University of Hawaii, Hilo Branch.

To celebrate the one hundreth anniversary of the founding of the Hilo Boarding School, the trustees decided to honor the memory of its founders, David Belden Lyman and Sarah Joiner Lyman, by raising funds to build and equip on Kamehameha Avenue (a new location) the Hilo Community Center. The center was dedicated on April 3, 1937, for "boys and girls in need of social service who are not clients already of another organization," and Mr. John E. Beukema was appointed its director. In 1949 Mr. Beukema left Hawaii, and with changing conditions the program came to an end. The building is used, however, as a boarding home for boys working in Hilo whose own homes are in other parts of the Island. It also provides offices for various community organizations.

In 1954 the Hilo Community Center became the headquarters of a newly organized branch of the Boys Clubs of America. This new organization is administered and wholly financed by the Hilo Boarding School which, though no longer functioning as a school, still owns the property and still maintains its legal identity.[19]

Waiakea Social Settlement

In 1900, a group of women from the Hawaiian Board of Missions First Foreign Church interested themselves in finding means to counteract "rough influences" in Waiakea-kai, then a remote district from Hilo proper. The "roughness" was generated by a fishing fleet, the railroad shops, and the sugar mill. To teach "a better way of life," these women began in a church with classes for the Hawaiian women of Waiakea in cooking, sewing, and child care. In 1901 a tidal wave swept away the little church—all but the bell. Following this catastrophe the Waiakea Mill Company[20] deeded the land on which the church had stood for a new building, to become known as Waiakea Social Settlement. The old church bell was hung in the new structure.

As long as its functions had a religious motivation the settlement continued to receive support from the Hawaiian Board of Missions, but, with the establishment of churches in Hilo, the Waiakea Social Settlement widened its sphere of service to include current social needs as they became apparent.

One who was long associated with the settlement, Mrs. Eric Hartley (then Jean McConn), a trained kindergarten teacher, went there in 1924. During her years of activity Mrs. Hartley was not only a devoted teacher but in numerous ways performed social services that have since become the functions of governmental agencies.

For many years before Hawaii had a Juvenile Court or a probation officer, the circuit court judge in juvenile hearings would designate Mrs. Hartley as "guardian" of some wayward boy or girl. In the 1920s the first Child Health Conference on Hawaii was organized by Miss Jane Service, the first public health nurse appointed to that island (1914). The meetings were held at Waiakea Social Settlement, Mrs. Hartley co-operating with Miss Service in this program. Another program initiated at Waiakea was the summer recreational program for children. In later years this became the responsibility of the county.

Nowadays the majority of the inhabitants in Waiakea are not Hawaiian but of Asian ancestry. In keeping with the needs of the times the functions of the settlement today include classes of various kinds for young and old and a diversity of recreational programs. The director of the Waiakea Social Settlement in 1954 is Mr. Edward Hifumi Sato, who holds an M.Sc. degree in recreation from Indiana University. The Waiakea Social Settlement is currently supported by the Hawaii Community Chest and Council.

Father Louis Boys' Home [21]

Though this home is no longer extant, is was once an important resource to the circuit judge in disposing of boys' cases. For many years Father Louis had been the curate of the Roman Catholic Church of St. Joseph, in Hilo. In addition to his clerical duties, he served as probation officer and naturally came into contact with boys who were without suitable homes. He would take them into the rectory, providing for them out of his salary as probation officer. When their number grew beyond this accommodation, he built a home on the premises of the Brothers' School. It was opened in 1916 and was generously supported in succeeding years by the people of Hawaii.

In time Father Louis was retired and went away. Efforts were made to carry on the home, but, owing to conditions during World War II, the continuation of this program became exceedingly difficult. Among other conditioning factors was the trend away from institutions toward foster home placement for children. After due consideration, the Department of Public Welfare, which has a responsibility for licensing foster homes and child-caring institutions, withdrew the license of Father Louis Boys' Home in 1945.[22] Since then, dependent boys of Hawaii are generally placed in foster homes. Those classified as delinquent are committed to the Koolau Boys' Home on Oahu.

Salvation Army Girls' Home

Prior to 1922 delinquent girls awaiting trial were kept in the county jail. In that year, through the interest of the Hilo Women's Club, the Salvation Army Girls' Home was founded. Since then delinquent girls have been sent to Kawailoa Girls' Home on Oahu, and the Salvation Army Girls' Home in Hilo has kept dependent girls, who are admitted from any part of the island of Hawaii. The Department of Public Welfare controls the intake, and pays board for each girl. The home is under the supervision of the Salvation Army, and the Hawaii Community Chest and Council covers its administrative expenses.

Lima Kokua (Helping Hand)

This agency was organized in 1911 by a group which limited its membership to twenty. It had no connection with any religious, political, or social institution. It restricted its functions to child welfare and might be considered the first agency to organize such services on Hawaii. During its active years the Lima Kokua was responsible for the furnishing and upkeep of a room in the old Hilo Memorial Hospital for needy sick children. It also founded foster homes and paid for the care of children in need of such placement. The organization was active until 1919, when its functions were absorbed by the newly created Territorial Board of Child Welfare.

Hawaii Island Welfare Bureau [23]

In 1918 a group of men and women in Hilo organized the Associated Charities. By 1919 it became known as the Hawaii Island Welfare Bureau. In the general sense of the term it was not, as its name might imply, a casework agency, but a community chest collecting voluntary contributions for the support of its constituent organizations.

Miss Kate O'Reilly, the first professionally qualified caseworker employed on Hawaii, was the first executive of the Welfare Bureau. Her duties took her all over the island. In her consultations with various groups she emphasized the need for breaking away from the old type of charitable work (handing out money) and for developing a more constructive program of prevention,[24] attitudes reminiscent of the evolution of social service in England and America. In 1948 the Hawaii Island Welfare Bureau became the Hawaii Community Chest and Council.

Hilo Relief and Welfare Agency [25]

In 1936 the Hilo Relief and Welfare Agency was organized. Its director was Miss Lucia Gardner, a professionally qualified social worker. This voluntary social agency was dissolved with the establishment in 1937 of the Territorial Board of Public Welfare and County Public Welfare Commission.

Governmental Organizations

On Hawaii, as was true of the other islands, a territorial law mandated the county to establish a board of child welfare and old age pensions.[26] These boards were administered in the respective counties principally by voluntary agencies. The Board of Child Welfare and Old Age Pensions on Hawaii was administered at first by the Hawaii Island Welfare Bureau and then by the Hilo Relief and Welfare Agency.

Boards of Child Welfare and Old Age Pensions were dissolved in 1937 when the Territorial Board of Public Welfare and County Public Welfare Commissions was established. There are no voluntary family casework agencies in the territory except on Oahu. The Department of Public Welfare will therefore accept referrals on any island of persons who are not indigent.

Another integral territorial organization is the Bureau of Sight Conservation and Work with the Blind, which is represented on all the islands.

One People

Considerable sociological evolution has taken place since the original immigrants were brought to these islands for the purpose of industrial exploitation. In those early years, women as well as men labored long and hard in cane fields, under contracts which gave them only the bare necessities of living. At the expiration of their contracts some of these immigrants returned to their homelands; a number emigrated to California; some remained on plantations, and others moved into Honolulu.

Over the years fundamental changes were taking place on plantations, brought about by mechanization, fast communication between the Islands and the outside world, and not least by the unionization of plantation labor in the 1940s.

Organized labor obtained the abolition by 1948 of all perquisites—housing, fuel, water, and medical care. Wages were increased and employees began to pay house rent and utility bills, and to consult doctors of their choice, at their own expense. Some plantations have voluntarily made it possible for employees to purchase their homes.

The Hawaii-born descendants of immigrant contract laborers are American citizens. Many have multiracial ancestry. They are educated in American schools, and many go on to universities to prepare themselves for responsible positions. Descendants of contract laborers are well represented in the professions, in industry, and in politics.

[1] *Portraits and Biographical Sketches of American Protestant Missions to the Hawaiian Islands* (Honolulu: The Hawaiian Mission Children's Society, 1937).

[2] Ernest Beaglehole, *Some Modern Hawaiians*, University of Hawaii Research Publication 19, p. 16.

[3] C. S. Childs, *Report and Recommendations for Establishing Welfare Work on the Plantations Belonging to the Hawaiian Sugar Planters' Association*, Nov. 1919; copy loaned by Mr. Childs.

[4] Women of Hawaii, edited by Geo. F. Nellist (E. A. Langton-Boyle, 1938), II, p. 301.

[5] Ethel M. Damon, "Mabel Wilcox, Pioneer in Public Health," *Paradise of the Pacific Annual*, 1952, p. 26.

[6] Founded by Mr. and Mrs. Albert Spencer Wilcox in memory of Mrs. Wilcox's son, Samuel H. K. Mahelona, who died of tuberculosis.

[7] The fragrant mokihana berry is the emblem of Kauai. *The Mokihana Club, A Sketch 1905–1930* (privately printed), p. 4.

[8] Information from the Bureau of Public Health Nursing.

[9] See *9 Doctors & God*, by Francis John Halford, M.D. (Honolulu: University of Hawaii Press, 1954).

[10] Arthur L. Dean, *Alexander and Baldwin, Ltd. and the Predecessor Partnerships* (Honolulu: Advertiser Publishing Company, Ltd., 1950), p. 24.

[11] *Ibid.*

[12] Charlotte L. Turner, *Twenty-seven Years on Maui* (Makawao, Maui,

Hawaii: Wailuku Times Print), June 16, 1920; copy in library, Hawaiian Mission Children's Society.

[13] Established in 1910 as a tuberculosis, as well as a general hospital.

[14] Ellis E. Pleasant, "Maui Aid Association," *The Friend*, Dec. 1922, p. 268.

[15] Information regarding Hale Makua was obtained from Mr. Alvin Silva, personnel director, Wailuku Sugar Company, and Mr. Harold Yamaguchi, Young Buddhist Association.

[16] *Second Annual Report Catholic Charities* 1945, p. 18.

[17] *Notes of the Hilo Boarding School 1836–1935;* library, Hawaiian Mission Children's Society.

[18] When Samuel Armstrong (born in the Hawaiian Islands, son of the Reverend Richard Armstrong) founded in Virginia the Hampton Institute for negroes in 1868, he patterned it after the Hilo Boarding School.

[19] "New Hilo Center," *The Friend*, May 1937, p. 90.

[20] Dissolved in 1952.

[21] *History of the Catholic Mission in Hawaii*, S.S.C.C., 1927.

[22] *Second Annual Report Catholic Charities*, p. 17.

[23] John H. Beukema, "Origin and Growth of Social Work on the Island of Hawaii," *The Friend*, May 1941, p. 85.

[24] *Territorial Conference of Social Work*, 1921, p. 33.

[25] Lydia M. Blakeslee, "Social Work on the Island of Hawaii," *The Friend*, March 1939, p. 45.

[26] *T.H. Session Laws* (1919), Act 129, p. 72; (1921), Act 37, p. 52; (1933), Act 208, p. 253; amended 1933, Special Session, Act 39, p. 51.

Part II

XIII

The Hospital Flower Society

It was in 1890, in the age of the gay 'nineties, of the lancers, the polka, and the waltz. Occasional steamers were coming and going between the Hawaiian Islands and the outside world, but the sailing vessel was still a common mode of ocean passage. On land, horses and carriages were the means of transportation and to reach Waikiki or the Pali was a journey in itself.

The population of Honolulu, then 31,194, (appendix I) was chiefly composed—apart from native Hawaiians—of missionaries and their descendants; there were also those who came with the purpose of commercial exploitation (and their descendants); still others with no purpose. Among them all some were lonely and some were ill. There were poor sick Hawaiians too. It was an era in which the sick, (unless they were poor) or strangers did not go to the hospital.

To bring cheer to such poor and lonely persons "the ladies of Honolulu" were called by the Reverend Alexander and Mrs. Mackintosh [1] to a meeting on February 22, 1890, in the parlor of the YMCA. [2] The Hospital Flower Society grew out of this meeting. It was organized "to encourage the spirit of benevolence and to promote sympathy amongst the ladies of Honolulu with the sick in the hospital." [3] This hospital, The Queen's, was the only general hospital in Honolulu at that time.

The ministrations of the Hospital Flower Society consisted of weekly distribution of flowers. The flowers were furnished through a vendor, who deposited them within the entrance of the original building of Queen's. The ladies, arriving in their carriages—some of the younger ones on bicycles—would tie the blooms into stiff little bunches, pile them on ugly tin trays (there was little sense of flower arrangement in those days), and then proceed through the wards, distributing them as they

163

went. Occasionally the hospital superintendent requested them to call on a stranger in a private room.

It was the age of philanthropy, and the intent of the "ministrations of fragrant cheer" was to open the way to further service. The effectiveness of service depended as much upon the personalities of the members of the Flower Society as upon the physical or emotional states of patients. Some of the latter were grumpy, or too ill to respond, while others were lonely and looked forward to the weekly visitors. While some of the visitors hurried through the wards with no genuine feeling for the patients, others lingered by bedsides to extend their ministrations, particularly to strangers. A few visitors made interim calls, supplied reading matter, and wrote letters. Now and then they would take a patient for a drive or even have him convalesce in their own homes.

The society's chief means of support, the annual pencil sale, became a tradition in Honolulu. The pencils, good ones, bore the inscription, "Remember the Hospital Flower Society." They were ten cents apiece, but many a dollar was given for a single pencil. Many a parent, too, bought pencils by the box for children going to school or away to college.

Beginning in The Queen's Hospital, the Hospital Flower Society expanded its services to what is known today as Leahi Hospital. Fish, eggs, and vegetables, in addition to flowers, were taken to the Home for Incurables, as it was then called, but it wasn't so easy to find volunteers who could or would travel the long way over dirt roads to minister to "incurables." One still remembers the prickles of the pineapples carried through the heat and dust from the end of the car line to a stranger with tuberculosis. When he died, she helped his young wife with the funeral arrangements.

With the passing years medicine was becoming increasingly scientific, and only hospitals were able to give the type of care physicians were demanding. The well-to-do, as well as the poor and the stranger, now accepted hospitalization as a normal occurrence in illness. Also, flowers were being brought to the sick by relatives and friends. Except for the stranger, the need for the ministrations of the Hospital Flower Society was diminishing. Charter members had grown old, some had died, and younger women were assuming other responsibilities.

Meetings began to drag; at times it was hard to get a quorum. The Hospital Flower Society had seemingly run its course.

HOSPITAL SOCIAL SERVICE

In the fall of 1919, I returned to Honolulu from New York with the diploma of the New York School of Social Work. Toward its attainment, I had presented a paper entitled "Organizing Hospital Social Service in a Pioneer Field," Hawaii being that field. One morning in September 1919, I attended a meeting of the Hospital Flower Society. At that meeting the burning question was how to spend an accumulation of some $2,000. Though the original purposes of the Hospital Flower Society had faded over the years, dissolution meant liquidation of their funds—to what use could they put their $2,000?

I told the remaining members of the Hospital Flower Society, meeting that morning in 1919, about hospital social service—and they realized that here was a vital purpose for their funds. Succeeding chapters follow the development of medical social service in Hawaii. But first are noted its beginnings in England and its spread to America.

1 Mr. Mackintosh was a minister of St. Andrew's (Episcopal) Cathedral.
2 Then on the *makai-ewa* (seaward and toward the district of Ewa) corner of Hotel and Alakea streets.
3 *Constitution and By-Laws, Hospital Flower Society,* "Article I, Object," Honolulu County Medical Library.

XIV

The Beginnings of Medical Social Work

IN ENGLAND [1]

In Britain during the latter half of the nineteenth century there was an acceleration of social consciousness, a counterpart to the poverty and slums largely consequent upon the industrial revolution. A form in which this found expression was the London Charity Organization Society [2] founded in 1869. In 1875 Charles Stewart Loch, at the age of twenty-six, became its executive secretary.

Upon his graduation from Oxford University in 1875 Loch had worked as a clerk to the Royal College of Surgeons, at the same time reading for the bar. It was not the legal profession, however, to which he gave allegiance, but rather to the social and welfare programs of his day. He was a member of the Islington District Committee of the society and took up residence in that poor quarter of London. In recognition of his many services, Loch was knighted in 1915; he died in 1923.

An abiding concern of Loch was the relationship of poverty to illness. In the early years of his affiliation with the Charity Organization Society this concern was shared with a special committee of medical consultants. The doctors were uneasy about the apparent exploitation of free care by persons they thought able to pay for it; this not only deprived them of income but was so overcrowding hospital dispensaries as to threaten the standards of medical practice.

Originally hospitals in England were founded for the sick poor. Loch realized the wastefulness, however, of free medical care for patients who lacked the means for necessary food. A select committee of the House of Lords was appointed to investigate the overcrowding of hospital dispensaries. It accepted Loch's recommendation for the placement of a social

166

worker from the Charity Organization Society as Lady almoner to the Royal Free Hospital in London.

In the age when monasteries were the chief dispensers of relief a man known as the almoner interviewed all applicants for relief, whether material or medical, and to decide what should be done for them. A number of the large teaching hospitals in London, perpetuating the old tradition of the monastic foundations, called the members of their boards of management "almoners." To distinguish social workers from the earlier almoners the prefix "lady" was used. In later years "hospital" replaced "lady"; today the title "hospital almoners" is giving place to "medical social workers."

Miss Mary Stewart, a staff member of the society, was appointed in January of 1895 as the first lady almoner to the Royal Free Hospital. Her functions as laid down by the hospital authorities concerned the prevention of exploitation of free medical treatment, referrals to Poor Law authorities, and the encouragement of persons to join provident dispensaries.

After three months Miss Stewart reported that out of 150 patients only three or four could afford a private practitioner but a large number could, she felt, contribute a small sum regularly to a provident medical association. Within ten years of the first experiment in the Royal Free Hospital, seven other hospitals in London appointed almoners selected and trained by the Medical Committee of the Charity Organization Society. In time, hospital almoners in England progressed from under the aegis of the London Charity Organization Society through several stages of development to the present autonomous Institute of Almoners. It is the only recognized agency in Great Britain for qualifying medical social workers.

IN AMERICA

In America it was a doctor, Richard Clarke Cabot,[3] who more than any other physician gave social workers an awareness of the social aspects of medicine. In 1898, when Dr. Cabot was appointed physician to outpatients at the Massachusetts General Hospital in Boston, the disparity between the treatment for dispensary patients and that for patients who could afford private consultation in doctors' offices began to grip his imagination. He felt constrained to do something about it, but what and how? At that time he was a director of the Boston Children's Aid Society, where he came in contact with social workers. Impressed by their case studies and the type of histories they wrote, he decided to put a social worker in his clinic at the Massachusetts General Hospital.

In that era there were no academically qualified social workers, but there were trained nurses who had social vision. One was Miss Garnet Isabel Pelton, who worked at the Denison House Settlement in Boston. In 1905, through Dr. Cabot's influence, Miss Pelton became the first social worker in the clinics of the Massachusetts General Hospital. Her duty was "to investigate and report to the doctor domestic and social conditions bearing on diagnosis and treatment, to see that orders were carried out and to form the link between the hospital and the many societies, institutions and persons whose aid could be enlisted."

Six months after taking office Miss Pelton resigned because of illness. Three others had followed her when, in October 1907, Miss Ida Maud Cannon became head social worker. Miss Cannon, a trained nurse, had come from Minnesota to Boston to attend the Simmons College School of Social Work (established in 1904) for the purpose of broadening her vision as a district nurse for the Associated Charities in St. Paul. In 1906 she met Dr. Cabot. He so inspired her that until she was graduated from Simmons she voluntarily gave all her free time to social service in the outpatient department of the Massachusetts General Hospital.

Previous to assuming the directorship of social service Miss Cannon visited St. Thomas's Hospital in London. Over the years she kept "a sense of comradeship" with almoners in England. At the end of thirty-nine years Miss Cannon retired (in 1945). She maintains her home in Cambridge, Massachusetts, and is widely consulted, even from Hawaii, regarding medical social work.

It is significant that in an earlier period of increasing emphasis on the scientific aspects of disease, a physician saw the importance of personal and psychological factors in illness. Dr. Cabot's ideas in this respect were not readily accepted by the medical profession. Social workers strove hard with him to prove their worth to the doctors affiliated with the outpatient department of Massachusetts General Hospital. A few physicians responded, others were too busy "running off a clinic"; some were antagonistic when approached about the aftercare of a patient; and some felt that responsibility ceased when a patient went out the door.

An exception to this attitude was Dr. James J. Putnam, chief of neurological services, who shared Dr. Cabot's conviction of the relevance of social factors to illness. During its first four years, social service at the Massachusetts General Hospital was entirely dependent upon the support, both moral and financial, of Dr. Cabot and Dr. Putnam. Miss Cannon realized this was not administratively sound, and was instrumental in establishing in 1909 the Supervisory Committee, to guide the policies of social service and to help secure its financial support.

The question of duplication arose—why couldn't social service in the hospital be administered by the Associated Charities? To clarify function is a salutary practice; in this instance it led to joint conferences of the hospital workers with those of the Associated Charities, Dr. Cabot presenting the physical, and the workers, the social aspects of a case; the result of these meetings was an acceptance of factors unique to each agency.

In that era social service was limited to outpatients, but in time doctors wanted its functions extended to ward patients. This was achieved in 1914, but administratively there was a division of functions. Service to ward patients was controlled and financed by the hospital administration, whereas the outpatient department remained under the governance of the Supervisory Committee to Social Service.

Prior to 1912 the apprentice method of learning on the job was the common means of "training" hospital social workers. In that year the Massachusetts General Hospital adopted the policy that students would thenceforth be required to take basic social work courses in a school of social work. In 1914 the Social Service Department began to collaborate with the Simmons College School of Social Work in training medical social workers.

That they might have an idea of the environments from which their patients came and to which they would return upon discharge, the Social Service Department at Massachusetts General began in 1912 to accept student nurses for periods of orientation. In 1913 Dr. David L. Edsell, professor of medicine at Harvard Medical School, arranged for medical students to discuss the social aspects of cases with a designated social worker from the hospital.

In 1919 the hospital assumed administrative and financial responsibility for social service; this functionally united the outpatient and inpatient services. Though the Supervisory Committee was divested of control, the trustees decided at the same time to continue it as an advisory committee to the Social Service Department.

Before the end of its first decade in America the concept of social service was spreading to other hospitals and other cities. It was strengthened considerably by Dr. S. S. Goldwater, superintendent of Mount Sinai Hospital in New York, who was president of the American Hospital Association in 1907–08.

IN HAWAII

Thus the seeds of medical social service planted in America (1905), ten years after they were sown in England (1895), matured into sturdy plants, spread to cities throughout the land and took root in Hawaii in 1923.

Hawaii, having remained essentially agricultural, did not at first contain the causes of widespread poverty which was an important factor in the establishment of medical social service in London and in Boston. In Honolulu it was the vision given the Hospital Flower Society—of social service in hospitals—which decided the members to spend the $2,000 laying idle in the treasury for the establishment of such a service in Honolulu. Its president, Mrs. Alonzo Gartley, was assisted in her efforts to do so by Mrs. Arthur Withington, a comparatively recent arrival. Mrs. Withington had been a social worker at the Massachusetts General Hospital and it was at her request that Dr. Richard C. Cabot wrote, in 1920, to Mr. Francis M. Hatch, president of The Queen's Hospital, as follows:

> It is fair to say that no up-to-date hospital in this country is now without social workers. In a general way, their function is to make the doctor's treatment effective, first by explaining it in simple words and in detail to the patient and then by seeing that the home conditions—financial, domestic, and others—are such that treatment can be really effective. In modern medicine drugs and surgery play only a part; the social, financial, and psychological conditions are almost as important.[4]

Prior to the establishment of the Territorial Government in 1900,[5] it was unlawful for anyone to land in Hawaii with less than fifty dollars.[6] But there were stranded seamen, and sick ones, too; there were a few tourists, some seeking health, others taken ill after arrival here; there were also the usual seaport ruffians. Geographically situated as it is, Honolulu at the turn of the century was becoming, in more senses than one, a melting pot of humanity.

SOCIAL SERVICE INTRODUCED INTO THE QUEEN'S HOSPITAL
(1923)

In 1922 the Hospital Flower Society wrote to the trustees of The Queen's Hospital,[7] offering to sponsor social service, with the understanding that if it proved successful the hospital would assume its support. Queen's accepted the society's offer[8] and I was appointed the social worker, reporting for duty on September 1, 1923. Thus Honolulu followed the pattern of London and Boston in the establishment of hospital social service by a community-based agency.

At the beginning of the 1920s, The Queen's Hospital was contemplating an enlargement, replacing the old building with a new one. This accounts in part for the delay in getting social service started there.

When I began, the new building was not completed and my office consisted of one drawer in an old typewriter desk in a corner of the temporary office of the superintendent, Mr. George C. Potter. I had no staff, so the cramped quarters were not too bad, nor was it unpleasant sitting on the ground under the trees or on a stone wall for other than bedside interviews. In April 1924, when the new Queen Emma Building was completed, social service was happily ensconced in an attractive office on the main floor.

The original idea of the Hospital Flower Society was to support social service in The Queen's Hospital as an experiment only; if this proved successful, the hospital would assume the service as its responsibility. A strong advocate of social service was Dr. Nils P. Larsen, then house physician and pathologist at Queen's. At a meeting of the visiting staff on July 15, 1924, Dr. Larsen stated: "Social service carried on for almost a year by the Hospital Flower Society has become a very necessary part of the Hospital and is very useful and helpful to doctors." At that meeting the following motion was carried unanimously: *"Resolved:* That the staff thoroughly endorse the work of the Social Service Department and consider it a necessary part of the Hospital."

On August 9, 1924, the directors of the Hospital Flower Society wrote to the board of The Queen's Hospital, asking their "intention regarding the future of social service." In the meantime, reports of the social worker's activities convinced the society that a longer period was needed to establish firmly what was still in an experimental stage. The society, therefore, wrote again to The Queen's Hospital, signifying their desire to continue a while longer.

On August 29, 1924, Mr. J. R. Galt, acting for Queen's, wrote in reply:

> From expressions of opinions from different members of the staff as well as the board of trustees, there seems little question but that the service is very valuable. In view of the present financial condition of the hospital with its constantly increasing expenses, the willingness of your organization to carry on this work for another year is most satisfactory.[9]

And so the society continued, not for one but for twenty-six years, never losing sight, however, of the ad interim nature of this arrangement.

On December 31, 1924, the Hospital Flower Society was incorporated "for the charitable purposes of giving relief to the sick and needy." In 1925 it broadened its constitution and by-laws to include "the organization and supervision of hospital social service." For a while the distributions of "fragrant cheer" were continued with more or less regularity by members of the Flower Society, but finally gave place to the more comprehensive program of social casework.

Before the Second World War, the Garden Club supplied the administrative offices with tastefully arranged flowers. The outbreak of the war and the call for volunteers elsewhere put a stop to this program, with one exception: below the paintings of Kamehameha IV and Queen Emma in the main entrance of The Queen's Hospital, the Garden Club continues to place a floral arrangement that is both distinctive and beautiful. (In 1954 this duty was assumed by the newly established Queen's Hospital Auxiliary.

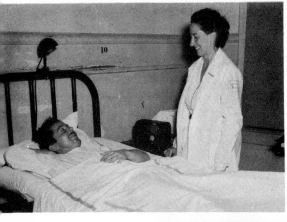

Left: A social worker in The Queen's Hospital in the early 1940's.

Below: The medical social worker.

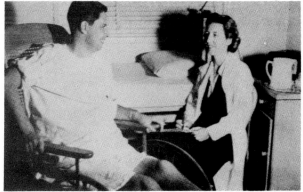

Below: The Queen's Hospital: Team work.

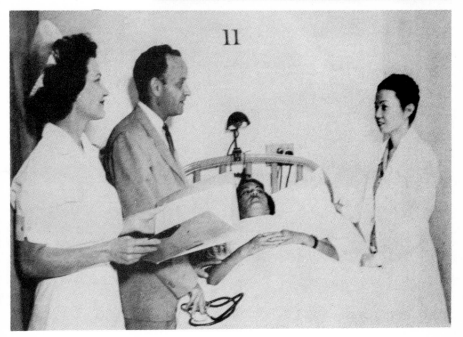

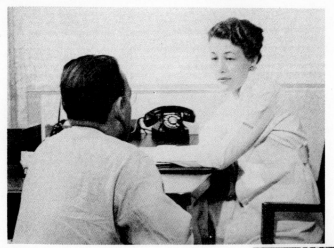

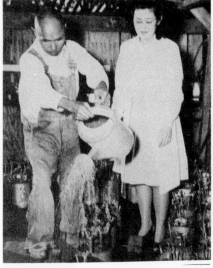

Above: The Queen's Hospital: "Tell me about it."

Right: Kuakini Home: They'll bloom by Christmas.

Below: Children's Hospital: "They are talking about me."

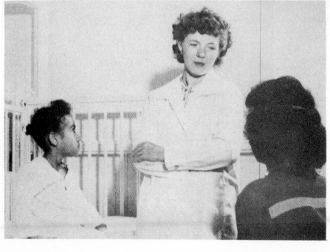

FOUNDATIONS

During 1923 and 1924 I worked alone but it soon became apparent that, despite extension of the working day and the working week, the volume remained greater than one person could adequately handle. As there was at that time no other professionally qualified social worker in Hawaii, we tried, without success, to find one on the mainland. In the fall of 1925 we employed a University of Hawaii graduate who had a real sense of service, Miss Jaunita Hess, to work as an apprentice.

In its active years, the Hospital Flower Society had included Leahi Home in its ministrations. The society now felt it should offer to establish social service there; in addition, it contemplated including Kauikeolani Children's Hospital. Expansion required additional workers, but where could we get them?

CULTURAL DETERMINANTS

At that time an understanding of the mores of our multiracial population and their readier acceptance of a worker of their own race was no less essential than training in a school of social work.

Hawaiian

It was important, for instance, to appreciate why some Hawaiians, even as late as the 1920s, had more faith in the *kahuna lapaau* (native doctor) and his treatment of the sick—with medicinal herbs, salt, and *lomi-lomi* (massage)—than in a doctor of scientific medicine; after all, the medical lore of the Hawaiians had been evolving for some thousand years before the white man introduced his type of medicine. Because so many waited until they were beyond recovery there were Hawaiians to whom admission to a hospital spelled death.

Japanese

With a large number of Japanese of the first generation in the population, naturally the majority of Japanese patients in hospitals were still living in accordance with many of the traditions of their homeland. Pidgin English, with a sprinkling of Hawaiian words, was their means of communication with non-Japanese people.

It was important, therefore, that we have on our staff a

Japanese worker, not only conversant with the Japanese language but also one who had an understanding of their customs, particularly those associated with health. One of the most important concerned marriage. In Japan marriage was not a matter of attraction between a certain man and a certain woman. It was possible that the contracting parties had not even a personal acquaintance with each other. Japanese parents arranged marriages for their children through intermediaries or "go-betweens."

The majority of Japanese immigrants who were contracted to work on plantations came to Hawaii as single men. Until the Immigration Act of 1924 prohibited further entries of aliens to the territory, it was customary for "go-betweens" to make marriage arrangements between the parents of a girl in Japan and a man in Hawaii, both usually belonging to the same prefecture in the mother country. The accompanying exchange of photographs gave rise to the term "picture bride."

The Japanese government required such a bride to be registered, before leaving Japan, as the wife of the man to whom she was destined. Hawaii required, immediately following the bride's arrival in the Islands, a marriage in accordance with the immigration law. Family histories were of great importance in arranged marriages; hence certain contagious diseases, being considered hereditary, were concealed lest they hinder opportunities for wedlock.

Today, immigration restrictions, the process of acculturation among the offspring of the first-generation Japanese, and the effects of World War II are diluting the practice of arranged marriages; the younger generation of Japanese ancestry are mating increasingly by personal choice.

Chinese

No less essential was an understanding of Chinese mores, such as the conflict in a Chinese mother's mind because the concoction advised by the temple priest (dried cockroaches, snake meat, and herbs) had failed to cure her boy's severe abdominal pain—caused, she was told, by the spirit of a disgruntled ancestor, who had one day crossed the youth's path on his way home from school. In desperation, the mother was finally persuaded to take her son to a doctor, who performed an emergency appendectomy. But human nature changes slowly. The patient, a high school student, told the social worker that he was not too sure that his China-born parents would, despite this experience, discontinue taking the advice of the temple priest.

EXPANDING SERVICES

In contemplating expansion of service to Leahi Home and the Children's Hospital, it was realized that if it was impossible to have both, racial rather than academic qualifications were the more desirable; nevertheless, it was essential to have a minimum of academically prepared staff. Toward this end I planned to visit the mainland, and in 1925 I spent a period in observation in both Leahi and the Children's Hospitals. The purpose of this was to acquire a knowledge of each hospital that would be helpful in recruiting social workers.

Leahi Home

In Leahi Home, as it was then called, I interviewed every one of the latest fifty admissions and visited most of the homes. Two outstanding needs were apparent: social service and occupational therapy.

A social worker could reduce preadmission anxieties by affording the patient or his family an opportunity to discuss problems incident to long hospitalization, act as a liaison between the patient and his family, or others, during his incapacity, and advise in planning for discharge from the hospital. As for occupational therapy, I noticed that, while a few patients of their own accord found wholesome occupation, the majority who were not bedfast sat around playing cards or indulging in idle chatter.

In accordance with two recommendations I made to the trustees of Leahi Home, they appropriated funds for a medical social worker to be supervised by the Hospital Flower Society [10] and for occupational therapy.

Kauikeolani Children's Hospital

The outstanding revelation at the Children's Hospital was the complete lack of recognition on the part of most attending physicians of the close relationship between the diseases treated in hospital and the home environments from which the children came. The doctors did not know whether mothers understood instructions about the care of their children and there was no system of follow-up. There were two instances of children who, although "discharged" for two weeks, had never been called for and were still in the hospital.

I visited the homes of the children discharged a year previously. Some homes were good, others bad; some were broken by death, divorce, or desertion of parents. Here were foci of future community problems. Obviously there was need for social service.

The trustees of the Kauikeolani Children's Hospital stated, however, that as the Hospital Flower Society's recommendation of a monthly salary of $175 for a social worker and the use of a car was in excess of what they paid their superintendent and her assistant, they feared serious dissensions if the society's recommendations were approved. They asked, therefore, that the matter of social service be held in abeyance.[11]

In January of 1926 I went to the mainland. It was a fruitful experience. I made the acquaintance of many leaders in the medical and social work professions, including Ida M. Cannon, the dean of medical social service. While in Boston, I engaged two professionally educated workers for our hospitals. Miss Miriam Buncher came in August 1926, for The Queen's Hospital, and Miss Margaret Frantz, in October 1926, for Leahi Home.

SEEKING RECOGNITION

At one time, as a means for getting recognition by the medical profession, a common expression among social workers was "selling ourselves." Some of us heartily disliked its cheap connotation, yet it did take salesmanship to win doctors and hospital personnel to the realization that sick people might have social and personal problems directly bearing on diagnosis and treatment.

In the formative years of social work most doctors considered it chiefly a service to "charity patients." This is understandable, for that was how it had begun in London and Boston. It was also an age when medical practice was strongly influenced by basic sciences and the effect these discoveries brought to bear on the medical profession.

On the other hand, medical social workers were still groping for essentials characteristic of a profession applicable to rich and poor alike. It was not until 1936 that functions appropriate to medical social casework were first spelled out in a *Statement of Standards* [12] by the American Association of Medical Social Workers. To meet these standards was the beginning, but only the beginning, of an evolving professional status for medical social workers.

Without referrals from doctors no other department in a hospital will accept patients for service, but had we waited, in the 1920s, for doctors to take the initiative in making all referrals to social service, I am sure that with the exception of the indigent, or what they called "charity patients," we would have spent our days in comparative idleness. We decided to "educate the doctors!" One means to this end was calling on newly admitted patients to certain hospital wards and reporting pertinent history to the attending physicians. This was a two-way service, for not only did it help doctors in diagnosis or treatment, but also it brought peace of mind to patients, especially strangers, when they knew there was someone to whom they could turn regarding matters of great personal concern.

Calling one evening on newly admitted patients in The Queen's Hospital, I noticed a young man, with both arms bandaged, trying to read *The Times* (London). In reply to my question, "Is there anything I can do for you?" he said, "Thanks very much. Will you write to my mother?" He told me that, as he was walking from work to his lodging late one night, an automobile had stopped alongside the curb. Three men had jumped out of the car, robbed him, and given him such a beating that he was injured internally and in both arms. He was the only son of a widowed mother, to whom he wrote weekly. He was anxious now on her account. "But even if I could use my arms," he said, "what could I tell her of my condition and how it happened?" I wrote her for him and kept in touch with the doctor. His condition improved, then worsened. The doctor advised an operation, but despite all that medical science could do, his body had been too much battered for survival. I arranged for a simple funeral service and had his ashes sent home to England.

Like many another patient, this young man had frequently

expressed his gratitude for the opportunity given him to talk to someone about his fears and doubts and hopes and to know that his family would be advised of results.

HOSPITAL SOCIAL SERVICE ASSOCIATION OF HAWAII (1927)

By 1927 general comments were being heard that the name "Hospital Flower Society" was outdated. It connoted to the current generation a fading era of indiscriminate philanthropy. We were led to believe that such a title might even act as a hindrance to sustained community support. Among the members of the Hospital Flower Society were some with strong emotional ties to a name which, after all, had stood for something since the days of royalty and had embraced royal membership. They were fearful, too, lest professional service do away with that of volunteers.

In 1927, nevertheless, by amendment of its charter, the Hospital Flower Society became the Hospital Social Service Association of Hawaii. The choice of title was consonant with that of the American Association of Hospital Social Workers, incorporated in 1918 as the national standard-setting agency in medical social work.

In 1933 the Hospital Social Service Association amended its constitution and by-laws to adopt the following purposes:

a) To organize and develop social service in the hospitals of the Territory, according to the standards of the American Association of Hospital Social Workers.

b) To act in an advisory capacity to the social service departments of hospitals as long as seems necessary or desirable.

c) To encourage the spirit of benevolence and to promote sympathy amongst the people of Honolulu with the sick in the hospitals.

The first two purposes give a professional aspect to the emerging functions of hospital social service. As for the third purpose, with its flavor of lavender and old lace, it was maintained out of deference to those members of the parent Hospital Flower Society who were fearful of a change in title. And yet with its deeper insight it might well remain as a fundamental purpose of all social work.

MEDICAL SOCIAL SERVICE ASSOCIATION OF HAWAII (1944)

Once more the charter was amended. In 1944 the word "medical" was substituted for "hospital" and it became the Medical Social Service Association of Hawaii. Again this was in accord with the national association which, in 1934, had substituted "medical" for "hospital" as more in keeping with the spread of medical social work to outpatients as well as inpatients and to other fields, notably public health.

The purposes of the association in the last amendment in 1944 are as follows:

a) To organize and develop medical social service in Hawaii according to the standards of the American Association of Medical Social Workers.

b) To give assistance and relief to the sick and needy.

c) To act in an advisory capacity to the social service departments of hospitals, and other institutions, as long as such is desired or advisable.

d) To encourage a spirit of benevolence and charity and to promote, among the people, sympathy with the sick and needy.[13]

SUPPORT

During the first several years of medical social service in Hawaii, the Hospital Flower Society assumed full responsibility for its support, except in Leahi Home. This was done through the pencil sales already mentioned and by special contributions, including that of the Stranger's Friend Society. Leahi Home, being territorially supported, was averse to any of its departments being financed by a voluntary organization and therefore included social service in its over-all budget to the government.

In 1926 the Hospital Flower Society applied to the United Welfare Fund (since known as the Honolulu Community Chest) for inclusion in the Fund's 1927 budget. The application was rejected. Theoretically, the Fund's reasoning was sound; practically, it was not.

The Funds' administrators contended that, if medical social service was as important as its proponents believe, a hospital should assume its support as it does that of other necessary functions. The society reasoned that, though certain services, e.g., nursing, were strictly intramural, medical social casework was both extra- and intramural; not infrequently it began before a patient's admission to the hospital and continued after his discharge or until the medical social problem was resolved. The Queen's Hospital felt it could not at that time afford more than a token contribution of $750 to the 1927 budget.

The rejection of the Hospital Flower Society by the United

Welfare Fund whetted the determination of its members to make their 1926 pencil sale a greater success than ever. The press was more than willing to further a cause with a sharp tang to it. (And incidentally, this publicity and the fact that we had been rejected by the United Welfare furthered a wider community understanding of the purpose of medical social work.) But the 1926 rejection by the Fund was no deterrent to a reapplication in 1927. Modernizing the name of our agency was a help.

At that time we had a men's advisory committee, representative not only of hospital boards and physicians but of the United Welfare Fund as well. Just as in history a common idea regarding similar subjects frequently occurs in the minds of widely scattered persons, in Honolulu the Men's Advisory Committee formulated an opinion similar to one formerly expressed in Boston in like circumstances. Their idea was that it would be more economical for medical social service to function from an already established agency—locally, the Social Service Bureau.[14] Again, as in Boston, by defining the respective functions of family casework and medical social work, enough unique factors were found to bring about an agreement that medical social service is an integrant of a medical institution.[15]

The trustees of The Queen's Hospital are traditionally opposed to public appeals, save for building funds; they were therefore hesitant that an appeal be made toward the support of their social service. For this reason the Men's Advisory Committee advised the inclusion of other hospitals in the Hospital Social Service Association; this would, they thought, strengthen the organization and, at the same time, reduce the sensitivity of Queen's on this point.

To this end the Hospital Social Service Association in 1927 addressed letters to the Kauikeolani Children's, St. Francis, and the Japanese hospitals, offering to organize, supervise, and support social service in their respective institutions during an experimental period.[16] All three accepted the association's offer.

PROVISIONAL MEMBER, UNITED WELFARE FUND

Reinforced now with five constituent member hospitals— Queen's, Leahi,[17] Children's, Japanese, and St. Francis—the

HSSA applied to the United Welfare Fund for inclusion in its 1928 budget. This time the application was accepted, but with two provisos: First, support was to be limited to the three years 1928 through 1930. It was thought that, by that time, the experiment would have so proved itself that each hospital would assume responsibility for its own social service. Second, the association was to make no public appeals either during or following the three-year period.[18]

As 1930 and our deadline with the United Welfare Fund approached, the HSSA asked the intention of its member hospitals regarding the future of social service. They all expressed the desire that it should continue but, with the exception of Queen's, none went so far as to assume any part of its support.

In the minds of the directors of the association, there was no doubt of the value of social service to these other hospitals, but three years had apparently proved too short a time to convince their administrators. The directors of the association, therefore, asked the United Welfare Fund for an extension of support. The request was refused, with a reminder of the condition that the HSSA would make no public appeal for funds either during or after the stipulated three-year period.[19]

Never were truer words uttered than "the female of the species is more deadly than the male"—if she is sufficiently aroused. The women of the HSSA were thoroughly aroused. Seeking legal counsel they were advised that, by the terms of their agreement with the United Welfare Fund, they could make no public appeal either through the press or by reactivating their pencil sales; but there was nothing illegal or unethical in making private appeals through personal letters.

And this they proceeded to do. Since The Queen's Hospital had by now assumed most of the cost of its social service and Leahi had withdrawn in 1928, the HSSA needed but $4,220 to cover its program in the other member hospitals for 1931.

The United Welfare Fund was on the eve of its drive and became alarmed lest two simultaneous campaigns, even though one was "private," would result in unfavorable community reaction. The chairman of the association's finance committee, Mrs. Paul S. Winslow, used good strategy to persuade the association not only to desist from its campaign, already started, but also to help the Fund in achieving its goal. For this gesture of good will, the United Welfare Fund gave the

HSSA $500, with the warning, however, that it was not an earnest of future allotments! [20]

The response to private appeals already under way more than met the 1931 budget. By 1933 the Japanese and Children's hospitals had begun to contribute toward the support of social service. For seven years the HSSA raised its own budget. Helping the association to do so there were, in addition to many personal contributions, those of various foundations and trusts. The S. N. and Mary Castle Foundation, the Juliette M. Atherton Trust, Charles M. Cooke, Ltd., the George N. Wilcox Trust, and the McInerny Foundation all contributed over the years, and some continuously, toward the furtherance of medical and psychiatric social service in Honolulu.

Permanent Member, United Welfare Fund

But the exclusion of the HSSA from the United Welfare Fund was neither co-ordinated nor constructive community welfare planning. Finally convinced of this fact by the association's president, Mrs. J. Platt Cooke, the United Welfare Fund accepted the HSSA as a permanent member in 1937.

The Honolulu Community Chest, as it is now known,[21] still contributes toward the support of social service in The Queen's, Kuakini, and Children's hospitals.[22] St. Francis Hospital withdrew from the HSSA in 1934.

ADMINISTRATION

In the beginning the Hospital Flower Society appointed an advisory committee "to assist the social worker"; later this group was known as the case committee.

It was usual in those years for social agencies to have case committees; their function was to discuss cases with the workers, offering suggestions for treatment. They were a means also for gaining community support of the particular agency. As the practice of casework became increasingly professional, laymen had less to offer as case consultants, but more to offer in other respects.

From the case committee of the Hospital Flower Society there developed a board of directors for the Hospital Social Service Association of Hawaii. The board included men, among whom were the administrators of the associated hospitals. In addition to financial support, the concern of this governing body was with standards of practice, personnel qualifications, and liaison as occasion arose between the social service department and the hospital administration.

The Hospital Social Service Association, and the Hospital Flower Society before it, consistently respected the over-all authority of the hospitals in which it functioned. This was not put into writing until 1945. Because of succeeding administrative changes in our member hospitals, it was decided in that year to put this policy in writing. The following resolution was therefore adopted by the association, by then renamed the Medical Social Service Association of Hawaii, on April 10, 1945: [23]

1. In consideration of such financial support as from time to time is agreed upon between the Medical Social Service Association and any one of its affiliated hospitals, the Association will furnish to that hospital medical social service by professionally qualified staff.

2. The Board of Directors of the Medical Social Service Association, in which all of the corporate powers of the Association are vested, requires the Director of Social Service, and the Staff furnished each hospital, to be responsible in that hospital to the medical director in all matters pertaining to the medical care of patients, and to the administrator in all matters not so designated.[24]

Copies of the resolution were sent to the administrators of the respective hospitals. Never in the twenty-five-odd years of this arrangement was there any conflict of authority.

SOCIAL SERVICE INTRODUCED INTO THE JAPANESE HOSPITAL
(1928)[25]

The seed of social service was planted in the Japanese Hospital on January 15, 1928. Established in 1900 by *isei* (born in Japan of Japanese ancestry), the atmosphere was inherently Japanese; the majority of attending physicians were not many years removed from their native homeland. Japanese was the common medium of speech and was the only language used in writing medical records. Their School of Nursing was conducted in Japanese. It was essential that a social worker be conversant not only with the Japanese language, but also with Japanese etiquette. For instance, like the nurses, the social worker must know how to bow appropriately when approaching anyone in authority, and it was most important that she have an appreciation of what health meant in regard to particular customs, notably planned marriages.

In 1928, professionally educated social workers of Japanese ancestry were not to be found in Hawaii nor anywhere else. Repeated attempts were made by correspondence to find such a person on the mainland or in Japan. If both could not be had, academic training was not as important in that period as familiarity with the mores of Japan.

The HSSA decided, therefore, to give in-service training to a nurse; she would at least have a hospital background. Island girls of Japanese ancestry were being graduated from The Queen's Hospital School of Nursing. A position in social service was offered to one. She accepted but resigned shortly afterwards. Miss Masae Ibara (Mrs. Steven S. Chinen), her successor, was also a Queen's alumna. Although she lacked academic background, Miss Ibara was at home in the Japanese language and traditions, and had the capacity to accept responsibility.

Before World War II the Japanese Hospital was governed and supported by the Japanese Benevolent Society, which also administered material relief to their nationals in need. The society therefore looked upon the social worker as an adjunct in this respect and would refer to her Japanese people applying for help from all over the island. Except for an older woman, Mrs. Tsuru Kishimoto, employed at the International Institute of the YWCA, Miss Ibara was for years the only Japanese social worker in Hawaii.

Before qualified workers of Japanese ancestry were obtainable, Miss Ibara helped workers and doctors at The Queen's, St. Francis, and Children's hospitals with non-English-speaking Japanese patients or parents. Occasionally Leahi or Shriner's Hospital would call her for the same purpose. Her sphere of service in the Japanese Hospital included also the adjacent Japanese Home of Hawaii.

In early 1940, Miss Ibara resigned from the HSSA, but by this time young women of Japanese ancestry were graduating from accredited mainland schools of social work. We were, therefore, able to raise our standards accordingly and to employ workers who held degrees in social work.

SOCIAL SERVICE INTRODUCED INTO THE KAUIKEOLANI CHILDREN'S
HOSPITAL (1928)[26]

The first social worker at Kauikeolani Children's Hospital
was Miss Constance Barnes, who had previously been employed by the YWCA on Kauai and who, in preparation for
this job, had taken three months of orientation in medical
social service at the University of Pennsylvania Hospital, Philadelphia. When Miss Barnes began on March 1, 1928, Children's and St. Francis Hospitals were small enough that one
worker could divide her time between the two institutions.
In 1930 Miss Barnes resigned in favor of Miss Dora Chung,
who had recently been graduated from Simmons College
School of Social Work, Boston. In 1932 the HSSA was asked
to release Mrs. Zane (nee Dora Chung) to help in developing
a territorial program in sight conservation. Not until 1942
did we succeed in getting another professionally educated
medical social worker for Children's Hospital. In the meantime, a pattern was being established there for using social
workers without professional education.

Hospital administrators, taking their cue from their directorate, frequently consider their chief duty to be economy, but
such an idea can be carried too far. This was true of the Children's Hospital during the years we could not provide the
hospital with professional social workers. Because those employed were not qualified, their salaries were low, a factor
agreeable to the administrator. It invariably happens that
unqualified workers are exploited as "extra arms." This was
true at Children's. So-called social workers ran errands, tended
the switchboard, upon occasion admitted patients, took discharged ones home and, in general, "did as they were told."
Several in succession were girls of Japanese ancestry and were
so useful as interpreters for Japanese parents who did not
speak English that the administrator stipulated this racial background for any social workers. Part-time workers were preferred because they could be obtained more cheaply.

Analysis of Social Service

All these problems added up to the need for a professional
analysis of social service in Kauikeolani Children's Hospital.

With the approval of the hospital's board of directors, this was made in 1938 by Mrs. Elizabeth Leong Lee, who transferred from The Queen's Hospital and worked full time for three months as the caseworker at Children's.[27] She made her study in accordance with the standards of the American Association of Medical Social Workers to determine:

1. Whether or not Kauikeolani Children's Hospital required the services of a graduate social worker instead of one with no formal training in social work.
2. Whether or not such a person should be employed on a full time or part time basis.
3. How the work could be improved.[28]

Mrs. Lee recommended that a full-time graduate social worker be employed, preferably one familiar with the cultural backgrounds of Hawaii's population, and that standards be in accordance with those of the AAMSW. She recommended inclusion of parents as well as patients in casework, weekly ward rounds with each staff doctor, the incorporation of social histories in medical records, a more extensive follow-up, and interagency referrals. Mrs. Lee stressed the need for a private office for the social worker, who had only a desk in the main office; and she particularly emphasized the need for secretarial assistance. The hospital was at that time entirely without such service; this lack became so acute, so far as social histories and records were concerned, that the board of the HSSA arranged for a meeting, in April 1939, with the trustees of the Children's Hospital. The result was not altogether satisfactory—a typist-telephonist was hired daily from 1 to 9 P.M., with allowance to the social worker of a certain number of hours per week.[29]

One result of Mrs. Lee's analysis was the approval by the Children's Hospital of a full-time worker, Irene Leong, with resulting improvement of social work. Miss Leong, however, was not then a graduate of an accredited school of social work, a requisite for permanent employment with the HSSA.

Professionally Educated Workers

In 1940 an Island girl, Jane Oleson (Mrs. W. F. Fleming), "always interested in hospitals and children," served a period at The Queen's Hospital for orientation to medical social service. This so strengthened her interest that she entered the New

York School of Social Work for postgraduate training. In November 1942 she became medical social worker at the Children's Hospital. But the association's luck was short-lived. Miss Oleson had married and, in November 1943, left to be near her soldier husband on the mainland. Until 1946 we covered the work at Children's with workers on part time from The Queen's and Kuakini hospitals.

In June 1946 Mrs. Esther Ryan, a professionally educated caseworker, joined the staff of the MSSA. Owing to a shortage of workers, Mrs. Ryan for six months divided her hours between The Queen's and Children's hospitals. In January 1947 she started serving full time at the Children's Hospital.

Mrs. Ryan had an understanding of child psychology; she knew, for instance, that for children requiring long hospitalization, great care is needed to prevent seeming neglect on the part of parents. It is natural for a mother encumbered with many cares to feel that her child is safe in the hospital and does not need her. He does. Mrs. Ryan did much with parents on this score. Where, upon occasion, a mother could not leave home, Mrs. Ryan would visit her there in order to glean home news to bring back to the child.

By 1947 Mr. John L. Moriarty had become the administrator of the Kauikeolani Children's Hospital. He recognized Mrs. Ryan's competency and despite crowded conditions in the existing building, Mr. Moriarty made it possible for her to have the privacy of a small office and secretarial service as needed. The old hospital was replaced by a new building in 1950. But Mrs. Ryan did not remain long. Knowing that the MSSA was contemplating withdrawal from its member hospitals, Mrs. Ryan, feeling her position was threatened, resigned at the end of 1948. Accredited social workers functioned in Children's until August 1949, but not again. This is not to confuse the hospital with the Rehabilitation Center of Hawaii, opened in 1953 on the same grounds and under the same administration. Here a professionally educated psychiatric social worker, Mrs. Mabel C. McConnell, is a member of its professional team. She gives supervision to a worker without professional education in the Children's Hospital. (In January 1958 Miss Helene Morgan, a professional medical social worker, was appointed to this hospital.)

Such, then, were some of the problems encountered in the

beginning of medical social work. The next chapter will describe the functions of social work in Hawaii, in accordance with the standards of the American Association of Medical Social Workers.

[1] Main sources for this material: Beck, I. F., A.M.I.A., with a foreword by Professor Alan Moncrieff, M.D., F.R.C.P. *The Almoner: A Brief Account of Medical Social Service in Great Britain.* Published by the Council of the Institute of Almoners, January 1948; copy in Honolulu County Medical Library. Cannon, Ida M. *On the Social Frontier of Medicine; Pioneering in Medical Social Work* (Cambridge: Harvard University Press, 1952). Correspondence with Helen E. Rees, Director of Social Studies, Institute of Almoners, London, 1953; Honolulu County Medical Library.

[2] Known since 1946 as the London Family Welfare Association.

[3] Dr. Cabot died on May 8, 1939, at the age of 72 years.

[4] Undated copy of letter in Hospital Flower Society File, 1890–1922, Honolulu County Medical Library.

[5] Ralph S. Kuykendall and A. Grove Day, *Hawaii: A History* (New York: Prentice-Hall, Inc., 1948), p. 297.

[6] *Laws of the Provisional Government* (1893–94), Act 66, p. 297.

[7] Copy of letter dated July 5, 1922, signed by E. M. Dawson, secretary, Hospital Flower Society; Hospital Flower Society File, 1922–27, Honolulu County Medical Library.

[8] Letter dated January 5, 1923, from Bruce Cartwright, secretary, The Queen's Hospital; Hospital Flower Society File, 1922–27, Honolulu County Medical Library.

[9] Correspondence between Mr. J. R. Galt and Mrs. Charles F. Eckart; Hospital Flower Society File, 1922–27, Honolulu County Medical Library.

[10] P. E. Spalding, secretary, Leahi Home, to Mrs. Clifford Kimball, president, Hospital Flower Society, Sept. 1, 1925; Hospital Flower Society File, 1922–27, Honolulu County Medical Library.

[11] Letter from Kauikeolani Children's Hospital, Oct. 20, 1926, signed by three trustees; Hospital Flower Society File, 1922–27, Honolulu County Medical Library.

[12] This "Statement" has been revised several times in the intervening years; the last revision was in 1949 (see chapter XV).

[13] By-Laws of the Medical Social Service Association of Hawaii, 1944, Article 1, Section 2, Name and Purpose; File: Constitution and By-Laws, Honolulu County Medical Library.

[14] In 1941 this name was changed to Child and Family Service.

[15] See chapter XVI for distinguishing aspects of medical social service.

[16] Correspondence between HSSA and Kauikeolani Children's, St. Francis, and the Japanese hospitals; Hospital Social Service Association File, 1927–37, Honolulu County Medical Library.

[17] In 1928 Leahi Hospital withdrew from the association to administer in all respects its own social service department. (Letter from P. E. Spalding, Jan. 23, 1928. Hospital Social Service Association File, 1927–37, Honolulu County Medical Library.)

[18] Geo. F. Hamilton, executive secretary, United Welfare Fund, to Mrs. F. J. Lowrey, president, HSSA, Sept. 13, 1927; Hospital Social Service Association File, 1927–37, Honolulu County Medical Library.

[19] Geo. F. Hamilton to Mrs. Fenwick, secretary, HSSA, Sept. 4, 1930; Hos-

pital Social Service Association File, 1927–37, Honolulu County Medical Library.

[20] Correspondence between Mr. J. R. Galt, president, and Mr. Geo. F. Hamilton, manager, United Welfare Fund and officers of the HSSA, October 1930 to January 1931; Hospital Social Service Association File, 1927–37, Honolulu County Medical Library.

[21] In February 1943 the United Welfare Fund became the Honolulu Community Chest.

[22] Contributions to these hospitals ceased in December 1957. (Ed. note.)

[23] *Minutes of Board Meeting, Medical Social Service Association,* April 10, 1945, p. 2; Honolulu County Medical Library.

[24] Prior to 1950 these were separate positions in The Queen's Hospital. Since then they have been combined under the title of Administrator and Medical Director. In Children's as well as in Kuakini, administration has always been the responsibility of one person.

[25] Following the entrance of the United States into World War II, on December 8, 1941, the name of this institution was changed to Kuakini Hospital. See p. 99 for brief history of this hospital.

[26] See pp. 99–101 for a brief history of the Kauikeolani Children's Hospital.

[27] At that time the bed capacity was seventy-five.

[28] Report of Survey of Medical Social Work at the Kauikeolani Children's Hospital, April 1 to July 1, 1938; Surveys, Medical Social Service, Honolulu County Medical Library.

[29] *Minutes of Board Meetings of the Medical Social Service Association,* Feb. 14, Mar. 14, April 11, 21, May 9, 1939; Honolulu County Medical Library.

XV

Standards

Professional Organizations

As an idea in human relations takes root and grows, its proponents tend to organize an association the better to clarify function and to standarize a profession. In England this was the raison d'être of the Institute of Almoners, the only recognized agency for qualifying medical social workers. In America hospital social workers, under the leadership of Ida Cannon, organized in 1918 the American Association of Hospital Social Workers for "intercommunication among hospital social workers and to maintain and improve standards of social work in hospitals and dispensaries." In 1934 this organization was renamed the American Association of Medical Social Workers.[1]

In establishing criteria for professional standards, social service in general was forced for several decades by the law of supply and demand to be flexible regarding academic education. This was evident from the large number of workers in all agencies who received in-service training on the job. As schools of social work and their graduates have increased in number, so have professional standards in education become more rigid.

Hawaii had a conditioning factor, additional to the law of supply and demand, particularly as it pertained to the sick among the older immigrants. As noted in the last chapter it was essential that medical social workers be familiar with the language and national traditions of their patients. As the older generations were passing away, however, their descendants were growing up with the same education as other American citizens. Some among them sought degrees in schools of social work.

The flexibility mentioned above is seen in the necessarily gradual development of standards by the American Association of Medical Social Workers. Although the association was
190

founded in 1918, for many years there were not enough schools of social work, nor enough professionally educated workers to meet the demand for them.

It was not until the 1949 revision of their standards that the AAMSW included as "a *minimum requirement* (italics theirs)" for "any staff member the completion of the full graduate curriculum in social work in an accredited school of social work."[2] I was a member of the AAMSW before accepting a position with the Hospital Flower Society—ancestor to the Medical Social Service Association of Hawaii. Employed staff members in succeeding years were also members of the national association.

There has never been a Hawaii chapter of the AAMSW. In the beginning there were not enough qualified caseworkers to form one.

In 1931–32, when I was on a year's leave, my substitute, Miss Willa Murray (Mrs. Robt. M. Breland), organized the Medical Social Workers' Committee of Hawaii[3] to maintain standards and promote interest in medical and psychiatric social work.[4] Membership was open to social workers from all our medical institutions, not all of whom had the academic requisites for memberships in national organizations. The original idea of this committee was to establish a Hawaii chapter of the AAMSW as soon as we had the required twenty-five members of the national association.

By 1950 we had not only the number required to form a chapter of the AAMSW, but enough members of the national association in Hawaii to attain the status of a region. The cost in effort and money, however, was more than most of these workers were willing to spend. At one time they thought of disbanding in favor of promoting a medical social service committee within the Hawaii chapter of the American Association of Social Workers. This did not materialize. In October 1951 the Medical Social Workers' Group was dissolved. While it lasted the group had some stimulating sessions, including the reviews of pertinent literature and analyses of functions.

American Association of Social Workers

Although at one time we did not have enough qualified medical social workers to form a chapter of the American Association of Medical Social Workers, there were enough workers in various fields to form a chapter of the American Association of Social Workers (incorporated in 1921). Mary Cady (general secretary of the YWCA) and I organized the Hawaii chapter of the American Association of Social Workers in 1935.

A requirement for employment by the Medical Social Service Association of Hawaii was membership in the American Association of Medical Social Workers or the American Association of Psychiatric Social Workers (founded in 1926), depending upon the worker's background and position. A worker not already a member of one or the other organization had to become so within a year of employment in order to retain her position.

At one time a worker of the MSSA was required to hold membership both in her own professional organization and in the more inclusive American Association of Social Workers,[5] the only national professional association to have a chapter in Hawaii.

The MSSA's policy that caseworkers must be members of their national organization held until 1947, when the classification of staff was revised. During the process of revision, in which both board and staff participated, recently appointed workers took the stand that enforced memberships in professional organizations savored of coercion—something to be eschewed in casework philosophy! The question was put to a vote and the majority of workers voted against the requirement. The board had the power of veto, but failed to exercise it; thus a long-established rule assuring high academic standards was abrogated. In the MSSA's 1947 revised classification of personnel, the only position requiring membership in the AAMSW and AASW was that of Director of Social Service.[6]

APPROVED FUNCTIONS

Because of the importance it set on high standards of practice, the Hospital Social Service Association of Hawaii amended its constitution in 1933 to include what had always been the policy: namely, that the activities of the HSSA should be in accordance with the standards of the American Association of Medical Social Workers.

Although there are not yet enough qualified medical social workers to make a social service department an essential in hospital accreditation, the American College of Surgeons responsible for accrediting hospitals is aware of the importance of social service and makes use of the criteria of the AAMSW when surveying hospitals that have social service departments.[7] In addition to the academic requirement previously mentioned, the following functions were adopted in 1949 by the AAMSW: [8]

1. Practice of social casework. This includes its nature, method of referral, recording, and statistics.

2. Participation in program planning and policy formulation within the medical institution.

3. Participation in the development of social and health programs in the community.

4. Participation in the educational program for professional personnel.

5. Social research.

Succeeding chapters indicate generally, though not categorically, the functions of the Medical Social Service Association of Hawaii as related to those approved by the American Association of Medical Social Workers.

---

[1] Since October 1955, the Medical Social Work Section in the newly organized National Association of Social Workers.

[2] *A Statement of Standards to be met by Social Service Departments in Hospitals, Clinics, and Sanatoria*, 3rd rev. (Washington, D.C., 1949), p. 7; Honolulu County Medical Library.

[3] Later known as the Medical Social Workers' Group.

[4] *Seventy-third Annual Report of The Queen's Hospital*, "Report of the Social Service Department," 1932, p. 44.

[5] The National Association of Social Workers was established October 1, 1955. This is a single new organization which includes the other national associations mentioned above.

[6] *Medical Social Service Association of Hawaii*, "Classification of Professional Staff," Oct. 14, 1947; Honolulu County Medical Library.

[7] Information received in a letter, dated August 17, 1951, from Paul R. Hawley, M.D., director of the American College of Surgeons. In December 1951 the Joint Commission of Accreditation of Hospitals was established. It is composed of the American College of Physicians, the American College of Surgeons, American Hospital Association, American Medical Association, and the Canadian Medical Association. The purpose of the commission is the promotion and maintenance of standards in medical and hospital service.

[8] *A Statement of Standards*, p. 3.

XVI

Practice of Social Casework

REFERRALS, RECORDING, STATISTICS

The first approved function of the American Association of Medical Social Workers mentioned in the preceding chapter is the practice of social casework.

Innumerable definitions of social casework have been formulated, but one which has wide acceptance is that of Father Swinthun Bowers: [1]

> Social casework is an art in which knowledge of the science of human relations and skill in relationship are used to mobilize capacities in the individual and resources in the community appropriate for better adjustment between the client and all or any part of his total environment.[2]

On the premise that generic concepts are common to all fields of casework, the dissimilarities occur in the areas of specialization. Whereas in a family agency, such as the Child and Family Service or the Department of Public Welfare, the functions are of a varied nature, that of medical social service is "limited to personal or social problems related to illness, physical handicap, and medical care."

In a family or general agency the principals are the caseworker and the client. In a medical organization there is another, and very important principal—the doctor. In the former, the casework relationship may be limited to two persons, the client and the worker; in the latter, the doctor is included with patient and worker. A further distinction is that a nonmedical organization is usually a self-contained unit, whereas a hospital is a configuration of numerous departments, of which social service is but one.

Unlike the other departments, social service functions extra- as well as intramurally. As with medical treatment, case-
194

work may begin before a patient is admitted to hospital, and continues after discharge, or as long as there is a medicosocial problem. Once we had to press this point when a president of The Queen's Hospital thought casework should not begin until after a patient was admitted to hospital and should cease upon discharge.

In the interest of a particular patient, the caseworker may need to collaborate with any one or more of the other departments within the medical institution. Her education for social work has given her a general understanding of illness, with emphasis on its psychosocial implications—the thinking and feeling and acting of those who need her help.

The relationship between client and worker and the skill with which this is controlled are important in all fields of social casework. In the medical field the relationship between doctor and patient takes precedence. The doctor's relationship is one of authority; he examines, diagnoses, and orders treatment; and the patient is willing, though he may have little conception of all these procedures, to do as his physician deems best. By contrast, the social worker's relationship has no authoritative basis other than the competence born of professional education and experience, and of participation in a medical team.

The aim of the medical social worker is to foster in the patient a sense of freedom, as well as independence in expressing himself, his wishes and foibles, his anxieties and fears. Some of these may be due to his misunderstanding of what the doctor has told him and his need for elucidation. The patient is not so much interested in diagnosis as in its implications. This is particularly true of illnesses or of states that provoke anxiety and require adjustments to a different way of life, such as tuberculosis, heart conditions, cancer, mutilations, amputations, or loss of sight. In this connection it is not only the patient who is affected, but also those nearest and dearest to him, who, in turn, react upon him, and with whom the caseworker should also establish rapport.

To foster independence is not to lose sight of occasions when the caseworker may have to assume an authoritative role to aid the doctor in carrying through treatment of an urgent nature, but, generally speaking, the patient is helped to make use of resources within himself, in his family or in his community, so that decisions and the right to accept or reject are in the last analysis his.

Competency in casework increases in direct ratio to the integration of the medical and social factors in illness, but teamwork between doctor and social worker [3] precedes integration, and this in turn is largely conditioned by whether the hospital is a closed or open institution as described in chapter X.

Referrals

A referral to social service may come in behalf of any patient, private or otherwise, and from any source within or outside the hospital. There is, however, an abiding rule that when an attending physician is not the referrer the social worker must apprise him of the source of the referral with the reason for it, and have his approval before proceeding with casework.

Although there is no disapproval of casework for patients whose accounts are paid by either the territorial or the county government, doctors in general are hesitant to accept it for their private patients.

A member of a local medical firm once remarked that there was no question in his mind that a professional social worker was better equipped than he to treat the social or emotional problems of some of his patients. "Why doesn't your firm employ a social worker?" he was asked. "Because the patient would resent anyone's coming between him and his doctor," was the reply. "If indicated, would you hesitate to refer a patient to another doctor in your firm—a pathologist, a dermatologist, or a surgeon?" "No," he answered, "but that's different." Perhaps the difference lies in this matter of relationship— the relationship of social worker to patient is, in competitive medicine, still a threat to some physicians.

The "Small Things" in Medical Social Work

The medical social worker has a responsibility not only for the diagnoses of psychosocial problems and collaborating with the doctor in plans of treatment, but also for such simple, direct services as helping a patient to meet the cost of treatment, obtaining a housekeeper to take care of children whose mother would otherwise refuse to be hospitalized, conferring with employers, writing letters, arranging for transportation, and providing for convalescent or domiciliary care. The value of this type of service lies in the optimum it helps to create for medical treatment.

An elderly widow was admitted one morning to The Queen's Hospital with pneumonia. By afternoon she had become so agitated about her unfed hens that it was essential for a social worker to go to her home in Kaimuki, feed the chickens, and arrange with a neighbor to carry on.

Although many of these activities can be done by competent volunteers, the professional worker remains completely responsible.

Recording and Statistics

A factor which conditions recording is the general attitude of doctors toward social histories. Many doctors think, with some justification, that social histories are verbose and will not take time to read them. Medical terminology makes it possible for doctors to record their histories succinctly on 4 x 5-inch cards. Without a comparable social casework terminology, description is the rule, and social histories tend to be voluminous by comparison.

In August of 1942, Ferris F. Laune, Ph.D., executive secretary of the Honolulu Council of Social Agencies, analyzed at our request the recording by the social workers in The Queen's Hospital. He made a random choice of cases listed on the workers' day sheets. His report was not complimentary, but it had a stimulating effect on the staff. As one worker remarked, "His analysis is like a shot in the arm." [4]

One result of Dr. Laune's analysis was the monthly critique of closed histories. Each worker put her comments in writing; these were discussed at staff conferences, summarized, and added to the case histories. The respective comments were such as, "Had the worker done this or that, the result might have been different." "Why did the worker do this or that?" "The record is informative and concisely expressed." "The record is neither concise nor informative." Letters and written referrals to other agencies were also scrutinized for content and mode of expression.

In the late 1930's the workers discussed first interviews with a view to establishing criteria—"a yardstick" they called it— for guidance in first interviews. This became useful in critiques of social histories. Critiques led to the next logical step, the classification of case histories. The shot in the arm was producing results.

For statistical purposes, we had been classifying records under two headings: "Casework" (subdivided into "long" and "short") and "Miscellaneous." It was a modified form of a system recommended in the late 1930's by the Children's Bureau and endorsed by the AAMSW. This form had been so involved that we were glad when, after a trial period, the proponents dropped it.

As we criticized histories, we found that our simplified classification had gone to extreme oversimplification. It was easy to designate as "miscellaneous" the simple direct services, such as feeding the chickens, but to classify histories as "casework" without designating depth of practice is meaningless, except for statistical counts. Nor do the qualifications "long" or "short" mean anything; one worker may take several pages to record a history for which another would use fewer pages and say more.

Provided their patient load is not unduly heavy, some workers can practice with comparative ease on intensive levels of casework, whereas others function better on superficial levels and can therefore carry a large caseload—both types of mind are needed to meet both types of social problem, one less deep-seated than the other. Unless qualitatively analyzed, however, numerical comparison of workers' caseloads may give a distorted impression.

Out of discussions on recording there evolved three categories—major, minor, and incidental, depending upon the depth of analytical study and the degree of treatment. We came to agree that:

Major casework is based on:

A. An intensive study with diagnostic thinking of a social or emotional problem that is pertinent to the illness for which a patient is under medical or psychiatric treatment. This has the aspects of a social diagnosis.

B. An evaluation of the findings on which to plan treatment. This is in the nature of a social prognosis.

C. Treatment in collaboration with the physician. Other interested individuals or agencies may co-operate.

Minor casework is based on:

A. Study and treatment on less intensive levels than major casework, either because the medical social problem is not so deep-seated or because only one aspect is studied and treated. It presupposes a degree of diagnostic thinking for identification of the social problem and such treatment as may be concluded within our own department or in co-operation with another agency.

B. Dealing with obvious and superficial evidences of maladjustment. This may involve only a few contacts or extend over long periods of time—similarly recording may be brief or extended. Whereas major casework presupposes both study and treatment and collaboration with attending physicians, minor casework, on the other hand, may be limited to study, e.g., the review of social and psychological factors influencing the physical and mental health of the patient, to the point of determining whether or not the case should remain with our agency or be referred to another; for example, the case of an unmarried mother, if referred to another agency would probably be minor in ours, and become major in the other. On the other hand, if it remains with us it may continue minor or develop into a major service. Another example is a social examination to determine whether or not home conditions are adequate for the convalescence of a given patient suffering with a particular illness—a child with pneumonia, an adult with a heart condition.

Note: A minor casework service may become major, but a major one can never become minor.

Incidental Service is based on:

Brief contacts to take care of a specific request; for example, cashing a check, informing an employer of an employee's illness, interpreting the functions of an agency to one who has come to us because he does not know where else to go; for instance, a person looking for a child to adopt. It is possible for an incidental service to develop into minor, or even major, casework.

As we progressed in our analysis we found recording was becoming more definitive. We could not, for example, classify a service major unless it fitted our definition of major casework. This in turn encouraged the staff to seek consultation with attending physicians. Recording was also taking on aspects of social diagnosis—and therefore was becoming more meaningful to doctors reading social histories.

This study on recording took place during World War II. At a meeting of the Social Workers' Committee of Hawaii the staff of the MSSA presented an analytical comparison of their new classification of major, minor, and incidental as contrasted with the old one of casework and incidental services.

Several mainland medical social workers attached to the American Red Cross were our guests at that meeting and took part in a lively discussion on what makes a case "major" and what "minor." The explicitness of the new method so impressed them that they declared it worthy of publication by the American Association of Medical Social Workers. Unfortunately it was not submitted for publication. Had this been done it might have contributed to further research in establishing social casework as an important discipline in the practice of medicine. It was another war casualty.

During the war medical social workers were, in common with all hospital personnel, frozen to their jobs. The war was no sooner over than resignations became the order of the day. Within a short time a completely new staff had taken over, bringing old habits to their new positions, and classification reverted to the former meaningless grouping of casework and incidental services.

TEAMWORK

But irrespective of good recording, medical social work in Hawaii, as elsewhere, has had to prove its value, step by step, to the much older medical profession. A means toward this end is teamwork between doctors and social workers, more difficult of achievement in open than in closed hospitals.

The Queen's Hospital

At The Queen's Hospital attempts were made to encourage teamwork by ward rounds, but these proved almost futile so far as the visiting staff [5] was concerned; some doctors came early, some came late, and occasionally, some came not at all. At one time succinct notes were written in the medical records of patients known to us, with the statement that detailed histories were available in the Social Service Department, but few doctors took advantage of this knowledge. At times we would take the initiative and ask an attending physician to read a social history.

One such case was that of a man suffering with acute recurrent dermatitis. His wife had been admitted to hospital numerous times for an obscure abdominal condition, which ended in a spleenectomy; two young sons increased family problems and debts were accumulating. The dermatologist did not request a social history. The social worker, to whom the patient had come for advice regarding his wife, related this history to the doctor and asked, "Do you think this man's social and emotional problems are an inciting cause of his dermatitis?" Though the answer was in the affirmative, medical treatment continued without consultation or collaboration with the social worker.

The Japanese Hospital

It was comparatively easy to bring about an acceptance of social service among the doctors in the Japanese Hospital. In 1939 they were leading in referrals. Although the majority were for financial arrangements, the worker took this opportunity to discuss with physicians other relevant social or emotional problems that came to light in determining who might be responsible for medical costs. The Japanese doctors, too, welcomed the social worker's knowledge and help in the use of available community resources.[6]

Kauikeolani Children's Hospital

Teamwork is also comparatively easy in a children's hospital. The Kauikeolani Children's Hospital, when supplied with a worker through the MSSA, was then small enough to make for a sense of team action between the medical staff and social service. Rounds with doctors became the rule; during these rounds there were instances when the caseworker, having made a visit to a child's home, was able to supply history pertinent to diagnosis and to give an appraisal of the suitability of the home, and the parents' understanding of the doctor's instructions for convalescence. The rounds also furnished the worker an opportunity to get medical information helpful to her in conferring with parents.

In 1947 a rheumatic fever convalescent ward was opened at the Children's Hospital. Mrs. Ryan, the social worker, had contact with every patient and participated in the weekly rounds of the professional team. As a result of this integration, arrangements were made for psychological or psychiatric consultations on children manifesting subnormal mental development or emotional disturbance.[7]

TOOLS IN CASEWORK

Social Service Funds

The Reverend George Johnston Ross, professor in the Union Theological Seminary, New York, was a visitor in the Islands in 1923 and was asked to speak at a meeting of the Hospital Flower Society. He advised the setting up of "a mercy fund" to help patients in need—with "no questions asked." This was an implicit principle, Dr. Ross said, in conserving the patient-worker relationship.

We did establish such a fund, known as the Social Service Funds. It was considered a tool in casework, with the emphasis on treatment rather than on its monetary value per se. Carrying this idea of a tool a bit further, an analogy may be drawn between the purpose of the Social Service Funds and the practice of medicine. A reputable doctor prescribes and treats in accordance with diagnosis, rather than with a patient's ability to pay; he does not perform a minor operation if a major one is indicated, nor curtail drugs that are necessary to recovery. As in medicine, so in casework—some patients recover with small expenditure; others do not, despite all that is done or spent in their behalf.

The sources of the Social Service Funds were many—some were expressions of gratitude, some came as memorials, others in response to a religious conviction. Once a man brought us $100, saying, "You won't remember me, but years ago, when I was a small boy, you helped my mother. We can show our gratitude now by helping someone else."

Another example was a young seaman, critically injured on shipboard. The attitude of the steamship company toward their responsibility so infuriated him that the doctor feared a mental complication. The caseworker was legally advised to get the young man to San Francisco, the home port of the steamer. He had no money, and speed was a factor in preventing a psychosis. His expenses were paid through the Social Service Funds. An attorney in San Francisco, to whom he was given a letter of introduction, managed a settlement out of court. In gratitude the sailor cabled Social Service three times the amount advanced him.

Sometimes smaller amounts would come over periods of

time. Thus there was one man who, for years, brought one dollar every month to social service at The Queen's Hospital, in recognition, he said, of blessings that had come to him and to his family.

It has become quite a custom, instead of sending flowers to funerals, to make contributions in memory of the deceased to some organization. This tradition was originated in Hawaii by the MSSA through published articles, talks to groups, and suggestions to those intimate with bereaved families. For years the Stranger's Friend Society (Chapter II) contributed $25 a month to the Social Service Funds.

Another source of income was through our alms boxes. The deep emotions of joy and sorrow often find expression in giving to those in need, but many would-be donors do not know how or to whom to give. The MSSA, with the approval of the administrator, placed neat alms boxes in the elevators of The Queen's Hospital, in which persons passing in and out could drop offerings. A similar box was placed in the entrance to the Kuakini Hospital. This was a source of income which we liked to think was helpful to those who gave as well as to those who received. The alms boxes at The Queen's Hospital are gone now; a new administrator removed them because "they made the elevators look untidy!"

The Social Service Funds call to mind the Old Testament story of the widow's barrel of meal and cruse of oil. The funds never failed, even when comparatively large sums of money were needed. This was true of a patient who had lost her physical stamina and, with it, her psychological grip. Casework here devolved on rehabilitation,[8] which would require about $1,000. One day I conferred with a businessman upon an entirely different matter. As I rose to leave his office, he said he was a tither and asked my assistance in helping him to spend an accumulation of tithes. I told him of this patient; he liked the idea of assisting someone to gain independence, and contributed a considerable sum towards the cost. The time came when she, in turn, contributed to the Social Service Funds; she also became a life member of the Medical Social Service Association.

But the picture did not invariably show a return in kind. Some to whom we made loans—when a loan, rather than a gift, was an element in casework—defaulted in their payments. The social worker, like the doctor, must sometimes take chances on recovery.

Special Nurses Fund

One day a young woman critically ill with pneumonia was admitted to The Queen's Hospital from a steamer en route from Australia to Canada. When the attending physician was asked if special nurses would help, he replied, "She's on the way out, I don't think it will make any difference"—but it did. The nurses who were engaged had a deep sense of dedication and said, "If nursing can save her life, we'll pull her through." They did. In a few weeks the girl was able to resume her journey. In the meantime, social service wrote to her family in Australia and received grateful letters in reply.

When this story was told to Miss H. Ethelwyn Castle, a member of the Medical Social Service Association, she established a Special Nurses Fund through monthly contributions to the Social Service Fund, and bequeathed $5,000 in trust to the Medical Social Service Association in memory of her mother, Mrs. Claire Eloise Williams (nee Coleman). It was Miss Castle's idea that others who wished so to memorialize relatives might make additions to the Special Nurses Fund. For some years another member of the MSSA gave an annual contribution of $300 to the Special Nurses Fund in memory of her mother. Once, when it was suggested that the interest from this fund might be more appropriately dispensed through the Nursing Office, Miss Castle very definitely expressed the wish that it should be the responsibility of no department other than social service and should be used solely in behalf of patients known to, or referred to social service. A special nurse was never engaged, however, without reference to the nursing office.

Lest the impression be given that we did not refer patients to agencies established to dispense relief, we did make such referrals—many of them—particularly those already registered in community agencies or in need of economic help over long periods. We did not refer when speed was a critical factor or when we knew that policies of certain agencies precluded the amount of aid which the doctor and the medical caseworker considered important. We also had to remember the importance of the caseworker-patient relationship and the possible effect of its severance by an inopportune transfer to strangers at a critical point in medical social treatment. A physician does not transfer a patient to another doctor without sufficient reason. Here, also, the reason had to be sufficient.[9]

[1] Director of School of Social Welfare, St. Patrick's College, University of Ottawa.

[2] *Social Work Year Book,* 1951, American Association of Social Workers, p. 461.

[3] Although only the physician is mentioned here, there are occasions when a team includes nurses or members of other related professions.

[4] Ferris F. Laune, *Survey of the Hospital Social Service Association,* August 22, 1942; Surveys, Medical Social Service, Honolulu County Medical Library.

[5] An honorary staff of practicing physicians, selected by the hospital, who act as supervisors or instructors of residents and interns (see note 7, chapter XVII).

[6] *Annual Report of Medical Social Service Association on Social Service,* "Japanese Hospital," 1932; Honolulu County Medical Library.

[7] *Report of Medical Social Service Association on Medical Social Service,* "Kauikeolani Children's Hospital," Jan. 1, 1947 to Jan. 1, 1948; Honolulu County Medical Library.

[8] Prior to the establishment of the Territorial Vocational Rehabilitation Service.

[9] The details of the Social Service Fund are given at greater length and filed in a folder—Special or Social Service Funds; Honolulu County Medical Library.

XVII

Participation in the Educational
Program for Professional Personnel

In promulgating standards of practice, the American Association of Medical Social Workers had as one frame of reference hospitals affiliated with medical colleges. Since Hawaii has no medical college, there are no medical students for "participation in an educational program."

The Medical Social Service Association of Hawaii did have, however, an educational program appropriate for students in social work, professionally educated workers, and student nurses. Education does not cease with the acquisition of a degree, so there were also programs planned primarily for physicians.

STUDENTS IN SOCIAL WORK

When social service was becoming established in Honolulu's hospitals during the 1920s, I was the only academically qualified worker in Hawaii; in-service or apprentice training was therefore the only resort for the time being. It was only for the time being.

The Medical Social Service Association of Hawaii, when still called the Hospital Flower Society, took the initiative in stimulating among Island girls an interest in social service as a profession.[1] Toward this end the society arranged a program of lectures, in which other agencies participated, on "Social Work as a Profession," to be given to senior students at Punahou and McKinley High Schools and to students at the University of Hawaii. High school students generally proved too immature for the subject matter; not so those of the university, where such lectures, in one form or another, continued for years.

206

One of the first college students to consider social work as a profession was Dora Chung (Mrs. Arthur Zane) who, upon her graduation from the University of Hawaii, entered Simmons College School of Social Work in Boston. She returned to Honolulu in 1929, the second Island-born woman, and the first of Chinese ancestry, to graduate from an accredited school of social work. A second worker of Chinese parentage was Elizabeth Leong (Mrs. Peter Lee). Elizabeth Leong had heard a lecture on "Social Service as a Profession" during her senior year at high school. While a senior at the University of Hawaii, she worked as a volunteer in the Social Service Department at The Queen's Hospital. In 1933 Elizabeth took her master's degree at the School of Social Service Administration, University of Chicago, and returned to The Queen's Hospital as a professional worker.

In 1939 Mrs. Lee was appointed medical social worker in the Bureau of Crippled Children, Department of Health. In accordance with a federal law, states wishing to participate in federal grants-in-aid had to abide by the ruling of the Children's Bureau that medical social service be included in this program. A purpose of the Hospital Social Service Association was to develop medical social service in Hawaii in accordance with the standards of the American Association of Medical Social Workers. The HSSA was glad, therefore, when this opportunity came to Mrs. Lee.

Two girls of Japanese ancestry, Edna Kanemoto (Mrs. Samuel Sakimoto) and Tsuneo Kinoshita (Mrs. Suyeki Okumura) were likewise so stimulated by lectures they had heard on social service as a profession that, following a period of in-service training with the HSSA, both went to the mainland in the late 1930s to become academically qualified as caseworkers. Upon their return to Honolulu, both became valuable members of the professional staff of the HSSA.

This does not mean that the Hospital Social Service Association of Hawaii, nor its successor, the Medical Social Service Association of Hawaii, did not employ mainland women. In 1926, two graduate social workers were engaged one each for The Queen's Hospital and Leahi Home.

A staff is generally stronger if the personnel is not limited to the immediate geographical area; but in Hawaii the effect may be detrimental if too much dependence is put upon mainland recruitment.[2] The question was sometimes put to a *malihini* (stranger) worker, "How long did it take you to become oriented in Hawaii, and to feel comfortable in your work?"

The answers gave periods of one to two years and over. Adjustment requires not only physical, but also psychological transplanting to the Islands. It takes time, too, to gain a working knowledge of the functions of allied community agencies. With little intent to take root, the majority of mainland workers leave just as they are becoming most valuable to a local agency.

This frequent turnover is both costly and disrupting. There are, for example, instances when policies or procedures adopted after months of careful thought and deliberation among the professional staff have been summarily dropped by succeeding workers with little or no consideration of what brought these policies about, and offering no equally meaningful alternatives. An example of this was the work put into recording and statistics as explained in the previous chapter. Nevertheless, at one time social agencies in the community had no alternative but to recruit qualified workers from the mainland.

School of Social Work, University of Hawaii

By the late 1930s, however, a school of social work was taking shape at the University of Hawaii. In 1948 it was accredited by the American Association of Schools of Social Work as a one-year school awarding a Certificate in Social Work. By January 1950 it had an accredited two-year curriculum leading to the degree of Master of Social Work.[3]

Until then it was impossible to include both the generic and special subject matter required in medical social service. When this was achieved the Social Service Department at The Queen's Hospital lacked sufficient staff to give supervised field work. By 1952 it was able to do so, and for several years had from the University of Hawaii School of Social Work a student for field work placement.[4]

Social Service at Leahi Hospital had the same problem regarding supervision and has not been able to accept student placements.

In 1953 the Territorial Hospital began to accept students

from the University of Hawaii's School of Social Work. At first they were supervised by the school (at best an unsatisfactory arrangement) and then by the Hospital's Social Service Department. Owing to shortage of staff this program was suspended in the fall of 1953.

Interest in medical social service as a profession needs a great deal more stimulation. Were more students made aware of its opportunities, turnover and the orientation of mainlanders to our medical institutions would cease to be such an acute problem. This depends, however, on the inclusion of a medical social work sequence in our School of Social Work and approved standards of social service in hospitals co-operating in field work placement.

PROFESSIONALLY EDUCATED WORKERS

"Reading maketh a full man; conference a ready man; and writing an exact man." We did them all.

Through the purchase of relevant books and related journals the MSSA encouraged its staff to keep abreast of current thought in medical social service. The book reviews, for which respective staff members took responsibility, were an added incentive.

The social workers from Queen's, Kuakini, and Children's hospitals came together for weekly conferences. Occasionally physicians and workers from other agencies were invited to meet with us. Programs included a wide range of subjects—interviewing, case histories, recording, classification, personnel policies, reviews of pertinent literature, and writing for publication.

As construed by the staff, writing included case histories, reports, and letters and papers for publication. Discussions in this regard concerned content, succinct expression and clarity, such as to be understood by the lay mind, respected by the professional mind and worthy of publication in a reputable, scientific, or social casework journal.

Beginning in the middle 1940s and continuing for some two years, the MSSA published a monthly bulletin which had wide circulation among professional (including doctors) and nonprofessional groups. The turnover in staff at the close of World War II caused the demise of the bulletin.[5]

Institute in Casework

In August of 1953, Miss Eleanor E. Cockerill, professor of social casework at the School of Social Work, University of Pittsburgh, came to Honolulu to conduct an institute in casework. This was the culmination of well-laid plans started under the guidance of Mrs. Evelyn R. Walker, Director of Social Service at The Queen's Hospital. The institute was not limited to medical social workers.

STUDENT NURSES

Nurses in their day-by-day contact with sick persons should know where to get help for patients who are obviously upset emotionally. It is to give nurses an awareness of where this help may be had that courses in the social aspects of medicine were given to student nurses at The Queen's Hospital.

The students were taught that although certain nursing techniques like bedmaking, bathing, and pulse and temperature taking are standardized, patients themselves cannot be standardized. Each is different from any other; these differences stem from physical and mental heritage, cultural origins, and social environment, and not all people react alike to the same stimuli.

One year, one assignment toward the end of the semester was to bring to class written questions regarding social problems the students had observed in the wards, or about which patients had talked to them. The following are some of their questions:

A cardiac patient who is better but does not want to be discharged evidences increased symptoms whenever the doctor or supervisor comes round; what should be done with him?

A widower with an inoperable cancer has five children to support; how can he manage?

A woman, ten years a widow, with children ranging from 16 to 24 years, is pregnant. Because of the connoted disgrace, keen hostility has arisen between the children and their mother, also toward the father of the unborn child. What can be done to prevent a family smash-up?

A twenty-six year old man has come from the mainland to work in the Navy Yard. He is engaged to be married. He has had five operations for a brain tumor and the prognosis is bad. He feels that to tell his fiancee of his condition would make her want to marry him out of pity and he would rather die than that. What can one do to help him?

A patient who is totally blind from a gonorrheal infection has spent all his savings in paying for medical care; are there no territorial agencies to care for such cases?

A maternity case is disowned by her family because she has married outside her race. What can be done about it?

In Japan it is legal for a man—when there is no son to perpetuate the name—to adopt his wife's family name. In Hawaii illegitimate children are registered under their mother's name. A Japanese man here wishes to adopt his wife's family name. Would he have to go through legal procedure to legitimatize his children?

An unmarried mother wants to keep her baby but cannot afford to. Are there any social agencies to aid her?

After every visit by the husband of a certain patient, her temperature rises or she cries—what can be done about it?

Why must patients pay their hospital bills a week in advance?

Why does the community have to support two organizations, the Child and Family Service and the Department of Public Welfare?

A patient emotionally upset because of a marital conflict confides in the student. She advises consultation with social service, but he refuses and she is frustrated. (*a*) Should she tell her supervisor? (*b*) If the latter is indifferent, then what?

A student is quite sure that a certain patient needs social service. She has spoken to her supervisor but the latter is indifferent. What should the student do? [6]

Please explain how a patient can be highly intelligent, yet emotionally disturbed about his illness.

Such questions as these emphasize the close relationship which nurses have with sick persons under their care. If aware of the functions of social service, they are, as members of the medical team, in a strategic position to further collaboration with the social service department. When the department included a psychiatric social worker, a course in mental hygiene was also given to student nurses.

Somewhat later than at Queen's, courses in the social aspects of medicine, and in mental hygiene, were given to student nurses at the Kuakini Hospital.

Kauikeolani Children's Hospital had no school of nursing as such; student nurses from St. Francis, Kuakini, and The Queen's hospitals affiliate there for pediatric nursing.

At the time Mrs. Ryan was the social worker in Children's, she gave one lecture to each new group on the social aspects of pediatrics. This was not enough, but ever since the MSSA withdrew from its member hospitals, the students have not received even this much. During her tenure, Mrs. Ryan commented on the marked difference in comprehension of social and emotional factors in illness between the girls from Kaukini and Queen's, where there was social service, and those from St. Francis Hospital, in which there was no in-patient social service department.

THE MEDICAL PROFESSION

"Educating doctors" to a recognition of social casework as a diagnostic and treatment resource is a slow, uphill process. The general lack of collaboration by doctors with social workers derives mainly from: the newness of professional social work, its threat to doctors where medicine is competitively oriented, and the threat of a weakened patient-doctor relationship by the addition of another personality.

Previous chapters describe various programs initiated by the MSSA to bring about greater co-ordination between the medical and social casework disciplines. In one such program the workers invited particular consultants to staff conferences to discuss certain diseases with us: What is the cause of this patient's dermatitis? What emotional factors may be related to this one's gastric ulcer? To another's severe asthma? What is the reason for this patient's wish for repeated surgery? How can we prevent this one's regression into dependency? The medical social workers know that answers to many of these problems may not be found in a test tube or by X-rays, but rather in strains and stresses on the forces of heredity and environment.

But until the medical profession is convinced of its necessity as a diagnostic and therapeutic agent, social casework will continue as a stepchild of medicine, its practitioners tolerated but not generally accepted. Psychiatrists and internists who have more than a passing interest in psychosomatic medicine are exceptions to this attitude prevalent among the medical profession.

Joint Conferences with House Staff

It was comparatively easy to establish closer professional relationships with the house staff—the interns and residents.[7]

The workers could join them on ward rounds, and they were available when questions arose. At one time they were required by the medical director of the hospital to attend, in rotation, a monthly staff conference with the social workers to discuss cases of mutual interest. They were expected to read, before coming to a meeting, the social histories of those patients.

By 1941 these conferences took the form of quarterly luncheon meetings [8] with the interns and residents, one of them acting as chairman. Once when asked who among them had attended medical colleges in which the curricula included the social and emotional aspects of illness, only two out of nine answered in the affirmative. This was perhaps why the contributions of these two young doctors to joint meetings with the social workers were more meaningful than those of their colleagues who had not had similar courses in their undergraduate years. There is an increasing trend in medical colleges for the inclusion of social and emotional aspects in illness and recovery, taught by medical social workers with faculty status.

Cases were not the only subjects discussed with the house staff. Sometimes the social workers would question a policy; for instance, the habit doctors have of prenatally advising an unwed mother to have her baby adopted without seeing it. The house physicians were inclined to agree with this practice; the social workers countered that before delivery an unwed mother is in no condition emotionally to make decisions that may cause future regret or remorse.

One particular case aroused considerable feeling. This patient was a fourteen-year-old girl who had been admitted to hospital several times. Attending physicians were unable to determine diagnosis. The worker knew the girl was a twin who had exhibited personality problems at home and at school, but the doctors had not asked for a social history. "Would it have been helpful in determining diagnosis?" the worker asked. In chorus the young doctors answered, "Yes!" and then launched into the difficulties of getting practicing physicians to accept psychiatry. "Lots of them want the security of knowing everything." It was certainly refreshing to hear their comments!

At another conference with the house staff, an intern of Chinese parentage told a Caucasian social worker that a Chinese mother's attitude regarding surgery for her son was due to cultural patterns and to the fact that the caseworker had entered the situation unprepared. It called to mind another worker's experience when trying to explain to a Chinese woman, in pidgin English, why her husband's doctor had advised amputation of a leg. The patient had Buerger's disease, and gangrene had set in. As the worker was trying to make the wife understand the significance of the diagnosis, a young Chinese intern warned the worker to "lay off." He explained that the woman's resistance was due to a Chinese belief that the dead must be buried intact, and the loss of a limb would violate an ancestral tradition. The woman, in dire conflict, said she wanted to consult her children, born and reared in Hawaii; she returned with permission to amputate. The patient died in surgery. Death, however, was not the widow's chief concern; it was the reclamation of the severed leg—that it might be buried with the body. This woman might have suffered an emotional trauma had she been unable to fulfill this cultural obligation.

There is no doubt of the educational value of these joint conferences between members of relevant disciplines contributing to the care of patients in hospitals. Over the years, arrangements for such discussions changed. In time the lunch conferences with the house staff gave place to the practice of discussing social case histories with interns, residents, and younger physicians. Attached to the histories, put at the disposal of the doctors, are questionnaires regarding the content of the histories, as to their diagnostic and treatment values. This is one of several means by which the social service department sought to further collaboration between the medical and social casework disciplines.

Once while at Queen's, I was disturbed about an incident involving a doctor of the Visiting Staff, and it was serious enough that I sought the counsel of Dr. Harry L. Arnold, chief of Medical Service. I still remember his parting words: "Never forget that education and training alone do not make a doctor." Nor do they make a social worker.

[1] *Hospital Social Service Association: Annual Meeting, 1926,* "Report of Director of Social Service"; Honolulu County Medical Library.

[2] According to a survey made in 1940, 51.42 per cent of the professional personnel in casework agencies in Honolulu had been in their agencies less than two years; 83 per cent, less than four years. *The Honolulu Plan. Survey Supplement.* Special Study of Personnel Problems. July 1940. Developed by

Community Chests and Councils Inc., under the auspices of the Honolulu Council of Social Agencies and United Welfare Fund.

3 *A Graduate Program for Professional Study*, 1953–54, University of Hawaii School of Social Work, Honolulu, p. 7.

4 By the end of the 1954–55 academic year The Queen's Hospital was without adequate qualified social workers. This necessitated a suspension of the training program, hardly begun.

5 Bulletin of the Medical Social Service Association, Honolulu County Medical Library.

6 Students were told by the class instructor that they must have the approval of their nursing supervisor in making referrals to social service.

7 An intern is "a medical graduate serving and residing in a hospital preparatory to his being licensed to practice medicine." A resident has obtained his license but is still resident in the hospital. (Dorland, *The American Illustrated Medical Dictionary.*) The house staff is supervised and instructed by an honorary staff of practicing physicians selected by the hospital directorate.

8 *Minutes of Medical Social Service Association Staff Conference*, March 18, 1941; Honolulu County Medical Library.

XVIII

Participation in Program Planning and Policy Formulation Within the Medical Institution

Financial Arrangements

For many years doctors and hospital administrators have held the belief that the chief function of social service is to make "financial investigations" (social workers would say, "financial arrangements" or "means reviews"). Social workers resent this opinion of their profession; making financial arrangements, per se, is a clerical operation not requiring a degree in social work.

A means review conducted by a social worker, however, can be an effective method of integrating the medical and social aspects of illness. It can, for instance, reveal deep-seated personal problems which would not be expressed to a clerk and of which the attending physician might be unaware.

A case in point was that of a woman admitted to hospital with a badly bruised body and fractured arm, the result, her doctor said, of a fall. Mentioning cost as the reason for her reluctance to hospitalization, she was referred by her physician to social service for financial arrangements. The caseworker told the doctor in her subsequent report that there was no question as to ample financial resources, nor had his patient had a fall. Her injured condition was the result of a more than usually severe beating by her husband, but her concern had been to shield the family from notoriety. Referral to social service for financial arrangements opened the door for her to give expression to long-pent-up troubles. With the worker's help and her doctor's advice, she came to realize the necessity for a mental examination of her husband. The diagnosis was paranoia, and he was committed to the Territorial Hospital.

"Financial arrangements" have very different connotations in closed and open hospitals. Overhead in a closed government institution is not likely to present the acute financial problem that it often does in an open nonprofit one. No one who is ill is refused admission to Hawaii's open hospitals, but their administrators must be concerned with delays or defaults in payment. The well-being of human beings is so closely associated with money, or the lack of it, that it is quite natural for hospital administrators to look to social service for means reviews and suitable recommendations.

Ideally, all hospital admissions—with the exception of the relatively few emergencies—should be arranged for in advance, and in co-operation with the social service department. With few exceptions, the questions on a hospital admission sheet are of a social nature, some having important bearing upon the illness for which a patient is being admitted, but, though often suggested, the policy of advance planning for hospitalization is not observed.

Making financial arrangements was a function of social service in the three member hospitals of the Medical Social Service Association, as described below.

THE QUEEN'S HOSPITAL

The number of patients indicating difficulty in meeting the cost of hospitalization, referred to the Social Service Department at Queen's for financial arrangements, had by 1937 grown to a load necessitating a full-time caseworker. Though functioning from the Social Service Department, she kept in close contact with the Business Office. In recent years this function was spread among all the caseworkers in accordance with the allocation of patients—medical, surgical, obstetrical, psychiatric, etc. In former years this was a frequently debated question, but experience proved that the making of financial arrangements has enough unique factors to put it in a category of its own; and not all medical social workers have the particular skills which it requires. Specialization also brings thorough familiarization with the problem and knowledge of the resources within the hospital, such as endowed beds, and of those in the community, particularly governmental resources. The worker doing only financial arrangements can help to modify existing policies where indicated or bring new programs into existence. The Hawaii Medical Service Association is an example of the last.

Endowed beds were an important resource to social service. Not infrequently social workers come in contact with patients who are unable to pay the price of prolonged or costly illnesses but whose resources are in excess of the limitations set by governmental agencies for free care. For many such patients endowed beds have been the answer.

In The Queen's Hospital, and dating back to the days of the monarchy, beds have been endowed over the years by individuals or national societies. By 1953 they totaled seventeen. The beds are all in wards, not any particular ward, nor any particular bed. Prior to 1951 patients occupying endowed beds could be attended by their personal physicians.

Until social service was introduced into The Queen's Hospital (1923), nominations for endowed beds were channeled chiefly through the hospital's administrator; an exception was the four beds of the Strangers' Friend Society, which reserved the right of nomination. These beds were used more often than any of the others; in fact it was not uncommon for the other beds to remain unassigned for months, or even years, the reason being not that they were not needed as that this was a resource little known in the community. With the advent of social service there came to be, at times, a waiting list for endowed beds. Before 1951 a patient occupying an endowed bed could have all the necessary services with which Queen's is provided. Depending upon circumstances, arrangements were sometimes made with a beneficiary to meet part of the cost of hospitalization. If for medical reasons a private room was indicated and there were no other resources, Social Service would pay the difference out of its Social Service Funds.

But "times change and we are changed in them"—the expense of administering a hospital has increased in ratio to the development of scientific medicine, and the costs of living generally, so that the interest from the original endowments does not meet prolonged hospitalization. This fact led to a decision by The Queen's Hospital in 1951 to reduce occupancy of endowed beds to within the limits of total income from the endowments. In 1951 there were 15 endowed beds; each bed was, therefore, allotted one-fifteenth of the total endowments. If a patient remained in hospital for a longer time than the one-fifteenth would cover, some other means had to be found to meet the extra cost. Patients are still referred to social service for means reviews, but final approval for an endowed bed no longer rests with social service but with the hospital's administrator—a regressive policy, for it slows up, sometimes by many hours, the reduction of a patient's anxiety.

Another quite as unfortunate decision is that, though a patient may still retain his personal physician, the latter may no longer charge for his services; otherwise the patient must accept staff service. Psychologically speaking, this is an unwholesome policy. Where doctors are paid in accordance with a fee-for-service, there is a common supposition that those who can pay the fees receive more attention than those who cannot. Even if no more than a token payment is made to their doctor, this is enough to give some patients a sense of security. Here again, if the suggestion was made by social service, it was not uncommon for a doctor to reduce or even cancel his charge.[1]

KUAKINI (FORMERLY JAPANESE) HOSPITAL

It was important that the caseworker in this hospital understand the tradition and implementation of the *tanomoshi*, a custom practiced among the early Japanese immigrants when in need of money. Originating in Japan and predating contact with the West, the *tanomoshi* in the beginning had a religious motivation, usually to supply money needed for pilgrimages to sacred shrines. It gradually developed into societies or clubs for mutual aid. This was true in Hawaii.

In accordance with the rules of *tanomoshi*, a man who needed $100, for example, would gather nine friends to form an association. Each member, including himself, would pay into it $10 a month for ten months (the amount put in was actually $1,000). The promoter always drew the first month's receipts, or $100. In each succeeding month the other members would bid for the $100. If the highest bid in the second month was $2 the bidder would have to pay each member (other than the promoter) $2 thus reducing his net return by $16, or to $84. After each member has drawn, he does not receive interest from the successful bidder during the remaining months, though he continues to make monthly payments of $10. The last member to draw, at the tenth month, thus receives

$100 plus the interest paid by the other members during the course of the tanomoshi.

Membership in a *tanomoshi* demanded that the monthly payment be considered almost a sacred obligation. A caseworker making financial arrangements for the medical care of a Japanese patient had to appreciate how vital it was to him to avoid default in his *tanomoshi* payments.[2]

The *tanomoshi* has faded, along with many other traditions of the first-generation Japanese in Hawaii. In the early decades of the Japanese Hospital, those in need of financial assistance might get it through a *tanomoshi*, the Japanese Benevolent Society, or from friends coming from the same prefecture in Japan.

Indigent Japanese could also apply to the city and county for free medical care, but prior to 1933 all city and county patients had to be hospitalized in The Queen's Hospital. The social worker in the Japanese Hospital at that time was Miss Masae Ibara (Mrs. Steven Chinen), an alumna of The Queen's Hospital School of Nursing. During the years she was at Queen's, Miss Ibara had come in contact with Japanese patients hospitalized there on city and county service.

She knew them to be unhappy there. They could not express themselves in English, they missed Japanese food, and they were not allowed to be attended by relatives in accordance with Japanese custom. It was chiefly due to Miss Ibara's initiative that Dr. Robert B. Faus, City and County Physician in 1935, induced the Board of Supervisors to include the Japanese Hospital in an appropriation for the care of the sick.[3]

There has been no social worker at the Kuakini Hospital since 1953,[4] so that investigations for eligibility for City and County service are made at the City and County Health Unit, located at the Punchbowl Street entrance to The Queen's Hospital. On July 1, 1958 it became a unit of the Maluhia Hospital.

KAUIKEOLANI CHILDREN'S HOSPITAL

In bygone years beds had been endowed by individuals in the Kauikeolani Children's Hospital for the benefit of "poor children," but by the time social service was introduced there (1928) the city and county was paying for the hospitalization of indigent minors. It may be assumed that income from endowments was used for overhead costs. The social worker conducted means reviews and referred indigent parents to the city and county financial investigator.

The Queen's Hospital

In 1923, when social service was introduced into The Queen's Hospital, Dr. Nils P. Larsen, as medical director, was responsible for training the house staff—the interns and residents.

This meant provision for check-ups on free bed patients such as is provided in outpatient departments, but prior to 1947 no general hospital in Honolulu had an outpatient service. Persons in need of outpatient care could obtain it, subject to financial investigation, at Palama Settlement, where a comprehensive dispensary service had been building up since 1915. So long as a patient was not hospitalized—and disregarding distance—attendance at Palama was a simple matter; but if upon examination there, hospitalization was indicated, procedure became complicated. It entailed further examinations by different doctors in unrelated institutions, together with the possibility of disagreements over diagnoses and treatments.

Upon discharge from hospital, the indigent in need of follow-up care had to return to Palama Settlement to get it, but he was also asked to come back to Queen's in order that the house staff might check their work. Sometimes they were told one thing by the hospital doctors, and another by those at Palama. Sometimes they would get back to Palama before the arrival of the mailed reports from a hospital; and sometimes, despite reports and telephone messages, patients did not return either to hospital or to Palama. Then arose the question of whose responsibility it was to get them back, particularly cases of educational value to interns and residents. As one social worker said, "It's a hopeless mess, and will remain so as long as we have such a disjointed service." Medical care was inefficient so far as outpatient service was concerned.

Conscious of the hiatus between in- and outpatient services, separated both geographically and administratively, Dr. Larsen requested the help of social service in organizing a Surgical Follow-up Clinic; so that, at the least, results of surgery could be appraised. The clinic was held one Sunday a month, in the Social Service Department, one worker being assigned to this duty. Her function was chiefly that of "rounder upper," to get patients to return for check-ups. In those years doctors were concentrating chiefly on the scientific aspects of illness but, as a worker remarked, "If we are alert, we can push in the relevant social and emotional problems of particular patients." It was not, however, integrated teamwork.

Two other clinics were organized at The Queen's Hospital in 1940 and 1941—a diabetic and a prenatal clinic, respectively —in both of which a social worker was a member of the consultant team.

The prenatal clinic was one of several maternal health conferences in various sections of the city, established and participated in by the Bureau of Maternal and Child Health, Department of Health.

The diabetic clinic was entirely a Queen's project. Its purposes were to help private physicians with advice regarding the care of diabetics, to help in reducing diabetic hospital admissions, and to provide means for the care of indigent diabetics. Dr. Morten E. Berk, senior resident at the time, was medical consultant. The integration of the medical, social, and dietary disciplines was excellent. Virginia Ott Herbst, social worker, and Lilian Elsholtz Page, dietitian, and Mrs. Alexander Fritschi, a volunteer, collaborated with Dr. Berk in an analysis of two hundred and thirty-two diabetic patients. Their study was published in the Hawaii Medical Journal.[5]

In July 1947, the dispensary at Palama Settlement closed with the opening of outpatient departments in The Queen's and St. Francis hospitals.

At Queen's the medical team in the outpatient department does not include a social caseworker but nevertheless collaboration was good between the out- and inpatient service. All unmarried mothers were automatically referred to an inpatient caseworker. Other patients (including children) who indicate social problems were also referred to a qualified caseworker. There was, besides, a screening by social service in the orthopedic clinic for the purpose of evaluating a patient's ability to profit by rehabilitation. There is no longer a social worker in the diabetic clinic.

Kauikeolani Children's Hospital

At the time The Queen's Hospital organized its follow-up clinics there was no pediatric service at Queen's therefore Queen's interns and residents rotated for this experience at the Children's Hospital. So that here, too, they might see the results of their treatment, a monthly Sunday follow-up clinic was organized at Children's in 1929. But it was not easy to persuade parents to bring their children back for a check up. If they needed further medical care as outpatients, they would have to be taken to Palama Settlement—so why bring them to the hospital "just for the doctor to look see. Waste time."

Following the analysis of social service in the Children's Hospital, when a full-time social worker was employed, a special effort was made to present relevant social histories to doctors. This proved so successful that it became necessary to hold two follow-up clinics a month at the Kauikeolani Children's Hospital. Follow-up clinics came to an end at The Queen's and Children's hospitals with the depletion of house staffs caused by World War II. The Children's Hospital established an outpatient service in 1949. Its professional team, however, does not include a professionally educated social worker.

Kuakini (formerly Japanese) Hospital

The earliest participation by social service in program planning and policy formulation in the Japanese Hospital was in 1929, when social worker Masae Ibara helped to organize a chest clinic. This followed the survey of public health in that year by Ira V. Hiscock, in which tuberculosis was found to be the leading cause of death in Honolulu.[6]

This clinic was initiated by the Japanese Medical Society and placed under the auspices of the Department of Health. As noted earlier, contagious disease was of particular significance in the family histories of Japanese, especially in its relevancy to matrimony.

Miss Ibara was a member of the Chest Clinic team. In simple Japanese language she talked to the patients about tuberculosis, of the favorable prognosis if treated in time, of the importance of care at the Leahi Home, and the examination of contacts. With these precautions there was little need, she explained, to fear tuberculosis in family histories.

Miss Ibara took the initiative in getting direct transfers of tuberculous patients from the Japanese Hospital to Leahi Home. Hitherto transfers from this hospital had to be routed through the Tuberculosis Bureau of the Department of Health by non-Japanese-speaking persons; at The Queen's Hospital the medical staff was privileged to transfer patients direct to Leahi. Now, with the same privilege extended to the medical staff at the Japanese Hospital, and social histories furnished by Miss Ibara, the process of transfer was greatly simplified.

There is no outpatient service as such in the Kuakini Hospital. In accordance with an arrangement between the hospital and the City and County Health Department, indigent Japanese who so desire may receive outpatient service at the Kuakini Hospital.

Joint Advisory Committee

In chapter XIV was noted the founding and guidance of medical social service in The Queen's Hospital by an extramural organization. Throughout its years of affiliation with the Hospital Social Service Association, the professional staff had a sense of support whenever crucial questions arose regarding their functions. A weakness, however, was the fact that the association's executive committee did not include representatives of the trustees of its respective member hospitals; consequently, when questions arose regarding the functions of the social workers, trustees could get unsubstantiated, or even prejudicial, reports from a hospital administrator, or medical director, who alone spoke for all the departments of the hospital. The following experience is an example.

In October 1939 I was advised by the administrator of The Queen's Hospital to submit a request directly to Mr. Charles R. Hemenway, the president, for a much needed refurbishment of the social service department. In his reply, Mr. Hemenway said he was appointing an evaluating committee "to make a complete study and review of the hospital social service work done by the Association." [7]

In response to Mr. Hemenway's letter, I wrote to say that we should welcome such a study, and offered to co-operate in every way. The appointed committee consisted of five men—

three doctors and two laymen. They did not consult with any member of the social service staff. They met twice and wrote a lengthy report.

The report was completely subjective. The social workers were accused of not giving doctors the credit they deserved for "commonsense social service thinking" and for knowing as much or more than social workers about the social problems of families they treated. The committee felt that workers trained in large centers of the eastern states did not understand local social problems as well as the doctors. Among the workers was "a militant group," they said, who "were strongly pink tinged," if not "deeply red" in their efforts to socialize medicine; they were also preoccupied with emotional problems and psychiatry; doctors with years of experience regarding emotional stresses of worry and fear in the development of symptoms were more competent, they felt, than social workers. In comparing disciplines, they said, the "nurse *asks*, the social worker *tells*." The most damning statement in the report was, "occasionally the social worker finding that the treatment ordered by one doctor was not up to their standards, would call another doctor not related to the case to try to get confirmation of the goodness or poorness of the therapy used."

As to "corrections" enumerated by the evaluating committee, they included arrangements for indigent "visitors from the Mainland or other Islands who do not rate City and County service"; tracing insurance contacts for widows, placement of children, and writing letters; contacting cancer and surgical patients for follow-up clinics; arrangements for special therapy —transfusions, surgery, psychiatry, X-rays, physiotherapy; eliminating complete family studies and only occasionally, at the doctor's request, going into the psyciatric history of a patient; eliminating voluminous reports; attaching records to charts except those of a confidential nature; giving the doctor a copy of these or telling him about them.

It was an abiding policy of the HSSA that workers were entitled to read reports which concerned them. The staff read this one, and wanted to face the evaluating committee with a rebuttal; but on further thought they agreed that, after all, we are a profession still very much in the making and this experience, constructively used, could be a blessing. It was obvious that doctors were generally ignorant regarding the qualifications of academically educated caseworkers for collaborating with physicians in medical practice. The workers thought the most constructive way to handle this experience would be through a joint advisory committee composed of the respective chiefs of medical, surgical, and city and county staffs; the administrator, the medical director and director of nursing, respectively, of The Queen's Hospital, the president of the HSSA, and the director of Social Service. To ensure its success, Mr. Hemenway, as president of The Queen's Hospital, agreed to appoint the members to the Joint Advisory Committee.

The Joint Advisory Committee held monthly meetings, including lunch, in the Interns' Cottage. The workers from the Social Service Department attended these meetings in rotation, each presenting, for general discussion, her particular function in casework, its pertinency to medical practice, and its related problems. Of the latter, selectivity was one. The worker on psychiatric service said that some doctors are resentful if they feel that a referral is rejected, but her caseload was so overweighted with alcoholics and others with seemingly poor social prognoses that she lacked time for the more promising cases. This worker commented later that the Joint Advisory Committee had given her a sense of support in working toward greater selectivity in caseload.

The worker on financial arrangements reported that, despite a ruling of Queen's to the contrary,[8] doctors were having admitted on private service patients unable to pay for hospitalization. From an analysis of her caseload, this worker said that eighty per cent of referrals came to her after, rather than before, admission. In some cases, patients were transferred to city and county service after surgery had already been performed by a "private" physician; thus the patient's anxiety was doubled by worry about his hospital bill and the fear induced by sudden transfer to a strange doctor. In stressing the value of having referrals precede admission rather than follow it, the worker on financial arrangements confirmed that additional problems often come to light in the process of a financial interview conducted by a social worker, which might otherwise have remained unsolved.

At these meetings, questions of policy were also discussed. At one, social service was twitted with "never being around when doctors make late afternoon calls." The response to this was a staggering of workers' hours so that there would be one on duty five days from four to six o'clock, and on Saturdays from noon to six o'clock. This plan proved the need for the establishment of such a policy but, following the outbreak of World War II and the consequent dearth of doctors, the plan, together with the Joint Advisory Committee, came to a sudden end in 1942.

The Joint Advisory Committee lasted a little longer than two years. Through it doctors and administrators gained some understanding of the functions of a social service department; it gave the social workers a feeling of support; and—most important of all—destructive criticisms might be brought to this committee and constructively handled. The committee's approval also strengthened the advancement of new programs or projects in hospital or community as indicated through the practice of social casework.

VOLUNTEERS

Volunteers have been associated with hospitals ever since hospitals came into being. It is as true of Hawaii as elsewhere that, long before there was any such thing as professional social service, countless unsung individuals had been giving of themselves in ministering to the sick. They add a plus to the functions of doctors, nurses, social workers, and others, in the form of the extra, but nevertheless important, things they do to round out medical care. There are occasions where, but for a volunteer, certain duties might remain undone for lack of employed staff.

Volunteers in the affiliated hospitals of the MSSA were under the general supervision of social service in the respective institutions. The group was co-ordinated by a chairman who was or became by virtue of this position, a member of the MSSA's board of directors.

The success of voluntary service depends upon good supervision and upon certain basic characteristics in the volunteer. She must really wish to serve in this capacity. Very little is accomplished, for example, by a woman who volunteers merely to fulfill a requirement of some organization of which she is, or desires to become, a member. A provisional member of one such organization, which required a certain number of hours in voluntary service, was once allotted the duty of circulating books in the Queen's Hospital. She wanted to know what to do with the book wagon if, while on the wards, her time was up before her rounds were finished!

Some persons want to pick and choose and are uninterested if a service is hard or dull; two young women resigned rather than take lonely folk for drives. On the other hand, when social service was once faced with the job of dismantling the home of a deceased patient, it was a volunteer who did the job—a long, hard, and dirty one—of sorting the accumulation of years.

When Dr. Malcolm T. MacEachern, associate director of the American College of Surgeons, was surveying Honolulu hospitals in 1936, he advised Social Service to organize hostesses for The Queen's Hospital. He did not define their function, so, when prospective volunteers asked to have the duties of a "hostess" explained, the reply was "we haven't the faintest idea, but let's keep a log and find out." These volunteers served in rotation at a desk inside the main entrance to Queen's and were required, before going off duty, to record the questions asked by visitors to the hospital, and what they had done while they were at the desk.

Some months later, at a meeting of the volunteers, the hostess log was reviewed. It related incidents both serious and amusing. One day a woman asked permission of the hostess to leave a sack by the desk while she called on a patient. Presently the hostess saw the sack move slightly, then higher and faster and faster, hopping right into the corridor. Upon recapturing and opening the bag, she found it contained a live rooster!

From analysis of the hostesses' activities, it was evident that their function was chiefly informational—to direct visitors to offices, rooms, or wards, and to tell some that the patients they had come to see were on the "No visitors" list. The hostess service became an information desk, which has continued ever since under the direction of Mrs. Arch W. Brown.

Returning to the early development of the volunteer program in The Queen's Hospital, the day came when the responsibility for recruiting, training, and supervising volunteers required the time of a special supervisor. In 1941 the association engaged for this purpose Mrs. Myrtle Schattenburg. Although

America did not actually participate in World War II until December of that year, preparations were being made against its possibility, and Mrs. Schattenburg, a registered nurse, was needed elsewhere.

Mrs. Schattenburg was succeeded by Mrs. Bertha Phelps as supervisor of volunteers. At the declaration of war The Queen's Hospital was fairly inundated with offers of voluntary service. Many of them were made by wives of men in the armed services who, in order to escape enforced evacuation to the mainland, had to prove they were necessary to the war effort. The Queen's Hospital, short of personnel, needed volunteers, but careful screening was necessary. At the suggestion of the HSSA the directorate of Queen's set up an integral department of volunteers with Mrs. Phelps, the supervisor, on the payroll. After the war voluntary service in all our hospitals was at a low ebb and Mrs. Phelps had left the territory.

Except for the information desk, voluntary service at The Queen's Hospital has until recently been negligible and spasmodic. In May 1953 The Queen's Hospital Auxiliary came into being. In the Children's Hospital the P.E.O., a philanthropic organization,[9] has for several years been taking responsibility for voluntary service. In the Kuakini Hospital and the Kuakini Home volunteer work is done by the Kuakini Hospital Women's Service Group.

OCCUPATIONAL THERAPY

The HSSA was responsible for launching occupational therapy in its member hospitals. In 1929 it engaged Mrs. Mabel Wood to teach patients at The Queen's Hospital how to weave *lauhala* (pandanus leaf) into attractive and useful articles. She also went to the Japanese Home of Hawaii for the same purpose. The work at Queen's was supervised by Mrs. Herbert M. Dowsett, a director of the HSSA, and at the Japanese Hospital by Mrs. Stanley Fukuda, a member of the Japanese Junior Service League.

In time we became aware that we should have to bring diversification into occupational therapy; not all patients were interested in *lauhala* weaving. In 1931, with continued and additional contributions, the HSSA employed Mrs. Irwin Spalding, an expert in handcrafts. She served under a special committee of the HSSA, of which Mrs. Dowsett was chairman.

By the end of 1931 the directors of Queen's established an occupational therapy department as an integral service of the hospital.[10]
Realizing the need for a qualified and registered occupational therapist, Mrs. Dowsett in 1933 passed the examination of the American Occupational Therapy Association and thus became Hawaii's first registered occupational therapist. She organized an accredited department at The Queen's Hospital, and was its full-time director from 1933 to 1946, at a salary of one dollar a year. Her department became a training center for volunteers in occupational therapy. With the exception of Leahi Hospital, which already had a department of its own, Mrs. Dowsett established occupational therapy in accordance with the standards of the American Occupational Therapy Association in most of the hospitals on Oahu.

Reading is more acceptable as an occupation to some patients than work with their hands. Through the generosity of Miss H. Ethelwyn A. Castle and several other members of the MSSA, books (fiction and nonfiction) and magazines, fresh from a bookstore, formed the nucleus of a very good library. Several times a week they were circulated about The Queen's Hospital by volunteers. As occupational therapy became established, Social Service transferred the patients' library to that department.

In this chapter the emphasis has been on participation by the Medical Social Service Association of Hawaii and its antecedents in "program planning and policy formulation within the medical institution." Medical social workers also have the responsibility for participation in community planning for services related to illness or the conservation of health. The staff of the MSSA participated in relevant community programs, sometimes in the role of leadership. The next chapter tells what the association and its workers did in this regard.

[1] Data regarding endowed beds were obtained from my experience as former director of social service; from the present director, Mrs. E. R. Walker; from the office manager, C. O. Drake; and from the administrator, Dr. Sumner Price, all of The Queen's Hospital.
[2] Ruth N. Masuda, *The Japanese "Tanomoshi,"* Social Process in Hawaii, vol. 3, 1937, pp. 16–19 published by the Sociology Club in collaboration with the Department of Sociology, University of Hawaii.
[3] "Kuakini Hospital, formerly Japanese Hospital," *Annual Report of Social Service to Hospital Social Service Association,* Jan. 25, 1936, p. 1; Honolulu County Medical Library.

4 Mr. Henry T. Tsuyemura, M.A., was employed July 1956. Resigned August 1957.

5 "An Analysis of The Queen's Hospital Diabetic Clinic," *Hawaii Medical Journal*, VI (Sept.–Oct., 1946), pp. 22–25, (Nov.–Dec., 1946), pp. 95–97.

6 Ira V. Hiscock, *Health and Welfare in Honolulu, Hawaii, A Survey*, United Welfare Fund (Honolulu, 1929), p. 67; the Honolulu County Medical Library.

7 Reference is made to the Hospital Social Service Association of Hawaii.

8 *Annual Report of The Queen's Hospital*, "Rules of The Queen's Hospital," 1939, p. 74.

9 Full name known only to the initiates.

10 *Hospital Social Service Association—Annual Report for 1931*, pp. 1, 2; Honolulu County Medical Library.

XIX

Participation in the Development of Social and Health Programs in the Community

At the suggestion of Dr. Harry L. Arnold, Sr., chief of medical services at The Queen's Hospital, I analyzed 6,070 case histories in our files in 1934. This naturally led to the questions—how many referrals came from physicians, and what were their reasons for referring patients to the Social Service Department?

The total number of doctor-referrals was 1,073. Of these, 696, or 65 per cent, were for means reviews and financial arrangements in meeting medical costs; 272 were for such direct services as follow-ups, interpretation to Japanese or Chinese patients by workers of the same racial heritage, home visits, notifying relatives of patients' conditions, finding donors for blood transfusions, obtaining permits for operations, finding employment, obtaining convalescent care, and arranging for transportation to the mainland. Only 105 referrals were for social histories.

The analysis revealed two basic factors: one, the lack of comprehension by the majority of the medical profession of the meaning of social casework; the other, the rising costs of medical care. The histories recorded the exhaustion of savings, the mortgaging of homes, the sale of choice possessions, or the borrowing from finance companies at 10 per cent interest, payable in advance, with nonpayment bringing the collector to the door. There were instances of conflicts in family life produced by illness and inability to pay for adequate medical care. (I wondered how much medical treatment was vitiated by the anxious states so produced.)

In accordance with the third of the approved functions of

232

medical social service, as stated in chapter XV, we decided to use our analysis of doctor-referrals (1) in an interpretation of social casework to the medical profession, and (2) to stimulate in the community a plan for meeting the costs of medical care.

Pertinent to the first decision, I read a paper, in April 1934, to the Honolulu County Medical Society entitled "Functions and Practices."[1] I described the function of casework as a discipline contributory to medical practice, which brings to the attention of doctors relevant psychosocial problems and, like medicine, is applicable to illness irrespective of the economic status of patients. But, I continued, if the analysis of social histories was any criterian, most physicians were of the opinion that the practice of social casework was limited to the indigent or medically indigent. However, as I remarked at that meeting, we welcomed doctor-referrals, no matter how trivial or irrelevant they seemed. A means review by a qualified social worker might disclose pertinent problems of a psychosocial nature that could not be seen or resolved by a test tube or X-rays, or effectively handled by drugs or surgery.

As to the second decision, the rising cost of medical care was an increasingly acute problem during the 1930s, and by no means limited to Hawaii. The financial crisis of those years was threatening Hawaii as well as the mainland and social security was becoming widely discussed. On August 14, 1935, President Franklin D. Roosevelt signed the Social Security Act. In that same year the Territorial Conference of Social Work[2] decided that social security, with a section on socialized medicine, would be the conference theme.

At hand was a copy of "Medical Care for the American People," published in 1932. It was the report of a privately sponsored and supported study of the costs of medical care, made over five years by a committee of fifty persons—physicians, health officers, dentists, pharmacists, nurses, social scientists, and representatives of the general public. The chairman was Ray Lyman Wilbur, M.D., at that time Secretary of the Interior. One of the recommendations signed by the majority of the committee was to meet the rising costs of illness through group payment by means of insurance or taxation, or both.[3] The local committee responsible for the section on socialized medicine at the Territorial Conference of Social Work used "Medical Care for the American People" as a guide.

Great care was taken in planning this section. Participants were chosen who could best represent the groups to whom the rising cost of illness was a major concern; namely, patients, doctors, and hospital administrators. We decided to concentrate on the middle economic group, since the county government was responsible for indigent patients and the cost of illness was of minor concern to the affluent.

Mr. Charles F. Loomis, then executive secretary of the Institute of Pacific Relations [4] was the moderator. His experience in round table technique was largely responsible for the objectivity of the discussions, which made the section on socialized medicine [5] the highlight of the 1953 Territorial Conference of Social Work. [6]

Committee on the Costs of Medical Care

The conference closed with the general agreement that Hawaii, too, was faced with a problem in medical economics, the solution of which needed thoughtful planning. To this end a holdover committee was appointed, [7] which, within a short time, grew to thirty-three members, representing the fields of medicine, education, nursing, social service, the ministry, hospital administration, and business. We called ourselves the Committee on the Costs of Medical Care. Mr. W. Harold Loper, then supervising principal of schools, became the general chairman.

For almost three years we worked at the idea of voluntary medical insurance. As we progressed, we became aware of the need to employ someone full-time to gather and analyze pertinent data and to act as secretary. Miss India Johnson ably carried this responsibility, the cost being met by contributions, including $200 from the Honolulu County Medical Society. Miss Johnson corresponded widely but could find nowhere a plan similar to the one contemplated here; namely, a project which offered medical, surgical, and hospital care, as well as doctors' consultations in both office and home.

HAWAII MEDICAL SERVICE ASSOCIATION

By June 1, 1938, the Hawaii Medical Service Association came into being and began to function as a voluntary nonprofit medical insurance organization.

In the beginning, the plan was limited to employed groups and to persons earning not more than $300 a month. Benefits were not to exceed $300 a year. As a safeguard of solvency, some illnesses were excluded.

The salaries of the teaching, nursing, and social service professions represented in that era the economic levels of the proponents of the plan. Therefore it was decided to stimulate advance membership among these groups since it was thought that, by education and training, they might be strong advocates of such a project. Our supposition proved erroneous. In January 1938 there were 1,220 teachers in the public schools on Oahu, but only 589 (less than half) had by then signified their intention to join a prepaid medical plan.

One might expect a greater sense of social consciousness on the part of social workers, who come into closer contact with illness, but they were no less apathetic. I have no figures at hand, only a vivid memory of their unresponsive attitude, even to the extent that, whereas some workers in various agencies wanted the protection of medical insurance, not enough of their colleagues would join to fulfill the required 75 per cent participation.

But despite ups and downs in promoting the idea of medical insurance, the membership of the HMSA increased from an initial few thousand to 100,000 in 1955 and is still going up. A large majority of the doctors in the territory are participating in the plan.[8] Maximum allowable income has also increased. The association pays doctors' accounts in accordance with a fee schedule, doctors reserving the right to make additional charges to those whose annual incomes exceed the maximum.

So much for the participation of the Hospital Social Service Association in establishing the first voluntary prepaid plan for medical care in the territory. But the fact is increasingly apparent that voluntary insurance is not the answer per se to the problem of medical costs. In order to remain solvent voluntary plans must exercise certain limitations, e.g., membership available only to employed groups,[9] and unavailable to persons over sixty-five years of age, or to those with chronic diseases—the ones who in general need protection most. Nor do voluntary plans meet the rising cost of services and administration of hospitals.

Hospital Service Study Commission

Nonprofit hospitals depend largely upon the fees of patients for support. Normally, only a minimum number of persons in a community is hospitalized at any one time, but the fees they pay include not only the cost of their care but also a "standby cost." This is to maintain against a possible emergency or epidemic the required number of vacant beds for many additional patients. As medical science expands, hospital services multiply, and so does the expense of administration. Thus, "standby costs" could so increase the price of an individual's hospitalization as to become an excessive burden, especially to the middle and lower income groups.

In 1945, Mr. Charles F. Honeywell, a director of The Queen's Hospital, took the lead by introducing in the legislature a bill whose purpose was to spread the "standby" or "ready-to-serve" costs over the total population, thus reducing the expense of hospitalization to individual patients.[10] During the same session, Representative Joseph Andrews introduced a more comprehensive bill, one that would cover through taxation the charges of both medical and hospital care to all people, irrespective of income.

These bills needed more time for consideration than was possible in a legislative session of seventy-four days. Governor Ingram M. Stainback was therefore mandated by a joint resolution to appoint a commission to study "the feasibility of establishing a Territorial system of health insurance." [11] For this task $50,000 was appropriated; it made possible the employment of a competent staff for research and technical work.

The governor appointed me to the commission, along with Charles F. Honeywell, chairman; Charles M. Wright, Nils P. Larsen, M.D., and Gerald W. Fisher. We soon learned that the subject required more knowledge than we possessed and therefore engaged a medical economist of national reputation —Nathan Sinai, Dr.P.H., director of the School of Public Health, University of Michigan.

Twice Dr. Sinai came to Honolulu to consult with the commissioners. From a heterogeneous mass of ideas, more or less conditioned by personal bias and limited knowledge, Dr. Sinai brought the group to face facts supported by authoritative research. Among these are the principles that medical care should be in accordance with the individual's need and not his ability to pay for it; that it should include both chronic and acute illnesses and all people irrespective of age, employment or dependency.

The commissioners found that 92 per cent of individuals and families in the territory had, at that time, incomes estimated at less than $5,000. We also learned that, according to studies made elsewhere, those with higher incomes have better health because they can afford to pay for it, whereas those with lower incomes spend a greater percentage for medical care.[12]

The commission gave due consideration to fundamental principles of medicine, e.g., free choice by patient of doctor and hospital, and vice versa; the sacredness of doctor-patient relationship; and freedom for the physician in prescribing treatment and consulting specialists. Policies of administration as well as of economy were discussed. Had each commissioner been asked, before the study began, to express an opinion on medical insurance, the answers would undoubtedly have been unanimously in favor of a voluntary plan. At its close and after much thought and earnest discussion, the five signed a report recommending a compulsory one.[13]

A carefully drafted bill providing for payment (within certain limitations) of physician's and hospital services through taxation, was introduced into the 1947 legislature. And what a reception it got!

The Territorial Medical Association, the Honolulu County Medical Society, and the Honolulu Chamber of Commerce were actively antagonistic. Press, radio, mass meetings, and special speakers became channels for fulminations poured upon an uninformed public. Its opponents succeeded in preventing the bill from being reported out of the committee to which it had been referred upon introduction to the 1947 legislature.[14]

GOVERNMENT'S RESPONSIBILITY FOR MEDICAL CARE

But the problem of adequate medical care for all people is not to be quelled by organized opposition. James Howard Means, M.D.,[15] reminds us in his book, *Doctors, People and Government*,[16] that medical care has a sociological base. In the process of evolution society will make demands in accordance with its requirements; it is not the doctors but society that calls the tune and where private enterprise is inadequate to meet medical needs, government takes over.

In July 1948 government had taken over in Great Britain; and in America organized medicine was fearful of a similar sociological evolution. The propaganda of Americans was full of misstatements regarding the British plan. One that persists is that in Great Britain patients do not have free choice of doctors nor doctors of patients—but they do.

Students of national health movements recognize the sociological base of medical care; they see this through governmental supplementation or control even though it be by slow stages. Tax-supported medicine, for example, began in the United States in 1798, when the United States Public Health Service was founded under the name "Marine Hospital Service" to provide hospitalization for sick merchant seamen.[17]

In the intervening years, government has assumed, with little evidence of co-ordination, increasing responsibility for treatment, research, education, and building projects in furthering medical care on federal, state, and county levels.

Several attempts were made during the Roosevelt and Truman administrations to establish a co-ordinated federal medical care program, but none succeeded in overcoming organized opposition. As Dr. Means wrote, "It is a chaotic situation." This is reflected in Hawaii by the agglomeration of various medical organizations: federal, territorial, county, and voluntary. By a territorial law enacted in 1945, private hospitals began to receive a "standby cost" of 50 cents per diem per ward bed, whether occupied or not. This subsidy has since been increased to 75 cents.[18]

Division of Hospitals and Medical Care for the Indigent and Medically Indigent

Another law was enacted in 1951 of wider but still limited coverage. It established within the Department of Health the Division of Hospitals and Medical Care for the Indigent and Medically Indigent.[19] The coverage of this division is broad—on the books. Medical and surgical expenses and the cost of mechanical appliances are included, but biennial appropriations do not always meet the demands.

The program is administered by the Territorial Advisory

Commission of ten members acting under the Board of Health, the law stipulating a minimum of four doctors of medicine. In 1953 there were six members, all private physicians. Although there is no doubt of the interrelationship of medical economics and social welfare, it is not mandatory for the Advisory Commission to include a qualified social worker. The director of the Department of Public Welfare is a member ex-officio but he is not necessarily a social worker.

As for eligibility under this law, people on relief, having been classified as needy, are automatically given medical care. The medically indigent are persons paying their own way in the community. They may have, or have had, some savings. They may even own a home and have a personal physician. They have been able to pay for comparatively minor illnesses, but only with great difficulty, if at all, for a major or prolonged one. However, to qualify as medically indigent they must submit to a means test.

Financial investigations under this law are the responsibility of the boards of supervisors of the counties in which applicants reside. In Honolulu, where there are no government physicians in the same sense as there are in rural areas, the indigent and medically indigent come under the care of a hospital's house staff. This means treatment by medical residents and interns, in the hospitals that have them.[20]

Where the medically indigent have to accept staff service, fear may be induced, the more so if the patient is at the time under the care of a personal physician. Also, the framers of this law failed to visualize the possibility that, in better days ahead when the patient is no longer a "medical indigent," he may have transferred his allegiance to an intern or resident who cared for him in the past and who is now a practicing physician.[21]

MENTAL HYGIENE

One of the earliest community needs apparent to the HSSA in the early years of medical social work was a better understanding of mental hygiene, in both its preventive and treatment aspects.

In the 1920s Hawaii had no psychiatrists in the accepted meaning of the term. Mental patients were treated by general practitioners or specialists in any field but psychiatry; if a psychotic person needed restraint, he was confined in a cell at the police station pending court hearing; if adjudged insane,[22] he was committed to the Oahu Insane Asylum, a veritable custodial institution, named by the Hawaiians *hale pupule* (crazy house).

Patients who had the means might be taken to more adequately equipped institutions on the mainland; the less acutely disturbed might be advised to take a trip "to forget it," disregarding the fact that changes of scene do not necessarily induce changes in mental patterns. Indigent mental patients were usually transferred from the police station direct to the Insane Asylum; if admitted to Queen's, it was only for short periods of observation, often followed by commitment to the Asylum.

This state of affairs was anything but a credit to the community. The Hospital Social Service Association decided to do something about it. With three exceptions, the association met with little encouragement from the medical profession. The exceptions were Dr. Robert B. Faus, Dr. Mon Fah Chung, and Captain B. W. Hogan,[23] who, while stationed in Honolulu, was in 1934 appointed honorary staff psychiatrist to The Queen's Hospital. These three doctors continually made effective use of social service.

In 1929 the National Conference of Social Work was being held in San Francisco, and some weeks later, the Territorial Conference of Social Work was to convene in Honolulu. Its executive committee, learning that Dr. Frederick H. Allen, director of the Child Guidance Clinic in Philadelphia and an executive officer of the National Committee on Mental Hygiene, was to participate in the National Conference, invited him to Honolulu, incidentally to address the Territorial Conference, but primarily to stimulate an interest in mental hygiene among our local physicians.

The doctors were, on the whole, indifferent; some were even derisive. It was Dr. Allen's opinion, however, that without more acceptance of mental hygiene by the medical profession it would be extremely difficult for us to make any headway. But we did make headway.

During his term of office (1921–29) Governor Wallace R. Farrington had Dr. Faus, City and County Physician, survey the Oahu Insane Asylum. Dr. Faus reported conditions so bad that a new mental hospital was erected on the windward side of the island. In 1930 the patients were transferred from the asylum on School Street to the newly built Territorial Hospital, in Kaneohe.

Clifford W. Beers Invited to Hawaii

But buildings alone are no guarantee of good standards in treatment. Governor Lawrence M. Judd, who succeeded Mr. Farrington, was also concerned about mental patients and "the way they were being handled at the Territorial Hospital." Mr. Judd had read Clifford Beers' *A Mind That Found Itself* and invited Mr. Beers to come to Hawaii to "help me improve our local conditions pertaining to mental cases." [24]

Mr. Beers came to Honolulu and gave a public lecture on February 8, 1931, at McKinley High School. The auditorium was packed. Clifford Beers told the story of his life in a simple, direct manner. Describing how he jumped out of a window in an effort to end that life, he said, "And the damned fools mended my broken feet without repairing the mind which compelled the jump!" Mr. Beers was confined for three years in mental hospitals, both private and state.[25] After his recovery in 1904 he returned to business, which he had always thought of as his life's vocation. But he came to feel that divine direction led him to expose the cruelty and ignorance he had experienced in mental institutions and to devote his life to obtaining greater understanding and more humane treatment of the mentally ill.

Following his lecture at McKinley High School, Mr. Beers privately expressed the opinion that he had made a mistake in coming to Hawaii without a psychiatrist, as so many people attending that mass meeting had gone there thinking he had the answers to their particular problems.

Advisory Council on Mental Hygiene

As a result of Mr. Beers' visit, the Advisory Council on Mental Hygiene was appointed by Governor Judd. It was composed of three laymen and six doctors.

During my leave of absence beginning in September of 1931, Miss Willa Murray acted as director of social service for the HSSA. Miss Murray, in consultation with the Governor's Advisory Council, recommended the employment of a psychiatric social worker and a stenographer to be attached to the staff of the Hospital Social Service Association.[26] The cost of this service was to be borne equally by the territory and private sources. But by this time the general financial depression had settled on Hawaii, putting a check on new programs, and the Advisory Council on Mental Hygiene disbanded.

The First Psychiatric Social Worker

In September of 1932 I talked with Clifford Beers in New York. He thought the demand in Hawaii for mental hygiene would have to come from the community rather than from the medical profession; also he thought we should not delay any longer to develop a favorable public opinion toward it. He advised the employment of a qualified psychiatric social worker, who would have the attributes of a pioneer—able to get on with the doctors and, at the same time, to stimulate in the community a desire for organized mental hygiene. Later Florence Brugger called on me. She was entering the New York School of Social Work for training in psychiatric social service, and expressed interest in the job.

Since we had already been so long on the project, we concluded that another year or two would not matter provided we got the right person for the task. Miss Brugger proved to be that person.

No program in mental hygiene could succeed without doctors' approval. In May 1934 Mrs. Richard A. Cooke, a director of the HSSA, invited to a luncheon meeting at her home several key physicians and the Men's Advisory Committee. The purpose of the meeting was to obtain approval for engaging a psychiatric social worker for a two-year demonstration at an estimated over-all cost of $6,282.

Despite a businessman's warning that the financial outlook for 1935 was so grave that no new service should be inaugurated for the time being, the net result of the meeting was the decision to engage the social worker if we could find the money. The association had faith enough in the importance of a demonstration in mental hygiene to ensure its support. This faith was strengthened by the aforementioned survey of public health in Hawaii made in 1929 by Dr. Ira V. Hiscock.

Commenting on mental hygiene, Dr. Hiscock had said:

There is no problem of public health which is more important and, at the same time, more difficult of solution than that which relates to mental hygiene. In the average family throughout a community, it is probable that the handicap due to mental maladjustments is as great as the handicaps due to all other defects combined.[27]

In due time Miss Brugger arrived in Hawaii and went to work in The Queen's Hospital on September 1, 1935. Though employed as a psychiatric social worker, her chief function in those pioneering years was one of interpretation in the broadest sense of the term, both inside and outside the hospital. She was an effective pioneer.

Within the hospital, her caseload was a general one, i.e., she took referrals as they came and conferred with attending physicians on mental or emotional aspects apparent in any of the referred patients.

Miss Brugger expressed herself dynamically, both in speaking and writing, and was therefore in demand by many community groups awakening to the need of organized mental hygiene. Very often after these talks, people would seek her advice about personal problems. She was sought as a consultant by social agencies and acted in this capacity for McKinley High School. Under the auspices of the HSSA, she organized the Mental Hygiene Committee, a study group of some eighteen members representing agencies, schools, and the community at large.

Collaboration with the Medical Profession

Dr. Faus, as city and county physician, was responsible for the commitment of indigent mental patients to the Territorial Hospital. Miss Brugger helped him by obtaining social histories of such patients or by suggesting substitute plans when commitment was not indicated. For this assistance, the city and county, at Dr. Faus' request, contributed $50 monthly to the budget of the HSSA. The Territorial Hospital in those years was administered by the Department of Health.[28] Its medical staff included neither a psychiatrist nor a social caseworker. Dr. F. E. Trotter, president of the Board of Health, was concerned about the meagerness of history forms regarding patients committed to the Territorial Hospital, and he obtained Miss Brugger's help in composing more adequate ones.

As to progress among doctors generally, out of 129 patients referred by physicians to Miss Brugger over a ten-month period in 1937, intensive casework was given to 78, 34 of whom were private patients. She noted that disturbed persons were being admitted to The Queen's Hospital with such provisional diagnoses as "manic-depressive, anxiety neurosis, behavior problem, hysteria, epilepsy, attempted suicide, alcoholic, nervousness, 'rest', and mental observation."

The following are a few examples of collaboration between Miss Brugger and the medical profession. A young woman was admitted for a major operation, and wanted it, but the case history of the patient revealed enough emotional disturbance for the doctor to cancel the operation. Another referral was for confirmation of a psychosis in a young man who had shot himself; the question arose, "Did the bullet cause his mental condition, or was he mentally disturbed before the bullet lodged in his head?" A third referral resulted in ruling out epilepsy from the diagnosis of a girl who had fainting spells.

Another milestone in the development of mental hygiene was the arrival in Hawaii of Dr. Franklin G. Ebaugh, professor of psychiatry, University of Colorado Medical School, to give a course in mental hygiene at the University of Hawaii in the summer of 1937.

Numerous social and health programs in the community, conceived and born of much thought and hard work on the part of organizations, have lacked the funds to carry them through. Over the years the Chamber of Commerce has aided many of these programs financially. So it was with the establishment of mental hygiene in Hawaii. The groundwork was laid by the Hospital Social Service Association and funds were provided by the Chamber of Commerce.

Of historic interest is the source of funds with which the Chamber of Commerce has done so much for community welfare. At the time of the bubonic plague epidemic in 1899, the government built a rat-proof wharf for transshipment of food from Honolulu to the other islands. A Chamber of Commerce committee made up of members of shipping firms had responsibility for operating the wharf. After the epidemic, the shippers, under the name of the Shippers' Wharf Committee, decided to remodel and rat-proof all wharves.

To finance this undertaking the shippers agreed to a levy of 15 cents per ton on imports (later reduced to 10 cents). In 1914 the Shippers' Wharf Committee decided to pay the tonnage levy to the Public Health Committee of the Honolulu Chamber of Commerce. From 1901 through 1949 it amounted to $2,264,284.36. The levy ceased in 1950.[29]

Survey of Mental Hygiene Needs

Dr. Faus, a member of the Health Committee of the Chamber of Commerce, and a strong ally of the HSSA, was instrumental in procuring means from these tonnage funds to finance a survey by Dr. Ebaugh of the mental hygiene needs in Hawaii. During this period the HSSA donated the full-time service of Miss Brugger to Dr. Ebaugh.

On August 5, 1937, Dr. Ebaugh made his report to the Honolulu Chamber of Commerce. His recommendations were:

1. Recodification of existing laws regarding the treatment of mental patients.
2. Complete reorganization of administration and treatment facilities of the Territorial Hospital.
3. The creation of a territorial psychiatric clinic.
4. The development of psychiatric departments and facilities in the general hospitals in the community.
5. Community education.
6. Creation of a mental hygiene committee under the auspices of the Chamber of Commerce, the Territorial Medical Society, and the Council of Social Agencies, which would assume responsibility for the promotion of psychiatric treatment resources and the development of better mental hygiene in the territory.[30]

In September 1937 the sixth recommendation was put into effect with the creation of the Hawaii Mental Health Committee. It was representative of the groups suggested by Dr. Ebaugh, together with Miss Brugger and Mrs. J. Platt Cooke, president of the HSSA. Mr. Frank E. Midkiff, representing the Chamber of Commerce, was chairman.

During the fall of 1937 Miss Brugger resigned from the HSSA to accept the superintendency of the Kawailoa Girls' Training School, and not until the following March was a competent successor found. Miss Martha Wood, who joined the staff of the association as its psychiatric social worker, increased the rapport with the medical profession begun by Miss Brugger and furthered the interpretation of mental hygiene to the community at large.

HAWAII MENTAL HEALTH CLINIC

In the meantime it had been decided to recall Dr. Ebaugh for the summer of 1938, to organize the Mental Health Clinic, space for which was given gratis in The Queen's Hospital. Again he was paid an honorarium by the Honolulu Chamber of Commerce; and again he had the full-time services, donated by the HSSA, of a psychiatric caseworker, this time Miss Wood.

The Hawaii Mental Health Clinic was in the nature of a demonstration to precede the introduction in the 1939 legislature of a bill to establish a bureau of mental hygiene.

When Dr. Ebaugh left the Islands in 1938 he had arranged with the Chamber of Commerce for the interim appointment of Dr. Edwin E. McNiel, the Chamber paying the latter's salary and also that of Miss Brugger, who resigned from the Kawailoa Girls' Training School and became psychiatric social worker for the Hawaii Mental Health Clinic.

By 1939 there was a firm foundation for the statutory establishment of mental hygiene. Except for one difficulty, it was a simple matter to get such a law enacted by the 1939 legislature. The difficulty was a divergence of opinion regarding policies governing the time and compensation of the director of the proposed bureau of mental hygiene. There was undoubtedly enough responsibility to engage the administrator's full time. A counter argument was that, to attract a competent psychiatrist, a high salary would be necessary; and, administratively, this could not be so high as that of the president of the Department of Health, where it was planned to place the bureau. The director should, therefore, be allowed to accept private patients and, to obviate criticism, this should be stated in the law.

In the latter part of 1938 I interviewed several leading psychiatrists on the mainland. Each was asked his opinion on the acceptance of private patients by the director of a bureau of mental hygiene. There was unanimous agreement that this would not be a sound policy. One psychiatrist in charge of a mental clinic in a general hospital said, in speaking of his own experience, that he had for a time taken private patients. He described the conflict caused by trying to keep office appointments on the one hand, with certain neurotic persons who had plenty of money, and on the other, with those who came to the mental clinic with greater need but less financial means. He felt he had to make a decision, so he chose the clinic. "My income is less," he concluded, "but my peace of mind is greater."

BUREAU OF MENTAL HYGIENE (1939)

After my return to Honolulu in 1939, the legislature being in session, a senator called me early one morning. He said, in effect, "I don't know where I'm at. Doctors are urging that the bill to establish a bureau of mental hygiene should include the right of the director to accept private patients, and you speak just as strongly against it." I told him the story of the mainland psychiatrist. The 1939 legislature enacted a law authorizing the creation of the Bureau of Mental Hygiene,[31] to be administered by the Board of Health and directed by a full-time psychiatrist certified by the American Board of Psychiatry and Neurology. It also provided for such professional and nonprofessional staff as would be deemed necessary by the Board of Health. Mention of the director's right to accept private patients was deleted from the bill; thus, granting him permission to accept private patients became the prerogative of the president of the Department of Health.

Legally the functions of the bureau included cooperative service regarding psychiatric problems with all territorial and county institutions and the conduct of in- and outpatient clinics for the examination, study, diagnosis, and treatment of cases of mental illness. Patients were to be charged in accordance with their ability to pay, but without undue sacrifice; and all money so collected was to go to the territorial government. Dr. McNiel was the first director of the Bureau of Mental Hygiene, and Miss Brugger, its first chief psychiatric caseworker. Both have since left the territory.

The bureau rented quarters at The Queen's Hospital until 1946, when it moved to adapted wooden barracks (remaining from World War II) on the campus of the University of Hawaii. Until 1946 it conducted both in- and outpatient services at Queen's; since then it has limited its functions to outpatients; this includes persons from the other islands for whom satisfactory living arrangements can be made in Honolulu.

As of June 1953, it was the opinion of the chief, Dr. Yan Tim Wong, that the Bureau of Mental Hygiene needed four psychiatrists. Other than himself it had none. A private practitioner was giving, under contract, a daily service of two hours at $10 an hour. Though in the past it had a child psychiatrist, it has none at present. The social service staff includes one resident psychiatric caseworker on each of the islands of Hawaii, Maui, and Kauai. There are four at headquarters in Honolulu.

Monthly clinics on each island were conducted alternately by the Territorial Hospital and the Bureau until July 1953, when they were discontinued. This is now the function of the Bureau of Mental Hygiene, through its psychiatric caseworkers and periodic visits of psychiatrists. By statute, the bureau is to charge for consultations in accordance with patient's ability to pay. In practice, this policy is disregarded, since patients who seem able to afford it are encouraged to consult private psychiatrists, whose fees are usually twenty-five dollars an hour. In 1946 The Queen's Hospital was licensed to include an inpatient mental health service, and in 1952 it opened an outpatient psychiatric clinic at an hourly rate of $5 for self-paying patients and $2.40 for patients referred by social agencies. An additional $2.40 is charged when psychiatric casework is included. Rates are determined by means reviews.

Mental Hygiene Society of the Territory of Hawaii

Just as important as treatment facilities for mental illness is prevention. This is fostered by education and, where necessary, by social action.

The Hawaii Mental Health Committee, organized in 1937 to effect Dr. Ebaugh's recommendations, passed through various vicissitudes until 1942, when the Mental Hygiene Society of the Territory of Hawaii was established.[32] It is a voluntary organization administered by twenty-five directors, representatives of various professions, and the lay community. The society is supported by membership dues, contributions, and the Honolulu Community Chest. It is affiliated with the National Association for Mental Hygiene. The activities of the organization are in the fields of education, community organization, and legislation. This last brings to mind the impasse mentioned in chapter VI between two tax-supported institutions in mental health, the Psychological and Psychopathic Clinic and the Bureau of Mental Hygiene. Because of this block neither organization was adequately staffed. The Mental Hygiene Society did much to bring about the unification of these two governmental organizations in 1955.

A means for furthering popular understanding of mental hygiene is "Mental Hygiene Week" during the month of May. This was established on the mainland by the National Association of Mental Hygiene. Hawaii quadrupled the schedule in 1953 by providing enough programs to fill an entire month. One of the most significant was the annual "Open House" at the Territorial Hospital.

The program was held in the modern Goddard Building, completed in 1950. During the day six lectures were given by members of the professional staff on the theme, "Yesterday, Today, and Tomorrow." Visitors were shown an old type of ward in another building and some of the mechanical restraints used in the yesterday of custodial care of the mentally ill. In the Goddard Building were to be seen evidences of today's greater enlightenment and more humane treatment of mental patients. The lecturers envisioned greater understanding for the tomorrows.

What follows concerns only services in the 1940s during World War II. Because of its significance to Hawaii's social work, the war years will be treated separately in chapter XXI. This chapter continues with community programs which the Hospital Social Service Association participated in or initiated.

EMERGENCY POLIOMYELITIS HOSPITAL (1943) [33]

In 1943 poliomyelitis was being reported from all the islands. As at that time there were no hospitals with facilities to meet the threatened epidemic, an emergency one was provided through the co-operation of public and private organizations, including the Hospital Social Service Association.

The Emergency Poliomyelitis Hospital was composed of quonset huts set up in the grounds of the Shriners' Hospital on Punahou Street. It was governed first by the Office of Civilian Defense and subsequently by a special board of Shriners. Mrs. Elaine P. Johnson became its administrator, a duty additional to that of administering a general emergency hospital (chapter XXI).

Though working extra hours, the HSSA accepted the added responsibility for social service in the Emergency Poliomyelitis

Hospital; three workers shared the program in addition to their own full caseloads. Concomitant with poliomyelitis are emotional, social, family, and vocational problems. These are manifested in the anxieties regarding the effects of crippling conditions, in the disruption of family relationships that sometimes occur, and the problems incident to vocational rehabilitation.

One or another of the caseworkers established contact with the families of all patients living on Oahu, irrespective of economic status. After admission to hospital, patients were kept for a time in strict quarantine, and it meant much to relatives to receive progress reports from the social workers, who were in touch with attending physicians. Visits to some homes revealed unwholesome factors—quarrelsome, separated, indifferent, or oversolicitous parents—particularly significant in planning for the return home of a child crippled by polio.

As for those whose homes were on the other islands, contact was maintained through correspondence. One such instance was the case of a little girl. To overcome her reluctance to leave her brothers and sisters, the pleasure of a plane trip to Honolulu had been so emphasized as to give the child a sense of superiority. So long as none of the other children were allowed to receive visits from parents, she seemed content. But when quarantine was lifted and the child found she was the only one in the ward whose mother or father did not come, she became silent and withdrawn. Coaxed to eat, she would vomit her food. The mother was sent for, and when she arrived she told the social worker the story of the plane trip, adding that when she and her husband returned home they had become fearful of having betrayed their child's trust. Eventually the confidence between the child and her mother was restored, but it took time.

In the Emergency Poliomyelitis Hospital, adults, as well as children, were treated. Very definitely in need of casework was one young man. Paralyzed from the waist down, he had become embittered and rebellious. Some time after the closing of the hospital and his return home, still brooding over his misfortune, he read of a surgical procedure for the feet of polio-paralytics supposedly giving them movement. The orthopedist felt improvement was questionable, but agreed that it was psychologically sound to try all possible means of physical help. The paralytic was therefore admitted to The Queen's Hospital, with expenses met by the Honolulu Chapter of the National Foundation for Infantile Paralysis.

The operation, so far as ability to walk was concerned, was not a success, but, from the standpoint of emotional adjustment, it was well worth while. He had been a patient, with all his material needs met, long enough to have developed the out-of-work habit and become content to frivol away the hours wheeling himself about the hospital in a specially constructed chair. Casework meant helping him to the realization that, though he was crippled from the waist down, there was no comparable crippling from the waist up, unless he himself brought this about by disuse of his mental faculties. Watch repairing seemed a good answer.

The Vocational Rehabilitation Service participated in this plan but it was uphill work to foster concentration in the patient. He would make one excuse after another; but as fast as he made them, the social worker met them. One day it was a lack of parts, which, he said, could not be purchased because of war conditions. Through the co-operation of the press, an appeal was made for old watches and clocks. Time-pieces poured into social service—big and little, baroque and plain, striking and silent; one clock at least was a museum piece.

Fortunately the young man was in a ward of convalescing patients; the nursing supervisor co-operated by allowing him an extra table for some of the timepieces, the rest being stored in the basement. When the ward was asked if the striking clocks disturbed them, there was an outburst of No's. "It's fun," the patients said, "listening to them and looking at them, especially the one which sends out a bird and a worm in the early morning."

In the meantime the patient's competency was gradually increasing, and hospital personnel and social workers encouraged this by entrusting him with the repair of their watches and clocks. From a morose, rebellious, what's-the-use attitude, this man, severely crippled by poliomyelitis, was helped to the point where he was able to make plans for a workbench and a full-time job. Nine years later he was still at his job of repairing clocks and watches.

Reports of the caseworkers to the governing board of the Emergency Poliomyelitis Hospital and to the Honolulu Chapter of the National Foundation for Infantile Paralysis proved an excellent channel for the interpretation of the social and emotional aspects of poliomyelitis. The Honolulu Chapter of the Foundation expressed their satisfaction by contributing to the budget of the HSSA with the assurance that they would pay the salary of a full-time worker, should one be needed; but the epidemic was subsiding, and the Emergency Poliomyelitis Hospital, opened in April 1943, was closed in July 1944.

In several hospitals, provision has been made against any further epidemic; but only in one is there accredited social casework, a factor of undeniable importance in the treatment of this disease.

CONVALESCENT-NURSING HOME

Early in 1943, Dr. Nathaniel M. Benyas, president of the Honolulu County Medical Society, came to the Social Service Department at The Queen's Hospital to ask me about an appeal he had seen in a newspaper. Social Service was seeking "a boarding home for an invalid gentleman." Dr. Benyas asked if our plea concerned a patient of his who needed similar care. Although it was a different patient, a discussion ensued concerning the need of a home to care for patients recovering from acute illness, as well as for the chronically ill, or patients whose conditions lasted over long periods of time but who did not need hospitalization. We talked, too, of the increasing number of elderly persons; of one old lady who had a special nurse and who had lived eight years in The Queen's Hospital; of another, who, with her maid, had moved into one of its suites; of a widower whose chauffer daily brought his car and took him to spend a few hours at his own residence where, however, he would not stay "because it was too lonely."

With the increase in population and in the number of the aged, this situation was growing more acute. The general hospitals were therefore becoming, in some respects, boarding homes for people who, though not acutely ill, had no other resort. Suddenly, the problem was greatly aggravated. With the outbreak of the war in 1941, a certain number of hospital beds had to be kept vacant against further emergencies; therefore the order was to "get rid of the boarders."

I felt the Hospital Social Service Association would help with its solution, provided the medical profession would co-operate. Toward this end Dr. Benyas signed questionnaires addressed to the members of the Honolulu County Medical Society, asking: (1) Had we had a suitable convalescent-nursing home, how many of their patients, admitted to any hospital during the previous twelve months, could have been discharged earlier? (Their answers gave a total of 596.) (2) How many chronically ill patients, employing special nurses in their own homes, could be cared for in a convalescent-nursing home, thus relieving the shortage of trained nurses? (The answers to this gave a total of 23.)

Upon the basis of replies to these questionnaires the HSSA took the initiative in the development of a convalescent-nursing home. Mrs. Charles F. Honeywell, president of the association, arranged a luncheon meeting at the Pacific Club, attended by hospital administrators, doctors, nurses, representatives of the American Red Cross and HSSA, and business leaders.

The discussion led to a consensus that as some provision was made on the various islands by governmental and voluntary agencies for the indigent and lower income groups, the need, generally speaking, was for a convalescent-nursing home for the middle and above-middle income groups.

For estimating the amount of needed funds we were advised to start with a capacity of not fewer than fifty nor more than a hundred beds. From an analysis made by Mr. Gustav W. Olson, administrator of The Queen's Hospital, the operating expenses without the overhead of a general hospital would be about $5 a day per bed. The Convalescent-Nursing Home eventually opened with only forty-three beds and at a higher per diem rate.

Residents within the income brackets we had in mind would presumably be accustomed to, and would want, the privacy of single rooms. On the other hand, irrespective of income, some persons would, for medical or psychological reasons, be better off in wards. Both types of accommodations would therefore be considered. We had a further type in mind.

On the mainland and elsewhere, small cottages or housekeeping units are provided for aging couples who desire as much independence as their health permits, but who want to be rid of the upkeep of their own larger homes. We considered developing a similar plan on the grounds of the proposed convalescent-nursing home. Interested couples might pay the costs of units, which would be subject to an over-all architectural plan with the understanding that, at their demise, the buildings would become the property of the home. They could then be allocated to persons of limited means who in other respects were eligible for the home. Subject to admission policies to be worked out, there would be no restrictions as to sex or race.

The planning committee decided that $350,000 would be adequate to get the home under way. But a necessary prelude to fund raising is a charter of incorporation. Toward this step a well-planned meeting was held on August 9, 1945, with Mr. Alan Davis in the chair. To some 200 persons had been sent invitations signed by doctors representing respectively the Public Health Committee of the Honolulu Chamber of Commerce, the Territorial Medical Association, and the Honolulu County Medical Society; and by three women, directors respectively of what had now become the Medical Social Service Association of Hawaii, the Nursing Service Bureau, and the Hospital Council of Honolulu. Speakers representing these groups spoke from different points of view on the need for a convalescent-nursing home.

The audience was told that, though there would be no building until the war was over, it was important to acquire legal identity through incorporation, in order to establish responsibility for contributions and bequests, and to keep the project alive. The vote was unanimously in favor of the motion to incorporate.[34] This was done in September 1945.

The objects and purposes of the Convalescent-Nursing Home as stated in the charter are:

1. To give convalescent care to patients convalescing from acute illnesses,
2. To give nursing care to those whose illnesses are of a chronic nature, and
3. To give domiciliary and nursing care to the aged who are without families or relatives who can or will take care of them.

In November 1945 a campaign was started to raise $350,000. It is doubtful whether any fund drive began with greater promise of success. The need of a convalescent-nursing home was emphasized in the press, both editorially and by full- and part-page publicity; ministers spoke of it from their pulpits; and talks were given to organized groups direct and over the radio. The early response was heartening. The question began to be heard, "Where is the home to be?" With rising costs and a larger population wanting land, it was not easy to find a site which had all the requirements envisioned for a convalescent-nursing home—sufficient acreage for expansion, for the housekeeping units that were mentioned in the fund campaign, and for division by ages and by the physical conditions of the residents. Healthful climate, inspiring view, and accessibility were other desiderata.

Acquisition of Property

We looked at several pieces of property and settled on one of 9.47 acres on Maunalani Heights. On this property was the recently built home of Miss H. Ethelwyn A. Castle. Miss Castle had deeded her estate to The Queen's Hospital for a convalescent home subject to the life interest of Mr. and Mrs. B. L. Marx, Sr., and their son, B. L. Marx, Jr. Mrs. Marx, Miss Castle's sister, had since died. Mr. Marx no longer desired to live on the property, and his son did not want to assume the heavy cost of its upkeep. The will provided that should The Queen's Hospital not accept the property, it was to be sold and the net proceeds added to a trust estate to be created under the terms of the will. At the death of two life beneficiaries of the trust, the income, and ultimately the principal, would go to the Honolulu Academy of Arts.[35]

Queen's was willing to release future title to Miss Castle's home, only provided that it would be used for the purposes named in the charter of the Convalescent-Nursing Home; otherwise, it would revert to the hospital. Mr. Marx donated his life interest in the property, and his son sold his for $30,000. Legal steps having been consummated, the property was acquired by the Convalescent-Nursing Home in May, 1946.[36]

In the meantime committees were organized to get construction under way; others to formulate policies relevant to admissions, to medical care, and to furnishings. The subject of furnishings was one of much debate. While some wanted the home furnished throughout by professionals and in accordance with modern design, others felt that residents who had private accommodations and who expected to stay in the home for the rest of their lives, should be allowed to have with them, as far as possible, the things with which they had long and deep association.

The founding of the Convalescent-Nursing Home was a more or less smooth progress toward achievement up to this point, but, after this, it was anything but smooth. The idea of a convalescent-nursing home had taken shape during a world war. While the war continued, materials and labor were restricted to military purposes. The war was scarcely over (August 14, 1945) when business was harassed with shortages of building materials, skyrocketing prices, and acute labor problems.

Untoward Community Reactions

On July 6, 1947, there appeared in the _Honolulu Advertiser_ the architect's sketch of the proposed Convalescent-Nursing Home, a formidable three-story type of institution. It was the signal for united action on Maunalani Heights by some 160 residents against an institutional type of building when they had been led to believe the home would be constructed on a cottage plan. Through the Maunalani Improvement Club, these residents petitioned the mayor and the Board of Supervisors to pass an ordinance protecting residential districts "against encroachment of undesirable types of business or projects moving into the same."

A public hearing was held at the City Hall on September 9, 1947. Mr. C. T. Oliphant, president, gave the history of the home, agreeing that originally the Halekulani Hotel type of construction with cottages around a central two-story building had been favored; however, this plan had proved impracticable, and costs had become so prohibitive that plans for a single unit structure were substituted.[37]

The supervisors took no action on the Maunalani Improvement Club's petition. Meanwhile, bids on the publicized structure were being called. They were so far in excess of anticipated cost that the Operating Committee decided to lay aside the original plan and to reduce the bed capacity by using the existing building with the addition of one wing.

In 1949 the project was faced with another united expression of opposition. This was in response to the passing of a resolution by the Honolulu County Medical Society on November 4, 1949, to debar residents of the Convalescent-Nursing Home from the right to treatment by doctors of osteopathy. The resolution brought about a strong reaction in the community which had been given to understand that, subject to admission and certain residence policies, inhabitants of the home could be treated by other than doctors of medicine. Enough feeling was aroused in the community to prevent the resolution of the County Medical Society from taking effect.

Convalescent-Nursing Home Established (1950)

With many alterations to the original plans, the Convalescent-Nursing Home was opened with a dedication by the Reverend Edward Kahale on January 6, 1950. At the beginning its capacity was forty-three beds, ten in private rooms (at $12.00 per diem), the others in wards of two, four, and six beds. No differentiation is made in attention or food between residents in private rooms and wards. Mrs. Elaine P. Johnson, R.N., who had worked tirelessly as executive secretary since the Convalescent-Nursing Home was incorporated, was now appointed the administrator.

Change of Title

At a special meeting on February 4, 1953, the Charter of Incorporation and By-laws was so amended as to change the name, Convalescent-Nursing Home, to Maunalani Hospital and Convalescent Home. The directors decided on this change because companies issuing prepaid medical insurance disapproved, they said, of paying for care in institutions not designated as "hosptials." The home was therefore losing "revenue urgently needed." This reason seems ill-founded. According to an analysis made by the Hawaii Medical Service Association in January 1953, the majority of medically insured persons in the territory are members of that organization. The HMSA approves, to the extent of its allowable maximum, the care of members in the Convalescent-Nursing Home.

A determinant for the change was undoubtedly the fact that a hospital is tax exempt, whereas a "home" may not be. Hospitals are also eligible for the territorial subsidy of 75 cents per ward bed per diem. Laws can be so amended, however, to embrace current needs in health and social welfare. The name matters little so long as the original purposes are maintained;

namely, (1) to give convalescent care to patients recovering from acute illness, (2) to give nursing care to those whose illnesses are of a chronic nature, and (3) to give domiciliary and nursing care to the aged.

[1] Margaret M. L. Catton, *Functions and Practices.* Paper read to Honolulu County Medical Society, April 1934; File: Cost of Medical Care. Minutes and reports made over several years, leading to the founding of the Hawaii Medical Service Association; Honolulu County Medical Library.

[2] Since 1950, Social Welfare Association of Hawaii. Dissolved in 1957.

[3] *Medical Care for the American People,* "Final Report of the Committee on the Costs of Medical Care" (University of Chicago Press, November 1932), p. xvi; Honolulu County Medical Library.

[4] Name changed in 1953 to Pacific and Asian Affairs Council.

[5] The term "socialized medicine" is giving place to "national health" as an expression less emotionally charged.

[6] *Territorial Conference of Social Work* (Honolulu, July 29–30–31); File: Cost of Medical Care, Honolulu County Medical Library.

[7] *Minutes of meeting, Dec. 13, 1935;* File: Committee on Costs of Medical Care, Honolulu County Medical Library.

[8] Information acquired at the office of the Hawaii Medical Service Association.

[9] The HMSA has recently opened services to individuals who join during annual membership campaigns.

[10] Charles F. Honeywell, "Civilian Hospital Needs," *Hawaii Medical Journal,* Vol. 4, July–August, 1945, p. 311.

[11] *T.H. Session Laws* (1945), Resolution 12, pp. 454–55.

[12] "Medical" here includes both hospital and doctor's care.

[13] *Report of the Hospital Service Study Commission* (Honolulu, Jan. 1947): Pursuant to Joint Resolution No. 12, *T.H. Session Laws* (1945); Honolulu County Medical Library.

[14] According to Dr. Sinai, the report of the Hospital Service Study Commission has been used as a model in several localities on the mainland.

[15] Formerly president of the American College of Physicians and professor of clinical medicine at Harvard Medical School. Chief of medical services at the Massachusetts General Hospital.

[16] James Howard Means, *Doctors, People, and Government,* an Atlantic Monthly Press Book (Boston: Little, Brown and Company, 1953).

[17] *Ibid.,* p. 108.

[18] Information acquired from the Bureau of the Budget and The Queen's Hospital.

[19] *T.H. Session Laws* (1951), Act 129, pp. 162–65.

[20] An interpretation of house staff is given in note 7, chapter XVII.

[21] A comprehensive review was made of national health services. This included both the British National Health Service and attempts in America for a similar plan to meet the costs of medical care. These data will be deposited in the Honolulu County Medical Library.

[22] Insanity is the legal term for mental illness.

[23] Dr. Hogan is now rear admiral in the United States Navy.

[24] Information obtained in correspondence with Lawrence M. Judd, May 13, 1953; File: Psychiatric Social Work, Honolulu County Medical Library.

[25] Clifford W. Beers, *A Mind that Found Itself,* 7th ed. (New York: Doubleday & Company, 1948).

[26] *Annual Report of the Hospial Social Service Association,* 1931, pp. 2, 3; Honolulu County Medical Library.

[27] Ira V. Hiscock, *Health and Welfare in Honolulu, Hawaii* (New Haven, Conn.: Quinnipiack Press, 1929), p. 133; Honolulu County Medical Library.

[28] Administration later passed to the Department of Institutions, created in 1939. *T.H. Session Laws* (1939), Act 203, p. 313.

[29] Clarence L. Hodge and Peggy Ferris, *Building Honolulu, A Century of Community Services,* Honolulu Chamber of Commerce, 1950, p. 84; Honolulu County Medical Library.

[30] Franklin G. Ebaugh, speech given at Chamber of Commerce luncheon, Young Hotel, August 5, 1937; File: Mental Hygiene, Psychiatric Social Service, Honolulu County Medical Library.

[31] *T.H. Session Laws* (1939), Act 257, p. 39.

[32] In 1954 the name was changed to Mental Health Association of Hawaii.

[33] For confirmation of the history in this section the reader is referred to the File: Emergency Poliomyelitis, Honolulu County Medical Library.

[34] File: Convalescent-Nursing Home, Honolulu County Medical Library.

[35] Statement by the president at the Special Meeting of the members of the Convalescent-Nursing Home, Feb. 5, 1953; File: Convalescent-Nursing Home, Honolulu County Medical Library.

[36] *Ibid.*

[37] *Ibid.,* copy of Mr. Oliphant's paper to the Board of Supervisors.

XX

Social Research

This chapter considers social research, the last of the approved functions established in 1949 by the American Association of Medical Social Workers. The reader is reminded that when these standards were promulgated, research in social work had not yet established criteria acceptable to much older professional disciplines. At that time (as spelled out by the AAMSW) research meant the "studying of problems which recur . . . in practice and being ready to collaborate in the social aspects of study projects undertaken by related professions in community planning." [1]

Applied to the Medical Social Service Association the recurring problem, still of greatest significance, is the gaining of acceptance by the medical profession of social workers as collaborators in medical practice. With the exception of psychiatric cases and, more recently, illnesses of a psychosomatic nature, doctors, generally speaking, still think of social casework as related primarily to the indigent or medically indigent, and to making financial arrangements for medical care.

Reviewed historically this opinion is understandable. Through centuries of scientific research, medicine has discovered causes of disease and methods of treating and eradicating them. In contrast, social casework, stemming from organized charity, has only since the beginning of this century evolved as a profession with an accepted body of knowledge and skills in technique.

In the mainland areas where there are medical schools, more progress is being made in social research than is possible in Hawaii, where there is no medical school. In a number of medical schools, students are required to participate in home care programs, the faculties including social workers. The purpose of the home care programs is to direct students from

260

the belief that sickness is "purely a physiochemical phenomenon" and to give them an opportunity to observe their patients in their home environments and to become cognizant of pertinent psychosocial factors in illness.

Previous chapters have reviewed intra- and extramural programs that evolved from studies and analyses conducted by the workers of the Medical Social Service Association. One of particular significance for its potential value in social casework has been related in chapter XVI—recording and statistics.

TOWARD COLLABORATION

Interns and residents in The Queen's Hospital are required to serve stated periods in various departments—medical, surgical, obstetrical, etc., but not in the Social Service Department. The social service staff was conscious of this disregard and decided to do something about it.

For some time the workers had been concerned about the number of patients who were referred to social service after surgery had been performed, some of whom had lacked comprehension of impending operations and were disturbed in consequence. The workers, therefore, planned a conference to which were invited the medical director of Queen's, the neurosurgical and psychiatric chiefs of staff, the resident on surgical service, and the president of the Medical Social Service Association. In preparation for this conference they read two articles—"Psychiatric Implications of Surgery," by Joseph J. Michaels, M.D., and "Psychiatric Understanding in Social Casework with Surgical Patients," by Eleanor Cockerill.

The psychiatrist and the neurosurgeon spoke of patients upon whom surgery is performed without sufficient objective evidence of disease, and whose symptoms could be traced to emotional disturbances—the desire to suffer, to be punished, or to punish another, or the wish for death in order to escape an intolerable situation.

Two case histories were presented by the social workers. One was a woman whose reaction to the marriage of her closest friend was a desire to die. Complaining of abdominal pains, she underwent major operations by more than one doctor, in more than one hospital. Her minister referred her to a social worker at Queen's. The worker learned from the patient that she had chosen surgery as a means to die, hoping she "would never get off the operating table." She did get off and with the help of sustained casework her emotional problem was resolved.

The second history concerned a young man recently arrived in Honolulu. He complained of such acute abdominal pains that he too underwent surgery. He had consulted one of the city's leading surgeons, engaged a private room at The Queen's Hospital, and been operated upon, assuring the Business Office that a wire to his mother on the mainland would bring ample funds to cover all costs. When there was no response to the telegrams the case was referred to Social Service. In correspondence with the Social Service Department of a hospital in the patient's home town, it was learned that this young man "had a mania for operations." After exhausting one city he would go to another, giving his mother's name and address as guarantee for payment of his bills. By the time he reached Honolulu his mother refused any further responsibility. The Queen's Hospital had to write off their bill, and the surgeon likewise was not paid. Asked by the social worker what the laparotomy had revealed, the doctor replied, "Nothing but a mass of adhesions." In the meantime the young man had left the Islands.

As to advance preparation for surgery, one doctor at the conference stressed the point that it depends upon the individual patient whether or not this is indicated. Another expressed the opinion that there are doctors too prone to surgery with whom a potential fee carries weight. With regard to children, the opinion was unanimous that the effect of surgery upon an unprepared child might lay the foundation for a psychoneurotic personality.

As the conference ended, the doctors and social workers agreed to collaborate in a study of 100 cases to determine the extent of patients' understanding of impending operations and to note pertinent psychosocial factors. Unfortunately this program, full of promise as a research project, was nipped in the bud by World War II, which called many physicians into the armed services and laid extra burdens on those who remained.

CONCERNING ADOPTIONS

The following study is a condensation of a thesis, "Adoption Laws of the Territory of Hawaii," [2] written in 1942 by a staff member of the Medical Social Service Association of Hawaii,

Miss Tsuneo Kinoshita (later Mrs. Suyeki Okumura), toward her degree from the New York School of Social Work, Columbia University. The subject was timely, for concern was mounting among social workers and agencies regarding the lack of adequate adoption laws in Hawaii.

Miss Kinoshita went back to the mid-nineteenth century in tracing so-called adoption laws, and farther back in describing *hanai*, the custom among Hawaiians of giving and accepting another's children. She cited Queen Liliuokalani, Hawaii's last monarch, as an example of a happy *hanai* child. But times were changing and legal safe-guards, particularly in the matter of inheritance, became necessary in adoptions, not only for Hawaiian children but also for children of other cultural backgrounds.

The Honolulu Council of Social Agencies expressed concern that there was no law requiring investigations by qualified persons as to the fitness of individuals petitioning for children in adoption, no interlocutory decree assuring adequate time for investigations, and no provision for the annulment of an adoption. In 1939 the legislative committee of the council attempted to have these faults corrected through the legislature then in session. The limited success of their efforts was the amendment to Section 4525 of the Revised Laws of 1935, whereby the "judge may in his discretion request the Board of Public Welfare [3] to make an investigation of any case." The amendment gave Public Welfare the authority to support or to oppose the petitioner in an adoption case.

In 1940 the Territorial Conference of Social Work appointed a legislative committee to consider, among other things, a revision of the territorial adoption laws. The committee was particularly interested in the enactment of an interlocutory decree, but the next session of the legislature (1941) adjourned without consideration of the bill.

Miss Kinoshita described the adoption policies of three hospitals—Kapiolani Maternity and Gynecological, St. Francis, and The Queen's hospitals.

The administrator of Kapiolani Maternity and Gynecological Hospital said that, as she did not consider adoptions a function of her institution, she did not show any interest in the matter lest she be swamped with requests of this nature; rather, she referred such inquiries to attending or staff physicians.

The administrator at the St. Francis Hospital expressed concern about the problem but was at a loss as to how to handle it. She cited several case histories of adoptions for which doctors had made the arrangements, or which the mothers had made after discharge, leaving their babies in the hospital as boarders, to be claimed later or given to persons who presented proper legal papers. The Catholic sister cited a case in which she had assisted with the adoption arrangements for one such baby boarder. It made such a deep impression upon her that she doubted if she would ever do the like again. An unmarried mother, upon discharge from the hospital, had asked the administrator's help in finding a home for her baby. The sister knew of a childless couple, financially independent, who had been happily married for ten years. They adopted the baby. Later the baby's maternal grandmother called on the administrator. She had suspected her daughter's pregnancy, she said, but had learned of the baby's birth only by accident. She was greatly disturbed when told of the baby's adoption stating she would gladly have made a home for him, "for, after all, he is my flesh and blood."

The Queen's Hospital was the only one in which there was a social service department. The worker assigned to maternity service routinely saw all staff [4] patients, and those on private service who were referred by their attending physicians. Concerning illegitimate births, or unwanted babies, it was the policy of the social worker to have at least one interview with the mother. If adoption or placement seemed the wisest plan, the case was referred with the mother's consent to either a private child-caring agency or to the Department of Public Welfare for more intensive casework and disposition.

In 1941–42 the worker made a study of 203 cases; among them were sixteen mothers, fifteen of whom were illegitimately pregnant and were considering giving their babies in adoption. After consultation with the caseworker, eight did have their babies adopted; of the remaining eight, one baby died and the rest remained with their mothers or the mothers' families.

Concerning unmarried mothers admitted to Queen's on private service, the worker commented on the fact that it was sometimes through a nurse that a contact was made between the social worker and the attending physician. This emphasizes the value to student nurses of courses in the social aspects of medicine.

Miss Kinoshita conferred with five prominent physicians, representing three racial groups. They expressed their opinions on various phases of adoptions and were in general agreement as to the necessity of a study of the prospective home and adoptive parents prior to placement. There was not the same unanimity as to how or by whom the study should be made.

Two of the doctors, realizing their limitations in this regard, referred cases in The Queen's Hospital to the social service department, in other hospitals to social agencies. Two doctors felt qualified to make their own adoptive arrangements; they had a somewhat negative attitude toward social agencies and were critical of the "interminable questioning by social workers"; one doctor blamed an agency for a breakdown in a case he felt he was handling constructively. Miss Kinoshita felt that physicians identify more with the person seeking a baby than with the natural mother or the baby and his future welfare.

Adoptive Caucasian babies are scarce in Hawaii [5] and it is not uncommon for persons to apply to mainland agencies for them, but much red tape is involved. "It is not infrequent," one doctor commented, "for the prospective adoptive parents to pay for the entire medical care of a mother and child without assurance that the child will be finally theirs."

The doctors who expressed their feelings were against placement in a foster home for a period of observation between the petition for a baby and the final adoptive decree. They minimized the risk of unsatisfactory development in comparison with the advantage of greater security to a baby with adoptive parents than in a foster home run for profit. One physician remarked, apropos of a possible risk in development, "You can't tell about your own, either."

Adoption cases were heard in chambers by the judge of the Court of Domestic Relations. It was not uncommon for an individual petitioning for a child to obtain a decree upon the first and only appearance in court. Decisions seemed largely influenced by personal appearance of and impressions made by the petitioners. Although the judge might, if he so desired, refer cases to the Department of Public Welfare for investigation, the practice was negligible. There seemed to be a feeling that Public Welfare was inordinately slow with such investigations.

Miss Kinoshita found no clearance of cases by the court with the Confidential Exchange. She consulted the exchange about fifteen adoptive families and found ten were registered with one or more social and/or health agencies. Illustrative case histories were given of glaring examples of what can happen to human beings because of inadequate adoption laws.

Though confining her study principally to Honolulu, Miss Kinoshita learned of another judicial circuit (unidentified) where there was strong integration of the legal and social aspects in adoptions. The judge in this particular circuit not only referred all adoption cases to the child welfare worker of the county for investigations, but gave due consideration to her report and recommendations.

Conclusions and Recommendations

Miss Kinoshita found that very few requests were being made of the Department of Public Welfare for investigations; the few that were referred "were usually quite involved and the petitioner's attitude already antagonistic."

Due to the speed with which decrees were granted and the nonuse of the Confidential Exchange, children under the care of social agencies had, in some instances, been adopted without the knowledge of the respective agencies.

Noted was a general attitude among nonsocial workers that persons socially or professionally prominent should not, or need not, be subjected to questioning by a social agency. As the Department of Public Welfare had been given responsibility for investigations—if the judge so desired—and would require a reasonable time to make them, an interlocutory statute no longer seemed necessary.

Miss Kinoshita concluded her thesis with a statement that left no doubt of the need for "interpretation and more interpretation to the community of accepted adoption procedures." Toward this end, and particularly as a means for interpretation to doctors, she recommended cerain pamphlets on adoption published by the Children's Bureau of the United States Department of Labor.[6]

RELIGION AS A RESOURCE IN SOCIAL WORK [7]

So far, the emphasis has been on the physical and psychological aspects of social welfare. There is another aspect of great importance—the spiritual.

One day in 1943 a social worker was discussing with an attending physician, at The Queen's Hospital, the case of a young man whose course was running steadily downhill. "Is there anything more that can be done?" she asked. "No," he replied, "the only thing that can help him now is spiritual help and that's something doctors and social workers know little about." "But we know where to get it," was her immediate response. She had reference to a current institute on "Religion as a Resource in Social Work."

This institute was initiated by a staff member of the HSSA and a Christian minister. They wanted to know to what extent religion could contribute to social casework. Through our interest the Territorial Conference of Social Work in 1942 appointed an interim committee on religion as a resource in social work. Participants in the institute were seven social workers, representatives of both group work and casework agencies including the HSSA, and seven ministers whose faiths included Jewish, Episcopalian, Roman Catholic, Methodist, and Congregational. Had it not been for the war which caused the internment of numbers of Buddhist priests, their faith also would have been represented.

The discussions centered on a clarification of the respective objectives and functions of religion and social work. Social workers and ministers took turns in preparing and introducing discussion questions.

At the start there was a general agreement that a gap existed between the two professions, committed alike to the development of personality and to helping people in trouble. Ministers are not in the habit of consulting social workers concerning their parishioners, and apparently it rarely occurs to social workers that clergymen have anything to contribute to casework. At a case conference, for instance, there may be gathered the social worker, the public health nurse, the physician, occasionally the school teacher, but the minister is conspicuous by his absence. Aside from the general exception of child placement—when an attempt is made to place children in homes or institutions of the parents' faith—religion today scarcely appears in social case histories, and the space allotted to it on face sheets is more frequently than not left blank.

The institute discussed concepts common to both professions, among them authority, adjustment, guilt, and conscience. Out of these discussions came the realization that social casework, drawing largely upon the sciences, is more or less circumscribed by heredity and environment, whereas religion, taking cognizance of the soul, transcends these determinants by a relationship to the supernatural—to God. Time and again this was borne in upon the group; that although religion is not so clearly defined as casework, it has an additional component—that man is more than heredity and environment; more than glands and complexes; that he has, in addition to body and mind, a soul.

It was further realized that, unless religion is an important element in the life of the social worker, he cannot use it effectively as a resource. It was also agreed that a client or patient for whom religion has significance will take his cue from the caseworker; if he feels it to be unimportant to the worker, he will remain silent on the subject—and spiritually hungry.

A significant feature of the study group was the radiation of its influence among the staffs of several agencies, who, though not participants, heard much about it and asked help of ministers in particular cases.

One worker, who candidly said that religion "left her cold," became sufficiently interested to try it out on an unmarried mother "as an experiment." The worker had had this case already during six prenatal and five postnatal months. In all this time religion had never been mentioned between them. Her curiosity now aroused, the social worker brought up the subject of baptism. No more was needed; the young mother talked at length about religion having been an important factor in her upbringing and how troubled she now was about the deceit she was planning, upon her return to the mainland, to account for her baby. She was thinking of telling her parents that she had married a soldier who was subsequently killed in action. Through this discussion, the social worker became sufficiently convinced of religion as a resource as to seek consultation with one of the ministers participating in the institute and to introduce him to the unmarried mother. The minister and the social worker helped her to tell her family the truth and to plan constructively for her future.

The case of another unmarried mother had been discussed by this group of clergymen and social workers. The workers were impressed with the consensus among the clergy in the group that unwed motherhood is no sin; it is when deceit becomes a factor that sin enters.

This led to an exploration of the difference in concept between sin and guilt. One to whom sin is meaningful may refuse to do some act, or to leave it undone, because for him such an act or ommission constitutes a sin—sin has a deterrent effect—whereas one having no religious conviction may do some act or leave it undone, and in consequence experience a sense of guilt so strong as to cause physical or mental illness.

Doctors, nurses, and social workers encounter attitudes of rebellion or anxiety relevant to an illness or injury, and sometimes they are at a loss to handle them. One such case was that of a defense worker, who, having stooped to pick up a paper, struck his head against a steel filing cabinet, smashed his glasses, and was admitted to hospital with an injured eye. He was very rebellious and tense—not the best frame of mind for medical treatment. A skillful social worker tried to resolve his stress, but to no avail. Every time she visited him on the ward, he would reiterate, "Why did this happen to me; why did it happen to me? Instead of going out with the boys, I stayed at headquarters to write letters. Other men drink and carouse; I don't. Why did it happen to me?" He lost the sight of his eye, and a mental condition threatened. The social worker was frustrated. She had heard colleagues talking about religion as a resource in social work and thought, "Perhaps, where I have failed, a minister might succeed." She therefore consulted a minister who had participated in the institute and who had considerable casework insight. He agreed to collaborate with her. Broaching the subject to the patient, she got an eager response. Several interviews between priest and patient followed and, with them, a slackening of tension, and acceptance of the handicap.

Another instance of religion as a resource in social work concerned a mentally deranged woman of the Buddhist faith. To all sects of this doctrine the rite of *Hoji* is of prime importance in its relationship to the departed. For seven days following the death of a Buddhist, a religious ceremony is performed daily by a priest, either in a temple or at the family shrine in the home. After the first seven days the ceremony is repeated (in temple or home) once a week until the forty-ninth day, and again at prescribed intervals over many years.[8]

Largely because of the war, when Japanese Buddhist priests were interned and the Japanese community generally was upset, the rites of *Hoji* were not performed for the departed husband of this mentally ill patient. The caseworker, in consultation with the psychiatrist, conferred with a priestess who came from her temple to minister to the widow in the hospital. The priestess contributed in no small way to the patient's recovery by lifting from her mind an overwhelming sense of unfulfilled responsibility.

As a final example, there was a patient with an inoperable cancer. His chief complaint was the fancied negligence of doctors and nurses but, medically, there was little they could do for him. He was querulous, lonely, and afraid. Visiting him was not a pleasant duty.

One day the social worker, somewhat irked with his continuous fault-finding, said to him, "It's not a doctor you need but a minister." She was taken aback by his immediate affirmative response. He had a keen intellect and stipulated it must be a minister "who can argue." The social worker interpreted this to mean that, through argument, he hoped to gain assurance of immortality.

The worker asked for a particular clergyman of the institute to visit this patient; the priest did so, "usually," as he expressed it, "in the gloaming." Through their discussions, peace of mind came to this man as he faced the inevitable end.

As was noted earlier, a radiation from the Institute on Religion as a Resource in Social Work was felt by social workers who were not members of it. For example, not all the workers of the HSSA were participants in the institute but they were unanimous in their choice of a book to review for staff discussion. It was *The Art of Ministering to the Sick,* by Dr. Richard C. Cabot and Chaplain Russell L. Dicks, both of the Massachusetts General Hospital.[9] The two men, working closely together, became so impressed with the strength to be gained through an alliance between doctors and ministers, that they collaborated in writing this book.

Though primarily addressed to ministers, *The Art of Ministering to the Sick* has value also for doctors and social workers. The appendices contain several case histories written by Chaplain Dicks which drew from one of our staff the comment, "He writes just like a caseworker—the reference, by whom and for what; his interviews with the patient, and his treatment."

A report of *The Institute on Religion as a Resource in Social Work* was published in 1942.[10] It brought from various places on the mainland requests for suggestions in organizing comparable study groups.

Ministers of all faiths visit our local hospitals in behalf of their parishioners, but there is little or no conscious relationship between them and the medical profession and scarcely any with social service. Each practitioner treats some part of the human being—one his body or mind, one his soul or spirit, and the third treats him in his relationship to pertinent environmental factors.

The problem is how to close these gaps so as to make all healing more complete. We know from the experience of some ministers and doctors that this has been done with notable results.[11] Perhaps another generation of social workers will be inspired to take leadership in another institute, not called "Religion as a Resource in Social Work" (the title of the first) but "Religion as a Component of Social Work," and because man is physical as well as spiritual, they will include physicians as participants with ministers.

Such an institute can point the way toward closing the gaps —a way that will bring about an alliance of physicians, social workers, and ministers in purposeful consultations, one with the other, about those cases that indicate the need of treating the patient's mind and spirit, as well as his body.

[1] *A Statement of Standard to be met by Social Service Departments in Hospitals, Clinics, and Sanatoria* (1949), p. 6.

[2] On file at the Honolulu Council of Social Agencies.

[3] Known since 1941 as the Department of Public Welfare.

[4] Admitted through the City and County Health Department and as such without a private physician.

[5] According to population statistics, Caucasians are in the minority (see Appendix I).

[6] See chapter XI for later legal developments concerning adoption.

[7] File: Religion as a Resource in Social Work, Honolulu County Medical Library.

[8] Information obtained from the Venerable Ernest S. Hunt of the Soto Zen Temple, Honolulu.

[9] Richard C. Cabot and Russell L. Dicks, *The Art of Ministering to the Sick* (New York: The Macmillan Company, 1937).

[10] *The Survey Midmonthly*, 1942; Honolulu County Medical Library.

[11] Reverend Leslie D. Weatherhead, *Psychology, Religion, and Healing* (London: Hodder and Stoughton, 1951).

XXI

World War II

For several years before 1941 the threat of war hung over the Islands.[1] As early as 1939, in anticipation of an attack, defense workers by the thousands were coming into the territory, or were passing through to other Pacific areas. The men and families of the armed services had likewise mushroomed the population.

By 1941 periodic blackout practice had started, and housewives were being encouraged to lay up stocks of food in case shipping was cut off. Another emergency measure was a blood bank organized in June of 1941 under the leadership of Dr. F. J. Pinkerton and sponsored by the Honolulu Chamber of Commerce.

Many men were being drafted into military service, and some were trying to avoid it. In December 1940 Colonel Perry M. Smoot, adjutant general of the territory, and director of selective service, asked the aid of the staff of the Hospital Social Service Association in reviewing draftees' requests for release from training.[2]

Among men rejected by the draft boards were those with remediable physical defects. They also were referred to HSSA, or rather to a group organized by the association which included all the medical social workers in the city.[3] We held evening hours in the National Guard Armory. In reviewing the social histories of the rejectees our duty was to steer those who could not afford private physicians to sources of free medical service. A sudden halt was called to this project when, after two weeks, the federal government decided to assume the costs of remedying these defects. We wondered about those with chronic defects—eyes, hearts, slightly crippled. A good many were self-supporting, and most might have been benefited to a degree by medical treatment.

272

Despite the preparations and rumors, when war came it was a terrible shock. Japanese naval aircraft bombed Pearl Harbor, Hickam Field, and other military areas early Sunday morning, December 7, 1941, wounding 1,143 and killing 2,335, mostly military personnel.[4]

In the Social Service Department at The Queen's Hospital the monthly Sunday Follow-Up Clinic was in session. Not many yards away, in the Mabel L. Smyth Auditorium, Dr. John J. Moorhead, a visiting authority on wound surgery was lecturing to a group of doctors.[5] They soon found themselves attending the wounded at Tripler U. S. Army Hospital, and The Queen's Follow-Up Clinic immediately became a receiving station for the civilian wounded. Military law was declared and blackout and curfew regulations were ordered.[6] Hospitals were soon equipped against eventualities with blackout contrivances, air raid shelters, and ramps for evacuating patients.

AFTER PEARL HARBOR

The Queen's Hospital

Following the attack, social service made contact with every casualty admitted to The Queen's Hospital. All activities were geared to the needs of the moment: "see if my house is still standing, notify my relatives, feed my dog, advise my employer." We had also to explain why, in this emergency, visitors had to be discouraged.

Late in the afternoon of December 8, a mother with a tear-stained face came searching for her son, reported by the police to be at Queen's. There was no registration of his admission, so the mother was shown through the male wards to see if by any chance he had been admitted under a different name. Failing to find him we had to suggest at last that perhaps he had been killed and his body might be in the morgue awaiting identification.

Drills were instituted and every person, from the administrator to the orderlies, was required to attend them. Whenever a long siren blast followed by intermittent short ones broke over the air, we knew it to be an air raid warning. Day or night, each one went to his appointed station; doctors arrived from their offices or homes to assigned locations in Queen's; and to a ward set apart for the dying came the Protestant and Roman Catholic priests arranged for by social service. An eerie stillness descended until the all clear signal sounded and we could return, each to his accustomed occupation. Preparedness had to be maintained, although no further attacks ensued.

Until conditions became somewhat settled the Social Service Department acted as a clearing center. Many women were referred to social service who were eager to avoid the military edict that, unless necessary to the war effort, wives of nonresident men in military service would have to leave the territory. Most had no background "necessary to the War effort," but there were a few. One said, as she sat down, "I am a doctor's daughter, the wife of a doctor, and I have a degree in medical social work." We put Mary Stuppy to work at once.

The war had drawn so heavily upon professional nurses that civilian hospitals had to depend to a large extent upon nurses' aids. Many local women volunteered for this service. They were trained by and under the supervision of Mrs. Bertha Phelps, a mainlander living in Honolulu at the time.

One reflection of the war, as reported by Miss Virginia C. Ott (Mrs. Mark G. Herbst), caseworker in the Pre-natal Clinic at Queen's, was the increased number of babies born in civilian hospitals.[7] It was the custom among Oriental women to be delivered by midwives. Thirty of these were aliens, and as such were forbidden to be on the streets after curfew. Dr. Harry L. Arnold, Sr., territorial medical director of Civilian Defense, arranged for alien midwives to be taken to their patients' homes during blackout hours by the police. Nevertheless, deliveries in hospitals by private physicians rose in number as general employment and wages increased with the war.

For several years before the war, a social worker had been assigned full time to financial arrangements at The Queen's Hospital. As employment and wages rose, this caseload dropped from 1,680 in 1940 to 730 in 1943; but there were many social problems, particularly in connection with defense workers recruited from the mainland. The caseworker on the financial arrangements service, Miss Dorothy Kaemlein, remarked, "Men were apparently scooped up, with no questions asked as to physical or mental fitness." One was a man in his sixties who had false teeth, a glass eye, arthritis, arteriosclerosis, and a leg ulcer. If war workers severed their employment previous to contract termination, or if they became ill out of the line of duty, the contracting firms refused any financial responsibility; this threw on the hospital a load of uncollectible bills and on the community a load of dependency.

In addition to the defense workers who were actually ill there were numerous malingerers. Among these were mainlanders who had reacted emotionally to the bombing of Pearl Harbor by immediately applying for war work in Hawaii. Some had never seen an ocean until they were on the Pacific. They had left their homes as members of united families. Now, working twelve hours a day, seven days a week, crowded into barracks with incompatible associates and inhibited by curfew and blackout from companionship elsewhere, they became increasingly homesick and importuned doctors to certify them as physically unfit. Such certification would automatically entitle them to return home.

The Japanese Hospital

Human nature reacts to danger or tragedy with emotions that often lead to excessive or unreasonable behavior. Nowhere is this better realized than in a state of war. Among hospitals, the most pronounced reaction following the "blitz" was at the Japanese Hospital.

Before December 7, 1941, there was a band of golden characters over the entrance of a building opened in 1939. Translated, these characters said that His Imperial Majesty Hirohito, Emperor of Japan, had contributed to the cost of this new wing. Immediately following the declaration of war, the golden words disappeared, along with the name by which this institution had been known for forty-odd years. The Japanese Hospital became the Kuakini Hospital—named for the street on which it fronts.

Prior to December 7, 1941, the atmosphere of this hospital was predominantly Japanese. Attending physicians, for the most part, were born and trained in Japan; medical records were written in Japanese; and except when occasionally called in as consultants, Caucasian doctors did not enter there.

The war abruptly changed this milieu. The hospital was commandeered at once by the United States Army, which designated certain units as Army Provisional Hospital No. 3. The remaining wards and buildings were allowed to continue admitting patients and civilian doctors, but under the governance of an army doctor, Major Robert Hoagland.[8]

The golden band, which had reminded entrants to the hospital of an emperor's largess was removed; the word "Japanese" was obliterated from its name; and its administrator and all but one of its directors (a *nisei*) were interned. Everything possibly reminiscent of Nippon disappeared, including rice bowls and chopsticks—Japanese patients now had to use knives and forks and American china. Minutes and data of inestimable value concerning the Japanese Benevolent Society and Hospital disappeared or were destroyed.

In Japanese homes, prints and family shrines vanished from view; and, vanished from the streets was the kimono, which in the past had added so much to the color and attractiveness of Hawaii. Older Japanese women now went forth with an awkward gait in Western garb to which they were unaccustomed.

Nipponese radio programs and newspapers were suspended, the former for the duration, leaving those who could neither read nor understand English entirely without current war news, thereby increasing tension in the Japanese community.[9] Immediately following the outbreak of war, and during it, Miss Mitsuko Ariki, the social worker at the Japanese (Kuakini) Hospital, was nearly swamped with telephone and personal calls from Japanese residents all over the city, many seeking information about internees, or advice regarding family problems arising out of the conflict.

After peace was declared, Kuakini Hospital became again an autonomous institution under the same governing body, the Japanese Benevolent Society, but now renamed Kuakini Hospital and Home. It has become much more cosmopolitan in atmosphere.

Kauikeolani Children's Hospital

The effect of the war was most dramatic at the Kuakini Hospital, and least so at Children's. Miss Kaemlein, the social worker there, reported that because employment and wages were at an all-time high, referrals for financial arrangements had dropped considerably; but these very factors were, in some instances, proving unwholesome for family life—the father in the army and the mother taking advantage of work opportunities at high wages. Children were left to irresponsible neighbors, to older but yet too young siblings, or with no supervision at all between school closing and the mother's return from work.

Some children were left at the hospital without visits from their parents; some remained even past the date of discharge. It was not unknown, too, for parents to move without giving their new address, and the social worker had to search for them so that unnecessarily occupied beds might be vacated for acutely ill children. The worker had also to explain to parents that children left indefinitely in a hospital after recovery ran the risk of contracting new diseases.

In these cases, and where there was no mistaking the emotional reaction in young ones thus neglected, it was the duty of the social worker to help mothers to make a wise choice of sacrifice—either the freedom and the things that money could buy, or their children's well being, which money could not replace.

Sacred Heart Hospital

After the outbreak of war, the Office of Civilian Defense was responsible for planning expanded hospital facilities for civilians, in case of need. One of the largest institutions taken over for this purpose was Sacred Heart Convent on Nuuanu Avenue. Substituting the word "hospital" for "convent" it became known as Sacred Heart Hospital. The HSSA supplied social service.

Most of the patients admitted there were defense workers, among them lonely, worried, and frightened ones. Some wished their relatives to receive the kind of letter that a medical social worker can write; and families wanted such letters, giving physicians' reports in layman's language. Sometimes relatives had to be notified of death, and these letters called for details that social workers were able to supply.

The workers of the association participated in many community projects with the common purpose of winning the war. One of the most dramatic in which they gave leadership resulted from a Saturday afternoon call from OCD (Office of Civilian Defense) "asking" them to get 1,500 persons out of a congested strategic area in the Iwilei district within forty-eight hours. No instructions were given as to how to do it—the order was simply to get the people out. The population of Iwilei was from many racial backgrounds. It included the old and young, the sick and well, able-bodied and handicapped, and pet dogs and cats. All were apprehensive at the sudden uprooting. Some evacuees had friends or relatives in other parts of Honolulu but the majority were not so well off. The sick among them were taken to hospitals and the others to Kaiulani School (within two miles) until more permanent quarters could be found for them. Social workers from public and private agencies and from hospitals and volunteers working shoulder to shoulder got the job done before the deadline.[10] In the meantime, nothing happened at Iwilei!

In order to hold personnel, hospitals had been declared essential employers,[11] which froze all employees to their jobs. There was no problem of turnover in those days! Even so, departments were so short-handed that it meant much give-and-take and doubling up as needs arose. And despite the untoward emotional reactions during the state of war, there were also good ones, such as the *esprit de corps* among those facing common dangers.

The atmosphere of Honolulu on August 14, 1945, was in direct contrast to that on December 7, 1941. With the declaration of war on the earlier date, an ominous stillness prevailed and, unless in line of duty, citizens were warned to keep off the streets. In 1945 it was as though pandemonium had broken loose when, on August 14, there was a general outpouring of persons on to streets, joining the noisy throngs in reaction to the news—the WAR IS OVER . . .

1 World War II broke out in continental Europe on September 1, 1939.
2 *Staff Conference Minutes*, Dec. 16, 1940; p. 1; Honolulu County Medical Library.
3 *Annual Report of Hospital Social Service Association* (1941), p. 8.
4 Gwenfread, Allen, *Hawaii's War Years 1941–1945* (Honolulu: University of Hawaii Press, 1950), p. 5.
5 *Ibid.*, p. 29.
6 *Ibid.*, p. 394.
7 *Report of Virginia Chatfield Ott.* Annual Meeting of Hospital Social Service Association, Feb. 26, 1943; Honolulu County Medical Library.
8 Kuakini Hospital (formerly Japanese Hospital). *Social Service Annual Report, 1941;* Honolulu County Medical Library.

9 Since the military government needed media to publicize orders to Japanese residents, the two newspapers were resumed, but under censorship and under different names.

10 *Pearl Harbor, Before and After,* paper dated April 1942, with combined points of view of HSSA staff; published in American Association Medical Social Workers Bulletin, May 1943. Honolulu County Medical Library.

11 Allen, *op. cit.,* p. 340.

XXII

The Growing Edge

Dr. Richard Cabot, whose name is closely associated with the beginning of medical social service in America, likened the growth in character, and knowledge, and wisdom, to new cells from the edge of a bit of muscle.[1] In Part I of this history instances are given of new organizations or programs growing from out the cells of older ones. This growing edge was applicable to the Hospital Flower Society, the parent cell of medical social service in Hawaii. But as the growing edge of human tissue dies if deprived of proper media, so will social service die if deprived of appropriate cultivation—consistency with high standards, constructive handling of frustrations, and the acceptance of community responsibilities indicated through practice. These are of the essence of growth in a progressively developing function in social casework. If they are disregarded, an organization withers and dies.

A threat to the life of medical social service in Honolulu came as an aftermath of World War II; all our hospitals experienced a general unrest accentuated by professional turnover. As it affected social service, by 1946 there was, with the exception of the director, a turnover of 100 per cent in the Medical Social Service Association's staff of eight, marriage and returns to the mainland being the chief reasons. The turnover was not limited to social workers; hospital administrators were also resigning or retiring, and new ones were jealous of their authority.

Withdrawal

The date of my retirement as director of social service had been set for September 30, 1948. In the minds of those most closely associated with the association, questions arose as to its future. After 26 years of service, had it fulfilled its mission and should it now dissolve, or had subsequent needs become
280

manifest for which the association should take responsibility? The question of dissolution had never been lost from sight. It first appeared in written form in the 1933 revision of the constitution and by-laws of the Hospital Social Service Association, wherein a stated purpose of the organization was "to act in an advisory capacity to social service departments in hospitals as long as seems necessary or desirable." If it dissolved, what guarantee would there be for maintaining standards, and what of its capital funds of some $30,000? Thinking was influenced by the opinion of Dr. Malcolm T. MacEachern, Associate Director of the American College of Surgeons, who came to Honolulu in 1936 for the purpose of hospital accreditation.

The directorate of The Queen's Hospital asked his judgment as to whether or not social service should be continued under a community-based board. Dr. MacEachern reported as follows:

As a general principle, all activities concerning the hospital should be under the control of the governing body rather than an independent group, but exceptions are made to this principle in sponsoring or carrying on medical social work within the hospital, particularly where the interest of a larger group is desired, and when the financing of the service is not entirely assumed by the hospital. Apparently the Hospital Social Service Association is a most excellent organization, working harmoniously with the management and governing body of The Queen's Hospital. It is hoped this interest and support will be continued, thus tying up with the hospital a greater community interest. It would, therefore, seem that the present plan in its organization, administration, and functioning should not be disturbed, but rather that the work be extended.[2]

Dr. MacEachern conducted a hospital institute during this visit. The following is quoted from his remarks on social service:

If an organization is doing good work and filling a need, let it continue; if it has weak spots, strengthen them; if in no way it is desirable, give it up . . . you may be understaffed and crowded for space, but your medical social service is the best I have seen in any city in the United States of the same size as Honolulu.[3]

But that was prewar 1936, and this was postwar 1948 with all the vicissitudes of the intervening years. It was thought, therefore, that an analysis made by a medical social worker unrelated to the Medical Social Service Association would help in making a decision as to whether or not the time had come for the Association to disincorporate. In July 1948 Mrs. Alice Clendenning, associate professor of Medical Social Work, University of Pittsburgh, came to Honolulu for this purpose. She remained here five weeks but her report was not rendered until February, 1949.[4]

Mrs. Clendenning recommended liquidation of the MSSA. Realizing this would take time she advised the Association to "employ a full-time, well qualified medical social worker for a two year period . . . to assist the hospitals on a consultative and advisory basis in the development of their own integrated departments." She made a third recommendation: namely, that each hospital have an advisory board for its social service department. But pressures were great and too much time had been lost. Two hospital administrators wanted immediate full control of social service and there was no interim period. The Association did not obtain such consultative services as Mrs. Clendenning had suggested.

At the annual meeting of the MSSA on July 12, 1949, this motion was adopted:

1. That the Association accept in principle the primary recommendation of the recent survey that the Board work toward the objective of liquidating the Association and ceasing to be a separate agency entity.

2. That the Association accept the offers of the several hospitals to take over the functional operations of the social service departments of the Medical Social Service Association of Hawaii as of July 15, 1949.[5]

The Association did make this transfer on July 15. At that time its capital funds amounted to $31,000.76.[6] Until these were disposed of the MSSA had to maintain its legal identity as a corporation.

A special meeting was held on November 26, 1951, to consider a legally prepared resolution,[7] whereby the Association would dissolve by dividing and transferring its financial assets to the hospitals with which it had been affiliated. The resolution failed of passage. The administrators of The Queen's and Children's hospitals refused to accept a stipulation in the charter of the MSSA to the effect that medical social service must be in accordance with the standards of the American

Association of Medical Social Workers.[8] The objecting administrators did not want to be so bound by professional standards and the majority of the members of the MSSA did not want to lose what had been established in this regard. In 1953 a new directorate was appointed. The president, Mrs. Robert E. White, is the granddaughter of the dedicated Mrs. Mackintosh, who was among those who attended the meeting at the YMCA, 63 years before, when the Hospital Flower Society was organized.

With capital funds in excess of $30,000, and no program, the Medical Social Service Association of Hawaii became moribund. But metaphorically speaking it has a growing edge. This edge was revivified in 1954. In that year the Pan-Pacific Surgical Association held its triennial Congress in Honolulu. At a hospital institute the question was asked, "If now there is general agreement among the medical profession that social and psychological factors have a bearing on diagnosis and treatment, why is a social service department not an essential in hospital accreditation?" Two visiting doctors, Dr. Robin C. Buerki, administrator of Henry Ford Hospital in Detroit, and Dr. Arthur W. Allen, associated with the Massachusetts General Hospital, speaking from personal knowledge, strongly endorsed the inclusion of social casework in medical practice, but until there are enough *qualified* social workers, they said, a social service department cannot be made an essential in hospital accreditation.

Professional Education

Those visiting doctors acknowledged the need for a more holistic approach to illness, a recognition that disease is not a purely physicochemical phenomenon but may be the result of inordinate social and emotional pressures. They were of the opinion, however, that social caseworkers in medical practice presupposes professional qualification, but qualification means education and education means teachers and teachers mean expense. This gave the MSSA the idea of spending their assets in providing for a professor in a medical social work sequence at the University of Hawaii, School of Social Work.

The association appointed a committee to work in collaboration with Mrs. Katherine N. Handley, Director of the School of Social Work. An offer was made to the University's Board of

Regents to the effect that the Medical Social Service Association of Hawaii would be responsible for the salary of a professor in medical social work for five consecutive years, if during that time the association could act in a consultative capacity with the School of Social Work. President Gregg M. Sinclair, in a letter dated May 31, 1955, informed the Association that "its offer was gratefully accepted by the Board of Regents." [9]

At the joint request of the MSSA and the School of Social Work for assistance in planning a medical social sequence at the University of Hawaii, the National Association of Social Workers sent Dr. Ruth Cooper, associate professor in the School of Social Work, University of California, to Hawaii in December 1955. Dr. Cooper visited hospitals and institutions and conferred with hospital administrators and physicians. The hospitals included those which formerly were members of the Medical Social Service Association of Hawaii—Queen's, Kuakini, and Children's. Dr. Cooper found that they were either without social workers or had none that were professionally qualified to collaborate in a training program. She got the impression, however, that some administrators and physicians were interested and, therefore, recommended the inclusion of medical social service in the curriculum of the School of Social Work. [10]

In September 1957 Miss Evelyn Cochran, associate professor in the School of Social Work, College of William and Mary, Richmond Professional Institute, joined the faculty of the University of Hawaii as associate professor in the School of Social Work; but education for medical social service is not limited to the classroom, it must include facilities in hospitals and medical institutions for practice under competent supervision. As this concerns general hospitals in Honolulu, the only acceptable one in 1957 is Tripler U.S. Army Hospital. Its executive officer, Lieutenant Colonel Camp, has masters' degrees in both hospital administration and medical social work. Four students expressed an interest in medical social work, but Tripler could take only two.

In seeking a reason for this recession in standards of social service in civilian general hospitals, one notes that social service is the only department in a hospital which has an extra- as well as an intramural focus. In addition to inpatient service, caseworkers are concerned with the psychological and social environments of referred patients. They also have responsibility for furthering relevant community-sponsored resources, the needs for which become apparent in patient-connected services. In her report Dr. Cooper strongly disagreed with the MSSA's thought of dissolution; pointing out its contributions in past years she emphasized a continuing need for citizen leadership in promoting adequate social and health services.[11]

With this broad orientation of medical social service it is scarcely possible to have adequate governance of a social service department if it is the sole responsibility of the hospital administrator. Governance is more intelligent if shared with others of various points of view. Had it not been for the Medical Social Service Association of Hawaii medical social work could not have developed in Honolulu as it did during the active years of the Association. The MSSA followed the pattern of the Massachusetts General Hospital in the establishment of social service by a community-based group, but failed to continue in that pattern. When the MGH assumed control of social service it expanded what had been a supervisory into an advisory committee. This committee is appointed by the Board of Trustees and includes members of that body, as well as the director of the hospital and chief of social service. Other members are representatives of the major clinical and nursing services; at least two social workers from the community and representatives of other pertinent interests. The function of the committee is advisory to the chief of social service and the hospital administrator on such subjects as organization, personnel, functions, and programs.[12]

In conclusion: the MSSA has a growing edge. That it not wither and die as a bit of human tissue would die, if deprived of proper nutriment, depends in large measure upon the medical profession and their practical, as well as their academic acceptance of the importance of psychosocial factors in diagnosis and treatment. Because of the extra- as well as the intramural focus of social service, advisory committees to hospital administrators are recommended in the governance of social service departments. It is here that the Medical Social Service Association of Hawaii could prove its value, anew—by helping to establish social service in hospitals presently without it, acting in an advisory capacity to hospitals where it is established, and deepening the conviction among doctors of the importance of social casework in the practice of medicine.

Finally, Dr. Cabot's metaphor of a growing edge—character, knowledge, and wisdom—is applicable to social welfare in general. So concludes the first comprehensive history of social casework in Hawaii.

[1] Richard C. Cabot and Russell L. Dicks, *The Art of Ministering to the Sick* (New York: The Macmillan Company, 1937), p. 14.

[2] Malcolm T. MacEachern, Jan. 15, 1937; File Surveys, Honolulu County Medical Library.

[3] Gleanings from Malcolm T. MacEachern's visit and the Hawaii Hospital Institute, Aug. 1936; Files Surveys.

[4] Alice Clendenning, *Survey of the Medical Social Service Association of Hawaii* (1945); File Surveys, Honolulu County Medical Library.

[5] Medical Social Service Association Annual Meeting, July 12, 1949; Honolulu County Medical Library.

[6] Auditor's Report, Tennant and Greaney, Jan. 1 to July 31, 1949; File: Medical Social Service Association of Hawaii, 1947—, Honolulu County Medical Library.

[7] *Resolution, Medical Social Service Association;* File: Medical Social Service Association of Hawaii, 1947—, Honolulu County Medical Library.

[8] *Constitution and By-Laws, 1890–1944;* Honolulu County Medical Library.

[9] It was subsequently learned that in accordance with policies of the University of Hawaii, initial contracts are limited to one year, renewable if services are satisfactory.

[10] Ruth Cooper: *Report of Educational Consultation Visit to Hawaii* (Dec. 7–28, 1955). Copies: University of Hawaii, School of Social Work; Honolulu Council of Social Agencies. Honolulu County Medical Library.

[11] Cooper, pp. 10, 11.

[12] Information submitted by Miss Josephine C. Barbour, chief of social service, Massachusetts General Hospital.

Appendix I

TOTAL POPULATION FOR THE COUNTY OF HONOLULU BY YEAR AND BY RACE

CENSUS COUNTS

Census Year	Population	Hawaiian	Part Hawaiian	Caucasian	Chinese	Japanese	Other
1890	31,194	11,096	3,615	14,067	13,995	15,418	
1900	58,504	10,567	6,716	21,612	13,724	27,128	
1910	82,028	10,735	10,459	30,735	16,930	44,467	10,201
1920	123,527	12,103	16,359	57,702	22,068	69,585	25,106
1930	202,993	...38,543...		82,516	24,567	83,387	29,243
1940	258,256	...59,265...		94,248	29,514	119,516	50,477
1950	353,020						

Department of Health
Bureau of Health Statistics

July 13, 1954

Appendix II

TOTAL POPULATION FOR THE TERRITORY
BY YEAR AND BY RACE
CENSUS COUNTS

Census Year	Total Population	Hawaiian and Part Hawaiian	Caucasian Including Puerto Rican	Chinese	Japanese	Other
1832	130,313	124,049				6,264
1836	108,579	107,354				1,225
1850	84,165	82,593				1,572
1860	69,800	66,984	1,600	700		516
1866	62,959	58,765	2,200	1,200		794
1872	56,897	51,531	2,944	2,038		384
1878	57,985	47,508	3,748	6,045		684
1884	80,578	44,232	16,579	18,254	116	1,397
1890	89,990	40,622	18,939	16,752	12,610	1,067
1900	154,001	37,656	28,819	25,767	61,111	648
1910	191,909	38,547	44,048	21,674	76,675	7,965
1920	255,912	41,750	54,742	23,507	109,274	26,639
1930	368,336	50,860	80,373	27,179	139,631	70,293
1940	423,330	64,310	112,087	28,774	157,905	60,254
1950	499,794	86,091	124,344	32,376	184,611	72,372

Department of Health
Bureau of Health Statistics

July 13, 1954

Appendix III

Name of Hospital	No. Beds	Type	Ownership	Closed	Open
Oahu					
Ann Pearl Convalescent Home	22	Chronic Nursing Home	Individual		X
Berg's Nursing Home	35	Chronic Nursing Home	Individual		X
Booth Memorial Home	25	Unmarried mothers	Salvation Army	X	
Ewa Plantation Hospital	45	General	Corporation	X	
Hale Mohalu	121	Hansen's Dis.	Territory	X	
Kahuku Hospital	30	General	Corporation	X	
Kaimuki Convalescent Nursing Home	19	Chronic Nursing Home	Individual		X
Kapiolani Maternity & Gynecological Hospital	115	Gynecology Maternity	Nonprofit Assoc.		X
Kaukeolani Children's Hospital	102	Children General	Nonprofit Assoc.		X
Kuakini Hospital	120	General	Nonprofit Assoc.		X
Leahi Hospital	606	Tuberculosis	Nonprofit Assoc.	X	

* To bring hospitals into relationship with population census counts, 1950 is the year taken for describing them. Naturally there have been changes in the intervening years, some institutions have dissolved and others have increased their bed capacities. An important new hospital was founded in 1958 by the Kaiser Foundation Hospitals. It is a general hospital of 150 beds, open, and classified as a nonprofit association.

289

Appendix III—Continued

Name of Hospital	No. Beds	Type	Ownership	Closed	Open
Maluhia Home	267	Chronic	City & County	X	
		Convalescent			
Manoa Convalescent Home	21	Chronic	Individual		X
Maunalani Hospital & Convalescent Home	42	Convalescent	Nonprofit Assoc.		X
		Chronic			
		Aged			
Oahu Sugar Company Hospital	52	General	Corporation	X	
The Queen's Hospital	385	General	Nonprofit Assoc.		X
Shriners' Hospital for Crippled Children	28	Orthopedic	Nonprofit Assoc.	X	
Southshore General Hospital	45	General	Corporation	X	
St. Francis Hospital	213	General	Nonprofit Assoc.		X
Territorial Hospital	1100	Mental	Territory	X	
Wahiawa General Hospital	60	General	Nonprofit Assoc.		X
Waialua Agricultural Co., Ltd., Hospital	44	General	Corporation	X	
Waimano Home—(hospital beds)	100	Feeble-minded	Territory	X	
Hawaii					
Hawaiian Agricultural Co. Hospital	37	General	Corporation	X	
Hamakua Mill Co.	11	General	Corporation	X	
Honokaa Plantation Hospital	20	General		X	
Kohala County Hospital	42	General	County		X
Kona Hospital	42	General	County		X
Laupahoehoe Sugar Company Hospital	28	General	Corporation	X	
Matayoshi Hospital	33	General	Individual	X	
Okada Hospital	6	General	Individual	X	

Name of Hospital	No. Beds	Type	Ownership	Closed	Open
Oto Hospital	8	General	Individual	X	
Pepeekeo Hospital	48	General	Corporation	X	
Puumaile & Hilo Memorial Hospital	137	General	County		X
	181	Tuberculosis		X	
Yamanoha Hospital	5	General	Individual	X	
Olaa Old Folks Home (Section of Hilo Memorial Hospital)	88	Chronic			X
Lanai					
Lanai City Hospital	26	General	Corporation	X	
Kauai					
Samuel Mahelona Memorial Hospital	83	Tuberculosis	County	X	
Waimea Hospital	36	General	Nonprofit Assoc.		X
G. N. Wilcox Memorial Hospital	76	General / Chronic	Nonprofit Assoc.		X
Maui					
Hana County Hospital	25	General	County	X	
Kula General Hospital	20	General	County		X
Kula Sanatorium	212	Tuberculosis	County		X
Malulani Hospital	110	General		X	
Pioneer Mill Company Hospital	64	General	Corporation		X
Puunene Hospital	112	General	Corporation	X	
Molokai					
Kalaupapa Settlement (includes 60 hospital beds)	300	Hansen's Dis.	Territory	X	
Maunaloa (Libby McNeill & Libby)	19	General	Corporation	X	
Molokai Community Hospital	32	General	Nonprofit Assoc.		X

Index

A

accreditation, 86–87, 102, 133, 146, 157, 190–193
  agencies, homes and institutions, 86–87, 133, 157
  hospitals, 102
  nurses, 146
  social workers, 190–193
Ackland, Ruth, 14
Addams, Jane, 149
adoptions, 60–61, 68–69, 74, 85–86, 97, 103, 132, **135**, 213, **262–266**, 267
  hanai 38, **85–86**, 97, 263
  hospital policies, 263–264
  territorial laws, 86, 135, **262–266**
agricultural development, 6, 54, **144–146**, 148, 150, 159
  pineapple, 54, 144
  sugar, 6, 100, 144, 148
alcoholics, 226
Alexander, Emily, 148
Alexander House Settlement, 148–151
aliens, 6, 17, 36, 38, 43–44, 54, 68, 101, 118, 145, 149, 158–159, 173–175, 183–184, 183–184, 213–214, 219–220, 269–270, 276
  Chinese, 6, 24, **43–44**, 101, 145, 149, **174–175**, 213–214
  Filipino, 6, 54, 145
  Japanese, 6, 17, 101, 118, 145, **173–174**, 183–184, **219–220**, 269–270, 276
  Korean, 118, 145
  Portuguese, 6, 24, 36, 38, 145
  Russian, 6
  Spanish, 6
Allen, Dr. Arthur W., 283
Allen, Dr. Frederick H. 240
almoners, 167, 168
alms boxes, 203

American Association of Hospital Social Workers, 178
American Association of Medical Social Workers, 177, 186, 190, **191–192**, 193, 194, 200, 206, 260, 282–283
American Association of Psychiatric Social Workers, 192
American Association of Schools of Social Work, 80, 208
American Association of Social Workers, 79, **191–192**
American Association for Organizing Charity, 42
American Board of Commissioners for Foreign Missions, Boston, 6, 8, 82, 100, 144, 146, 154
American Board of Psychiatry and Neurology, 247
American College of Surgeons, 99, 193, 281
American Hospital Association, 170
American Legion, 134
American Occupational Therapy Association, 230
American Red Cross, 45, 253
American Seamen's Friend Society of New York, 8
American Society for the prevention of Cruelty to Dumb Beast, 15
analyses and studies, 20–21, 47–48, 52–53, 67–70, 75, 88, 137–140, 141, 145, 222, 245, 262–266
  adoptions, 262–266
  child agencies and institutions, 20–21, 52–53, 88
  232 diabetic patients, 222
  100 Juvenile Court wards, 67–70
  mental hygiene needs, 245
  plantation welfare, 145
  public health, 75
  public welfare, 137–140, 141
  100 school children, 47–48
Andrews, Dr. A. L., 65

293